Capitalising on Culture, Competing on Difference

Both authors, already highly respected for their independent-minded approach to the relationship between culture and socio-economic performance, here hone their thinking into an invigorating contribution to the debate on what sort of society Ireland should become over the next generation.

Professor Joe Lee, Director, Glucksman Ireland House, New York University

The book addresses one of the key areas mostly ignored when assessing the DNA of successful business. A culture incorporating innovation, creativity, flexibility and learning nurtures an environment in which business can thrive. It offers a unique insight into the effects culture has on making Ireland a world-class economy and, in my view, is vital reading for every business person in Ireland and for anyone considering setting up business in the country.

Pádraig Ó Céidigh, Chairman, Aer Arann/Ernst & Young Irish Entrepreneur of the Year 2002

Their work highlights the need for a debate on how a national system of innovation is best supported by a diversity of ways of learning and knowing.

Professor Seán Ó Riain, Department of Sociology, NUI Maynooth

This book begins a great and important project: the reconstitution of a truly Irish culture atop a revived economy and people. It is necessarily thorough and written for the motivated. But for those of us who labour in the field of Ireland's future cultural development, it is a book we simply cannot do without.

Marc Coleman, Economics Editor, Newstalk 106-108 fm

Healthy communities, bursting with vitality, provide a foundation that fosters innovation. A real contribution of this book is that it illustrates why harnessing community resources could prove fruitful in creating a truly dynamic and prosperous Irish learning society.

Mary Redmond, founder of the Irish Hospice Foundation and The Wheel.

This farsighted and penetrating work offers a compelling argument for the importance of the Irish language as a part of a dynamic new economic and political culture in Ireland. It offers an exciting vision of how all the languages of Ireland can be used to create a resourceful and inclusive society and a sustainable economy in post-boom Ireland.

Professor Michael Cronin, Director, Centre for Translation and Textual Studies, DCU

The authors offer a timely assessment of how the innovation of the Revival shaped Irish life during the twentieth century. The book's special contribution is to argue that the creativity that led to a culturally distinctive Ireland after independence can support an economically sustainable Ireland a century later.

Frank Allen, Chief Executive, Railway Procurement Agency (Luas and Metro)

This is a work of superb clarity in how to push post-Celtic Tiger Ireland forward in outlining how we can change from a 'what we do is who we are' to a 'who we are is what we can do' society. It is an extraordinary tour de force that must be read by those who are interested in how Ireland can compete successfully and sustainably in our globalised world.

Danny McCoy, Director of Policy, Irish Business and Employers Confederation (IBEC)

Capitalising on Culture, Competing on Difference

Innovation, Learning and Sense of Place in a Globalising Ireland

Finbarr Bradley and
James J. Kennelly

Foreword by
Dermot Desmond

BLACKHALL
Publishing

This book was typeset by Ark Imaging for

Blackhall Publishing
33 Carysfort Avenue
Blackrock
Co. Dublin
Ireland

e-mail: info@blackhallpublishing.com
www.blackhallpublishing.com

ISBN (HB): 978-1-84218-163-8
ISBN (PB): 978-1-84218-149-2

A catalogue record for this book is available from the British Library.

Printed in Ireland by ColourBooks Ltd

Foreword

The future of Ireland will be determined by capabilities of the mind and soul. This ambitious book resonates with many of my own views on Irish competitiveness, learning and the nurturing of the innovative spirit. Its discussions revolve around elements essential to business success: intellect, aptitude, ability and commitment, coupled with a sense of belonging, whether to an organisation, community or society.

The issue of character is a central theme of this book. I see self-reliance as being related to character. Courage, which plays a big role in risk taking, is not the absence of the fear of failure but rather is the pursuing of a dream despite one's fears. Closely tied to character and courage is patriotism. It is a word I am not embarrassed to use. I agree with Taoiseach Brian Cowen who, invoking the memory of his predecessor Seán Lemass, said recently that patriotism is a combination of love of country, pride in its history, traditions and culture, and determination to add to its prestige and achievements.

Irish characteristics have positive implications for competitiveness. Distinctiveness is a valuable asset and can provide a solid foundation for the creation of a learning society. While knowledge is global, learning and innovation are most definitely local. Ireland will prosper if it can tie the benefits of international markets to local relationships based on quality and community.

I understand the frame of mind that integrates the local with the global. When establishing NCB in the early 1980s, I saw working on my own as an opportunity to establish my identity while competing with money brokers, all of them subsidiaries of UK firms. NCB grew by developing skills and innovations in dealing room technologies that the competition simply could not match. Although early on we linked up with an international firm, we retained our strong sense of Irishness, an asset we found a great advantage for innovative activities.

Our Celtic ancestors were skilled artists, with rich imaginations. A century ago, a driving vision spawned many creative initiatives in culture, language and sport. Some may wonder what relevance this past has for the contemporary business environment. Yet, as this book shows, the period before independence has intriguing lessons on how Irishness, knowledge, creativity and enterprise are related.

Older wisdom contains a deep understanding of human nature. While I believe there is enormous merit in tradition, it must not be frozen in time but undergo constant change and evolution. When I attended school in the 1960s, the teaching model was much the same as a century earlier. Not much has changed since! Students' minds are seen by many as a collection of empty vessels to be filled to the brim with knowledge.

I have had a keen interest in learning for many years and set up Intuition, a leading supplier of corporate e-learning content, in the mid-1980s to implement some of my ideas. I think the role of education is to nurture hunters of knowledge with learning opportunities through the active engagement of all the senses, emotions and feelings. Learning is a collaborative and reflective activity with learning communities and organisations central to value creation and sustainable competitive advantage. People learn by watching experts and sharing ideas or reflections with others within informal networks where ideas can be generated and tips exchanged. Here is where Irish social and cultural resources have many opportunities to excel.

An underlying concept in this book is that happiness and quality of life should be emphasised more in work and education. Young people should be encouraged to explore for themselves what makes them happy. True happiness is about much more than making money. Friendships, relationships, citizenship and public service are essential to development whether for a person, a country or the world. As the authors contend, the key is to identify what value, be it public or private, is created from resources, especially native human, social and cultural capital. I am delighted to see that value creation, such a rich dynamic concept, is central to the learning model Finbarr Bradley and James Kennelly propose. In every business I am involved in, the generation of value is a central feature.

The rationale in the book runs counter to current thinking on Irish education, business and social development. But even if its perspectives are those of the minority, I see little wrong with this. Indeed, real achievement doesn't come from holding what the majority believe; progress generally begins at the margins rather than the centre.

The authors anticipate developments not obvious today but that may in the fullness of time become conventional wisdom. Take their views on sustainable education. These fit in with a vision I had for a millennium project, the Ecosphere, to house an aquarium and simulate a tropical-forest habitat in the IFSC. If supported, what an engaging learning experience that could now be for young and old alike, particularly with the world's focus on climate change.

Finally, a most welcome feature of this book is that it applies the findings of academia to the 'real world', my own habitat. Too much university research, whether in science or business, is discussed among an inner circle or gets squirreled away in libraries instead of being made available to those in a position to apply the concepts in practice.

I recommend this work not just to policy-makers and business people, but to all with an interest in Ireland's continued development challenges in the twenty-first century. My wish is that it will provoke a debate about our future competitiveness and the health of Irish society.

Dermot Desmond, Dublin
May 2008

Preface

We have written this book for those who seriously ponder whether Ireland's economic success must necessarily come at the expense of its unique heritage, culture and natural environment. Some people assume future prosperity must lead to a further erosion of precisely those attributes that make Ireland different, special and 'itself'. We believe such a notion, while prevalent, presents an overly simplistic and ultimately false dichotomy. This book takes a different tack, arguing that national identity, sense of place, culture and language represent significant assets that foster innovation, creativity, entrepreneurship and meaning, and, in turn, sustainable competitive advantage. In a globalising world, 'the local' matters most!

Although we are business academicians by training, this book has a broad interdisciplinary approach that offers significant advantages over more narrow treatments. We feel such a holistic and ambitious approach is necessary for Ireland to develop as a true learning society. Economy and society, culture and competitiveness, the arts, science, technology and industry are intimately and intricately connected; everything is connected to everything else.

This book does not offer a cookbook of recipes, but rather takes a fresh look at how Ireland's competitiveness can be enhanced through embracing, rather than rejecting, the country's inimitable and distinctive advantages that are rooted in place. The emphasis is on the Republic more than Northern Ireland, but we hope not excessively so. This is the time when island-wide perspectives are most likely to bear fruit.

We would like to thank Gerard O'Connor of Blackhall Publishing for having confidence in this project, and Elizabeth Brennan for her heroic editing and thoughtful advice at various stages of the manuscript. Eileen O'Brien and Sarah Franklin provided great support at the critical final stage. Frank Allen, Jim Fitzpatrick, Brian O'Kelly and Chris Whann read a lengthy first manuscript and offered incisive comments and sensible suggestions. *Buíochas le Donla uí Bhraonáin as comhairle Ghaeilge.* Whatever faults remain, the book has much improved through all their efforts.

Skidmore College awarded a faculty development grant in support of this research; Amy Syrell of the Interlibrary Loan Department of the Scribner Library at Skidmore located materials efficiently, speedily and cheerfully. Lazy Days Café in Blackrock provided the ideal atmosphere to relax and 'reflect'.

We owe an enormous intellectual debt to Professor Joe Lee of New York University. His groundbreaking history of modern Ireland and his many other works had a tremendous impact upon our thinking. His encouragement of our efforts kept us going, and his enthusiasm, knowledge and generosity continues to be an inspiration to us. We would also like to thank the participants at the 2008 Grian Conference at NYU, and at the 2008 national meeting of the American Conference for Irish Studies, for their thoughtful questions and comments concerning the main ideas in this book.

We are deeply grateful to Dermot Desmond for agreeing to contribute a foreword and helping to fund the launch, and thank especially those people who kindly endorsed the book. The Kerry Group, in addition to its generosity in helping sponsor the launch, has also provided us with an inspiring example of a successful indigenous enterprise, globally successful and highly innovative, yet with a strong heritage and deep roots in Ireland.

Finally, the act of writing a book does not occur in a vacuum. Both of us would like to thank our families and friends for their special support. Jim thanks his wife Linda, and sons Brendan and Terence, for tolerating his absences from home while researching the book, and his mental absences while preoccupied with it. It has all been for a good cause. *Ba mhaith le Fionnbarra buíochas faoi leith a ghabháil lena mhuintir, a dheirfiúracha Clár, Siobhán agus Emer, a dheartháir Diarmuid, a neachtanna Niamh, Neasa, Sadhbh agus Doireann agus a nianna Oisín, Fiachra, Diarmuit agus Conn. Ba mhaith leis buíochas ó chroí a ghabháil lena chara Susan Ní Dhubhlaoich a d'éist go foighneach lena thuairimí agus a thug inspioráid dó thar na blianta. Go rathaí Dia iad go léir.*

If any reader has queries or comments on our work they wish to convey to us, please contact Blackhall Publishing at info@blackhallpublishing.com. Our website details are as follows: <http://www.intinn.ie> (FB) and <http://www.skidmore.edu> (JK).

Finbarr Bradley, Blackrock, Co. Dublin
James J. Kennelly, Saratoga Springs, New York
May 2008

I gcuimhne m'athar Mícheál (1916–2000) agus mo mháthar Máiréad (1919–1999) (FB)

Do Linda, agus do mo mhuintir go léir, san am i láthair is am atá thart, i gcéin is i gcóngar (JK)

Contents

CHAPTER 1

Overview – Culture and Place as Competitive Resources

> I doubt if any nation can become prosperous unless it has national faith; and one very important part of national faith is faith in its resourccs, faith both in the richness of its soil and the richness of its intellect; and I am convinced that as much wealth can come from the intellect of Ireland as will come from the soil and that the one will repay cultivation as much as the other.
>
> William Butler Yeats, 1926[1]

INTRODUCTION

The phenomenal growth that characterised Ireland's boom, the so-called Celtic Tiger, which lasted fifteen or so years, will not be repeated any time soon. Consumer confidence is plummeting, tax returns are dropping, unemployment is rising, house prices are falling and productivity growth is slowing. There are fears about long-term competitiveness and quality of life. The country is entering a new phase in its development, one where it competes not on investment and production costs but on *innovation* and high value-added services. The viability of the country's current enterprise, scientific and technological strategies is being questioned. Many wonder, for instance, whether spending huge amounts of money on Research and Development (R&D) is the correct approach for generating a spirit of innovation in business, public services and communities.

Ireland faces serious challenges not just to sustain economic success but to define the type of society it wishes to be. Although the economic accomplishments have been considerable, a holistic evaluation suggests there have been other substantial, although not easily quantifiable, aspects to Ireland's boom. Contemporary Ireland, while awash with capability, confidence and resources, seems uninspired and faces significant social and environmental challenges. It appears badly in need of the driving vision that characterised the period some thirty years before the creation of Saorstát Éireann (Irish Free State) in 1922. Often described as the Irish Revival or Irish Renaissance, it was an era of cultural cohesion, prodigious idealism, self-reliance, creativity and innovation.

Ireland today must identify where its competitive advantage lies, how this differs from its competitors and what inimitable resources or capabilities it possesses to deliver high value-added products and services. Learning communities and organisations are central to competitive advantage, so Ireland must foster these in order to create a learning society.[2] A core argument of this book is that culture, tradition and identity are powerful resources that lead to innovation, creativity, entrepreneurship and global advantage. Such qualities, founded on meaning, rooted in place and catalysed by a forward-looking public policy, can create conditions necessary for creation of the vaunted *knowledge* or *learning society*.

Ireland represents a twenty-first century experiment in the ability of a small country with an open economy to successfully negotiate the global economy. With recent power-sharing arrangements in the North, and immigration changing the island's ethnic make-up, now is the time to examine what a marriage of capability, culture and innovation might mean for Ireland over the coming decades.

Global Competitive Advantage

It is a truism that we live in a global economy. The tide of economic liberalism has spread ever higher and farther, with goods, services, capital and often people all in dynamic motion, searching at the furthest regions for greater financial returns. Capital flows increase in velocity, production locations shift with regularity, and nation states and their policy instruments appear almost irrelevant. Multinational enterprises, the primary instruments of globalisation, are rootless, stateless and footloose. In search of advantage, they create multiple options (based on production locations, investment opportunities or tax regimes), play these off against each other, and then exploit differences through a deft practice of arbitrage. The entire world is their playing field.

In this world of global markets, rapid transportation and high-speed communications, economic theory suggests local cultures and places should not be sources of competitive advantage. As cultural and political borders have eroded, free market liberalism represents the orthodox prescription for almost every national ailment. In the new global order, multinational enterprises place a premium upon mobility, flexibility and portability. Although cheerleaders for globalisation are fond of citing the old advertising slogan that claims 'Geography is history', such triumphalism may be premature. Within the orthodoxy of economic liberalism lies a contradiction. Even as the logic of the global economic system threatens to eclipse the policy-making power of the nation state, business strategy gurus increasingly argue that certain critical success factors, for firms and nation states alike, remain 'rooted' in place. In various, but perhaps not always explicit ways, the local seems to matter more than ever.

A country possesses a sustainable competitive advantage when it has value-creating potential that provides it with a long-term advantage not easily duplicated or imitated by other countries. While many of the accepted factors of competitive advantage are now interchangeable between locations, the most important factors – those least susceptible to imitation, copying, or substitution, and hence most valuable and sustainable – remain rooted solidly in physical, geographical and cultural space. The implication is that locations need to develop an understanding of the qualities that set them apart relative to alternative locations.

A clear emerging paradox is that, with globalisation, culture and geographical location are becoming *more* rather than *less* important.[3] In practice, as Harvard's Michael Porter argues, these remain central to innovation and competition: the more complex, knowledge-based and dynamic the global economy becomes, the more this is likely to hold true. He argues that the enduring competitive advantages in a global economy lie increasingly in local things – knowledge, relationships, motivation – that distant rivals cannot match.[4] Advantage lies in *difference* such as special places, shared values and a sense of national identity.

The evidence is clear: sustainable competitive advantage in the twenty-first century will be determined by *creating value* from resources that are rare, inimitable and non-substitutable.[5] Irish competitive advantage is therefore a function of how effectively the country fosters these resources. While tangible resources such as financial, natural and technological capital are certainly necessary, these are not sufficient to achieve a sustainable competitive advantage. Intangibles such as human, cultural and social capital are crucial. Such resources are rooted in individuals and in the social and economic fabric of the local communities in which they live. In other words, they are deeply embedded historically in the people, places and dynamic of a culture that constitutes a shared identity.

These 'rooted' resources create what we call a sense of rootedness or a *rooted Irish-global identity*. This facilitates innovation and continuous transformation by the application of knowledge in creative ways. Alongside a keen awareness of the international context and a strong sustainable ethic, this book contends that rootedness is a powerful competitive advantage. A nation's heritage and traditions, such as its language, literature, music and sport, in other words its cultural identity, help offer meaning in life and represent unique resources that, if properly harnessed, create an innovative society. Yet Ireland still suffers the consequences of ruptured roots from the loss of its language, primarily during the nineteenth century. To summarise, the best way for Ireland to generate a sustainable competitive advantage is through understanding and appreciating its inimitable resources, particularly intangibles, and implementing practical approaches to create value from these.[6]

Reconceptualising Irish Development

An increasingly accepted core component of competitiveness is sustainability. Sustainable development is one of the more complex concepts in modern society. As a radical new paradigm, it challenges humans to think medium and long term, rather than short term. Its ultimate goal is to protect and improve the quality of life lying at the heart of interactions between the economy, environment and society. These interactions are a system, seen as a group of interrelated and interdependent components forming a complex and unified whole. Sustainable development requires a systems way of thinking, where the focus is on the relationships among the system's components rather than on the components themselves.

Attempts are under way to evolve Ireland's development strategy from a focus on inward investment to indigenous innovation as a key driver of long-run economic growth. Yet finding ways of attracting foreign investment remains an important component of the overall approach. In a recent report called *Retuning the Growth Engine*, the American Chamber of Commerce in Ireland urged that the nation offer inward investors a new value proposition that had 'something distinctive in order to attract multinational companies' innovation investment'.[7] It also called for an educational system that is 'science-oriented and global in outlook'.[8] Such a recipe, while well conceived, is perhaps one that any number of countries competing for mobile international investment might emulate. An alternative, potentially transformative and paradigm-shifting proposition for building competitive advantage is to anchor learning and innovation to the concepts of sustainable development and sense of place.

A sense of place represents an emotional and complex attachment to a particular geographical and cultural space, a connection embedded in social networks and feelings. It is also rich in tacit knowledge.[9] Such knowledge embodies aesthetics, meaning and emotions that can often be critical motivators of creativity and hence innovation. Tacit knowledge is informed by people's sense of identity and place. A sense of place broadly encompasses elements of the natural, social and built environments, and a shared experience of history and community. In the case of contemporary Ireland, given the complex cultural dynamic (i.e. the 'two traditions' and the 'new Irish' immigrants), a sense of place is particularly important in providing the foundation or root system for a shared identity.

The challenge for a post-modern society like Ireland is the integration of humanity with the rest of nature. However, the relationship between the Irish, their sense of place and the natural world is unhealthily reflected in the country's perspective on resource use and its weak performance on a range of environmental issues such as biodiversity, waste management and materials utilisation. The prevailing attitude to nature and sense of place appears to be at odds with modern European thinking. Due perhaps to the early isolation of the Irish from the cultural forces that shaped ecological sentiments in Europe, and what Michael Viney calls 'the biological treachery of the famine', utility remains the benchmark of Irish attitudes to nature and the environment.[10]

Some see the Irish attitude as expressing alienation from the natural world. Liam De Paor holds that 'Ireland is a country of ruins, partly because abandoned structures were not removed, but simply left to rot; this expresses the alienation of the people. The landscape did not belong to them, and the old rent system penalised improvements in environment and amenities.'[11] Sensibilities towards nature in England, in contrast, evolved from intellectual and social conditions largely absent from Ireland. For its part, Ireland's tradition lacks the concepts of both the 'frontier' and the 'garden', two crucial images of the social mediation of the natural world. Christianity may have also fostered an antagonistic attitude towards nature. The Catholic Church showed scant interest in any form of natural theology for centuries. Non-human nature in Ireland scarcely elicited notice. The only experiences in Ireland regarded as valid were those that occurred solely as the result of negotiations within the human group.[12]

An underlying logic links a culture of sustainability, sense of place, resource productivity, a systems way of thinking, innovativeness and competitiveness. Of course, some will see little need for this way of thinking; in their view, Ireland has already arrived, and recent economic success supplies ample evidence. In the space of eighty odd years since the foundation of the State, Ireland appears to have moved from one extreme to another: from a place where sentiment, nationality and feelings were central features in the national vision to the polar opposite, where science, rationality and the economic marketplace dominate. This book posits an approach to Ireland's future development that harnesses the positive elements of both. It draws from the principles of social and environmental sustainability, international competitiveness, cultural distinctiveness, and a national ethos of creativity, innovation and quality, making the case that Ireland can develop in a way that is economically competitive, environmentally sustainable and socially equitable. But success in this endeavour implies that Ireland welcomes the richness in diversity of all traditions, including recent immigrants, while retaining its own distinctive placed-based resources.

Ireland's Learning Society

Evidence on whether the Irish approach to fostering innovation has been successful is mixed. Sociologist Seán Ó Riain argues that, for all of the undoubted economic success, Ireland's boom represented a missed opportunity to develop true innovation or learning capabilities. He blames this on a lack of sophisticated thinking about how learning actually takes place, especially concerning how social capital and properly resourced institutions foster innovation. As he puts it:

> The creation of new innovative capacities in the Irish economy could have gone much further but was limited by weak investment in social institutions of learning – the institutions which promoted innovation in the Irish economy emerged in the gaps and spaces left by the institutions focused on attracting foreign investment. At the same time, rising inequality could have been tackled much more decisively through redistribution through the tax and welfare systems, but more significantly by building a more inclusive set of institutions that supported learning and innovation.[13]

It is generally accepted that Ireland must now become a learning society capable of successfully facing fierce international competitive challenges. The Government is investing substantial financial resources to achieve this goal. The National Economic and Social Development Office (NESDO) defines a learning society as one that displays a *capacity* to learn and:

> . . . continually absorbs new ideas, knowledge and skills across a range of socio-economic activities, and fosters a culture of experimentation and creativity in turn with cultural patterns supportive of innovation and ingenuity, both existing and emerging. It might also be described as a society that creates both human and social capital.[14]

Simply put, a learning society represents a social milieu that facilitates innovation and continual transformation, teaching people how to create value themselves by striving to reach their potential. The Government considers this a critical component in developing a competitive edge in the global economy. It also represents an acknowledgement that the factors that drove Ireland's boom, particularly low corporate tax rates, an educated English-speaking workforce and reliance on foreign direct investment (FDI), will not ensure competitiveness in the future. However, public policy measures put in place to achieve a learning society may not be sufficient to do so.

A learning society cultivates high-quality learning organisations that help individuals to create value from *all* resources, whether tangible or intangible. Perhaps, during the boom, Ireland lost valuable resources, especially natural and social capital, that now damages competitiveness. Competitiveness depends critically on increased productivity, or output per unit of resource input. Because of practical difficulties, economists often use the value added per worker – labour productivity – as a proxy to measure productivity.[15] Total productivity (a broader concept than labour productivity) expresses the relationship between the outputs of an entity and its inputs, such as labour, capital, material, energy and all other factors needed for production. To enhance learning and innovation, attention should be concentrated on the productivity of *all* resources, in other words on the value that is truly created. The productivity of public services is especially important but difficult to measure in practice. In the private sector, productivity relates to profitability or efficiency, whereas productivity in public services measures the impact of spending on well-being or quality of life.

The role of communities as sources of cultural and social capital is crucial. The most valuable Irish resources are intangibles founded on capabilities, potentialities and social relationships. Learning environments based on a rooted Irish-global identity nurture quality, an aspirational work ethic and an empowered innovative community. National identity, language and traditions, rooted in place and fostered by a forward-looking public policy, provide the conditions necessary for development of a society that spurs innovation, creativity and entrepreneurship. Such a learning society, which recognises and capitalises upon the more tacit intangible resources resident in culture, language and social capital, could lead to an Ireland that is self-reliant if not self-sufficient, utterly unique while eminently cosmopolitan, and well able to compete in the global economy of the twenty-first century.

Learning from the Revival

The role of culture in fostering innovation is an object of increasing attention for academics, professionals and policy-makers.[16] Economic historian David Landes' conclusion in his groundbreaking book *The Wealth and Poverty of Nations* is: 'if we learn anything from the history of economic development, it is that culture makes all the difference.'[17] It seems essential that public policy fosters both *vision* and *capabilities* if Ireland is to develop in a manner consistent with its aspirations. However, policy documents published by Forfás (National Policy and Advisory Board for Enterprise, Trade, Science, Technology and Innovation) such as the *Enterprise Strategy Report*[18] or the latest Government *National Development Plan 2007–2013*[19] do not place much emphasis on the potential of linking Ireland's future as a learning society to the considerable cultural and social resources at its disposal.

This book takes a different tack in holding that a strong sense of identity, illustrated by difference and distinctiveness, is necessary for the cultivation of an innovative learning society. Demographic and social considerations make this an ideal time for reflection upon the present nature of Irish identity. In doing so, the book argues that contemporary Ireland, North and South, could benefit by drawing on the inspiration and ideals of the Irish Revival. The Revival encompassed a range of innovative initiatives in commerce, agriculture, theatre, literature, art, sport, language and natural science, all relating to a common theme: an awakening interest in Irish identity, broadly defined. The Revival fundamentally redefined Irish identity. It was a time of prodigious pioneering spirit, energy and idealism, characterised by a turbulent creativity and a spirit of self-help that led to changes in how Irish people related to one another and the rest of the world. The framework developed in this book – we name it the

New-Revival framework – draws on the thinking of the Irish Revival but applies it to the contemporary context of the emerging learning society.

During the Revival, many enthusiasts saw Ireland's natural, cultural and human resources, harnessed to a renewed sense of empowerment, as critical elements of an emerging ethic of self-reliance and innovation. Revival organisations such as Douglas Hyde's Conradh na Gaeilge (Gaelic League), Horace Plunkett's Irish Co-operative Movement, Michael Cusack's Gaelic Athletic Association (GAA) and the Irish Literary (later the Abbey) Theatre of Yeats and Lady Gregory were all cut from a similar cloth.[20] They collectively represented a broad self-help alliance that sought to transform the very fabric of Irish social, economic and political life. Despite a wide diversity in interests, the same individuals were often involved in projects across a spectrum of organisations, with a sense of Irish identity and national purpose the glue that bound them in a common enterprise.[21]

Serious reflection on the diversity of forward-looking ideas contested during the Revival should dissipate any idea that Irish nationalism was by definition inward looking, reactive and dreamily utopian. While the reality on the ground was often at odds with the founding vision, through the early decades of the Free State, and during the subsequent years of economic malaise and commercial lassitude, there remained a core vision of Ireland crafted in the Revival. This vision, widely accepted by most people for a long time, may still inform the policy choices of twenty-first century Ireland.

While a world apart in terms of their technological, political and social contexts, parallels between today's nascent learning society and the Revival suggest an opportunity for a fruitful symbiosis. Combining the spirit, effervescence, diversity, creativity and self-help ethos of the Revival with the development of resources necessary for building a learning society may produce a process of economic development that, while rooted in place, is socially, economically and environmentally sustainable; a nation that is globally competitive while distinctively Irish. It is easy to agree with Fallon that:

> How much more intelligent, and more constructive, it is to come to terms creatively with the past than to amputate it like a diseased limb, or put it under interdict! We are likely to find ourselves in the position of the self-conscious moderniser who, having thrown out his ancestral furniture and paintings or sold them off for a knockdown price, finds inside a few years that these have now become valuable, respected antiques and that he himself is much the poorer, financially as well as culturally. After all, at the risk of labouring the obvious, the past has produced us, and when we deny it we deny our own immediate ancestry, and even an essential part of ourselves.[22]

This book's thesis, while light years away from Éamon de Valera's notion of 'frugal self-sufficiency', nevertheless shares a similar appreciation of the valuable stock of indigenous Irish resources. Far from representing dead artefacts that are anti-modern and non-economic, these resources, if harnessed properly, represent dynamic and unique sources of global competitive advantage. Such a thesis is not an exercise in naïve nostalgia, nor is it an attempt to turn back the clock to some perceived pure and idyllic golden age. Rather, it is an appeal to utilise the core attributes of culture, tradition and sense of place in the creation of a new synthesis that will further Ireland's achievement of a 'successful society'.

No nation can be truly innovative if its people do not know and appreciate who they are, where they come from and where they are trying to go. This flies in the face of some economic thinking that suggests that confidence and independence are derived from the erosion of a sense of place, with rootedness antithetical to competitiveness. Yet, while knowledge is global, innovation is emphatically local. Countries and regions that can successfully combine the benefits of global markets with local relationships based on quality, sense of place and tradition are likely to prosper. Researchers on urban development, for instance, point to the special role of community and diversity as incubators of innovation. Those that emphasise trust and social capital are especially equipped to attract and keep the most creative people and enterprises, thereby generating the highest quality of life. Uniformity is not good for creativity; diversity in cultures and ideas brings about intellectual vitality. Places that succeed are those that are multiculturally diverse, yet also proud and respectful of the past, while possessing a strong ethic of sustainability. Such places are truly unique.[23]

TRANSFORMING EDUCATION

This book maintains that the Revival provides a blueprint for how Ireland's learning institutions can assist people in changing their mentality to achieve this advantage. John Dewey, the American philosopher, classified education as a process of living and not as a preparation for future living.[24] Developing a sustainable competitive advantage will require fostering a generation of sustainable innovators and lifelong learners. This is likely to lead to better stewardship of Ireland's unique natural and cultural capital, a richer path of *development* than economic *growth*, founded on the systemic relationships among human, social, economic and physical systems.

A common misconception is that the capacity for improving productivity, and managing change, innovation and competitiveness depends on the amount of money spent on R&D, especially within higher education institutions. It is assumed that spending vast resources on R&D, and linking this to a worldwide scientific and corporate infrastructure, will stimulate innovation and move the country further up the value chain. Likewise, the development of a learning society is often seen as limited to the work of education institutions. However, a range of institutions, organisations, networks and relationships – public, private and community-based, and rooted within the nation – influence learning and these can play a crucial role in developing a national system of innovation.[25] The creation of an Irish learning society must be based on the assumption that engaging in social practices is fundamental to its development. A strategy that devotes substantial resources to R&D, especially in science and technology at universities, may underestimate the contribution of the *local* character to learning and innovation.

How learning occurs, at individual, organisational, regional and national level is an important theme running through this book. Yet what matters most is not *what* people learn but *how* they learn. Learning is not an activity done just by individuals. Etienne Wenger noted the widely shared assumption that learning 'has a beginning and an end: that it is best separated from the rest of our activities, and that it is the result of teaching'.[26] The distinct challenge is to create potent learning environments that help students understand how to create, exchange, share and sustain value. Since value nowadays is largely co-created by parties involved in relationships, a mutual learning network should emphasise conversation in order to help students understand the contribution of each resource to value creation. Emphasis should be on fostering identity, relationships and meaning, through reflection and practical skills. Action learning and apprenticeship education can play an especially vital role.

The world is on the brink of a new industrial revolution, one transforming current notions about business, leading to a fundamental shift from the purchase of goods to the delivery of services, and reducing the importance of material acquisition as a measure of affluence.[27] This has enormous implications for Ireland since it is in services innovation that the country possesses potentially enormous and distinct advantages. Sustainable innovation will increasingly reflect integration, not balance. Therefore, third-level (and earlier) education in Ireland should help students think through the consequences of their actions. A key challenge is to help them appreciate that a trade-off between economic, social and environmental goals is not always inevitable. The fundamental aim is to enhance all three simultaneously through innovation that enhances value and service.

An exciting aspect, and one that presents a golden opportunity for Ireland, is that an ethic of service and an ethic of sustainability complement each other. But this opportunity will require radical rethinking in the self-conception of Irish educational institutions. The problems of both service and sustainability cut across many disciplines; even two disciplines working together is not sufficient. A rich dynamic environment means those from different disciplinary backgrounds such as business, the arts, engineering or science learn from each other while specialising in a particular area of interest. This is how the learner gets an opportunity to reflect on and explore his or her identity with others within the learning community, a central aspect of the development philosophy in this book. Learning programmes should not focus that much on individual subjects; instead, they should be built around interdisciplinary clusters that centre on resource productivity and value creation. Each cluster then helps students understand the contribution of that resource to the creation of value through the delivery of a service.

Global Opportunity

Globalisation was not unknown to the ancient Irish. During the Stone Age, axes travelled long distances from quarry sites in Rathlin Island off the Antrim coast, while Bronze Age Ireland participated fully in the industrial revolution of the time, trading across Northern Europe and into the Mediterranean.[28] George Sturt's *The Wheelwright's Shop*[29], a description of the working lives of craftsmen in nineteenth-century England, or Séamus Murphy's *Stone Mad*,[30] memoirs of a stone carver who became one of Ireland's greatest sculptors, show how quality, emotions, intuition and intimate knowledge of materials mattered in the lives of traditional craftsmen. In today's globalised world, however, much tacit knowledge is lost through the process of mass production. This can significantly curtail Ireland's innovative development and negatively impact its international competitiveness.

In the wake of the power-sharing agreement in Northern Ireland, the 'Global Question' has now superseded Ireland's

'National Question'. As Michael O'Sullivan notes in his book *Ireland and the Global Question,* 'most small developed countries share the same predicament as Ireland . . . their dilemma lies in balancing the impact of powerful external forces with independence of choice over the kind of society, identity, and public life they desire.'[31] O'Sullivan argues that, while Ireland must accept globalisation, it needs to adapt to it with strategic policy thinking. One response might be to give the Government a larger role in buffering the effects on society posed by the larger external risks the country now faces. Yet, unlike other small open countries such as Denmark, Irish Government spending has not grown in tandem with the pace of globalisation. This leaves the economy and society vulnerable.

This is a crucial juncture with respect to the next stage of development and the structure of Irish society. Yet, as with many policy issues in Ireland, globalisation has been treated with much pragmatism but perhaps not enough strategic thought. O'Sullivan fears that Ireland may squander its recent economic successes by delaying a serious examination of what its engagement with globalisation actually means now and what it will entail for the future.[32] Although Ireland has clearly embraced globalisation, and has reaped its benefits, it is not a global power. The pressure is therefore on Ireland to continue to adapt successfully through the constant development of sustainable competitive advantage. How it chooses to do so will make all the difference.

The current globalisation phase has so far been kind to Ireland, which is now among the most affluent countries in the world. Economic benefits, although not spread evenly, are at least spread widely among the population. The middle class has never been so large, or so well off. Young Irish, particularly those with advanced education, have never had as many employment opportunities, most of them at home. Material prosperity is now, perhaps, the most notable characteristic of the nation, replacing the saints, scholars and forty shades of green. There are downsides as well. The number of those left behind, economically, is still large. Crime has grown to levels characteristic of other developed economies, but unknown in Ireland until recently. The natural environment, while retaining much of its beauty, is under increasing threat. The Irish language is ebbing away in areas where recently it was the vernacular. Irish music and dance, although robust in many respects, is in danger of being 'hollowed out' and produced commercially to meet global demand, while losing its essential life-giving connections with people and places.

Ireland today sits in a crease in time, one that provides a genuine opportunity for the country to achieve its stated national aspirations of competitiveness, innovation, a high standard of living, cultural vitality, social equity and environmental sustainability. The nation is well positioned to take advantage of this opportunity. It is affluent, educated, confident and at peace. The 'bad old days' have largely evaporated, the national inferiority complex seems to have dissipated and there is a palpable sense that anything is possible. The key question now is: how do we turn this to national advantage?

The competitive strength of a small knowledge-driven nation lies in its ability to act quickly and in a coherent fashion, applying innovative methods and delivering high quality that leaves others behind.[33] This book holds that to achieve a successful learning society, public policy and its implementing institutions must be guided by a coherent approach founded on distinctiveness, difference, national identity, systems thinking and environmental sustainability. By marrying in this way the global with the local, and services with sustainability, Ireland has the opportunity to forge a unique development path, a model to be proud of and one that other countries might emulate.

Recent Irish economic successes are not the *end* of a long-delayed development journey. Rather, they are potentially the *beginning* of a different, more difficult, but ultimately more rewarding path towards a development trajectory that is distinctively Irish. Such a journey will be characterised by a renewed Irish identity rooted in a sense of place, globally competitive yet uniquely suited to the history and the aspirations of the people of the island, North and South. In an increasingly multicultural Ireland, with the entire island becoming virtually one economic unit and relationships improving between the political traditions, it becomes difficult to generate a sense of identity based on shared ethnicity, tradition or culture. Yet, just as the Revival emphasised the authenticity of place in defining Irishness, a shared sense of place can be the key to creating a common Irish identity today. In order to generate a spirit of enterprise, it is necessary to focus on this shared connection between people and the places in which they live. This will permit *all* to feel part of a common project or goal. A national purpose based on meaning, conservation, sustainability and sense of place represents an enormous competitive advantage in the coming era of fossil fuel shortage, climate change and potential social disharmony.

Chapter Outlines

> *Ní labhraíonn sí a thuilleadh liom, an áit seo,*
> *is níl aon bhuanaíocht ag mo theanga níos mó inti.*
>
> *Níor chuaigh mo phréamhacha síos ach fad áirithe*
> *is táid ag dreo anois cheal taca uaithi.*
>
> She no longer speaks to me, this place,
> and my language no longer finds sustenance in her.
>
> My roots only went down so far
> and now they are rotting due to lack of support from her.[34]

Figure 1 depicts (using the visual metaphor of a tree) the core argument of this book. The various resources represent potential. To the extent that such resources are embedded or rooted in the cultural and geographical space of Ireland, they have the potential to create unique and inimitable advantages specific to the country. These advantages may be harnessed to develop places, communities, institutions and enterprises that serve as incubators of innovation, entrepreneurship and, ultimately, sustainable competitiveness. This figure shows the reinforcing relationship between

Figure 1: Core Argument of Book

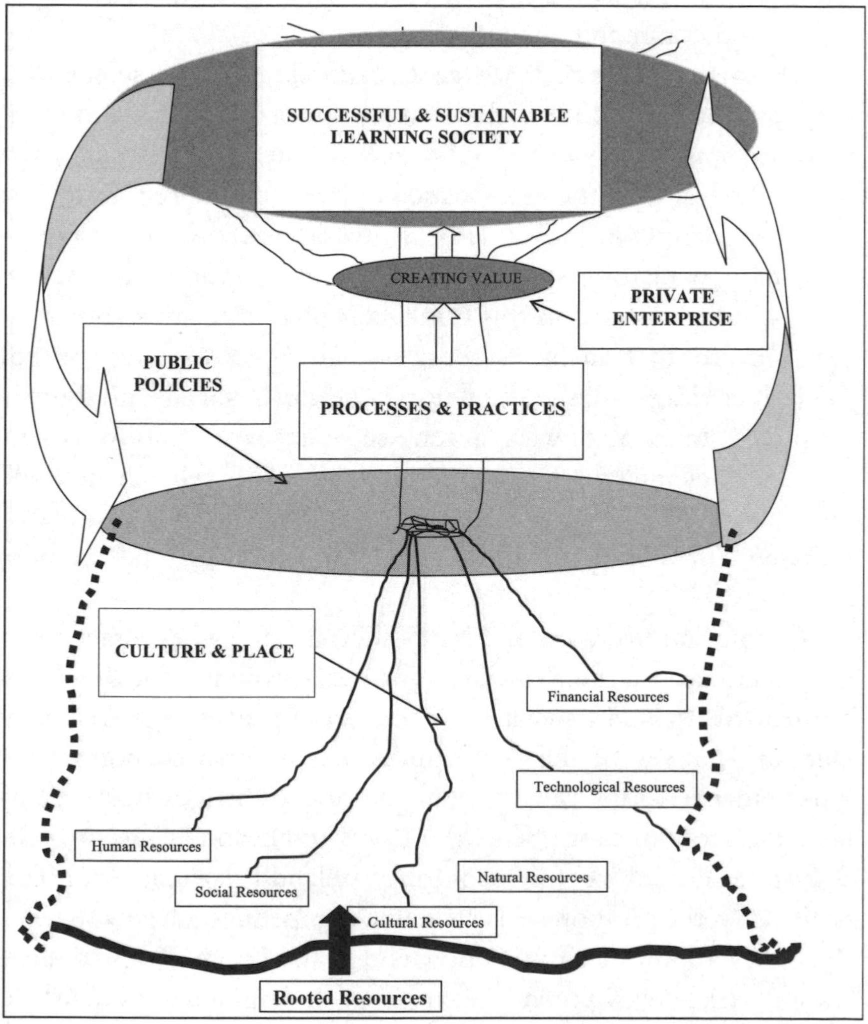

underlying culture and place, rooted resources, public policies, private enterprise and processes and practices. An equitable, culturally diverse, wise, globally focused but locally led society results if policies founded on creativity, resource efficiency and citizenship are put into practice. The focus is on value creation, which, as illustrated with the various feedback loops, ultimately leads to a sustainable and successful learning society. Such an approach infers a fundamental change in the self-conceptualisation of many public, private and community enterprises.

The main theme in Chapter 2 is the view that understanding the logic behind the Revival a century ago may foster an invigorating learning society in Ireland today. The defining characteristics of the Revival were the links made between cultural self-awareness and Irish identity in movements as diverse as economic organisation, natural history, sport, language and literature. A sense of place – also described in this book as rootedness – was an important feature that inspired these initiatives. Advocates of the Revival envisaged Ireland's natural, cultural, social and human resources, integrated with a renewed sense of empowerment, as critical elements of an emerging ethic of self-reliance and innovation. This chapter also examines the relevance of Revival thinking for competitiveness and innovation in the modern economy.

Chapter 3 introduces the New-Revival framework, drawing on the experience of the Revival, to set out a structure for the development of Ireland's sustainable competitive advantage. It begins with an overview of the development of the Irish economy from independence to the present, and the policy changes that precipitated the economic miracle of the 1990s and beyond. This provides a historical context for exploring Ireland's current economic challenge – the creation of sustainable competitive advantage – and the policy approaches to this now and in the future. Public policies for industrial development are currently undergoing a fundamental re-think. Now a high-cost economy, the country must rely less on FDI operating in low-skilled sectors, particularly manufacturing. Development depends on offering multinational corporations, especially those engaged in R&D and high value-added services, attractive and unique value-creating propositions to locate in Ireland. Indigenous companies must operate at higher levels of sophistication, identifying key niche areas within high-end global value networks such as high-tech services. Using the Revival as a guide, this chapter examines how Ireland might use its resources, both human and non-human, to achieve a sustainable and inimitable competitive advantage. The contention is that distinctive, potentially valuable resources should be identified and fostered in order to build a culture of creativity, applied science, resource productivity and meaning.

True innovation is really a state of mind and depends on people's attitudes and commitment. This is close in spirit to the guiding principles used by Horace Plunkett who linked character, co-operation, discipline, commercial capability and scientific practice. Chapter 4 argues that the challenge in developing a culture of creativity and dynamic learning is to create rich social relationships or cultural bonds. Without these, innovation is unlikely to occur. Learning and innovation are most effective when they take place within social networks or 'communities of practice'. The emphasis is on meaning, identity, action, application and practice rather than on academic science or theory. Ireland's present innovation strategy, which emphasises R&D especially within the third-level sector, ignores this local context of innovation. Generating relationships of trust, community and meaning is as crucial as science and technology for developing a learning society.

Chapter 5 proposes new approaches for educating in a learning society. Due to the way Irish education institutions (third level and earlier) generally see their mission, a radical transformation is necessary in how learning is conceptualised. Management and business education, in particular, will require reform in order to develop the type of global manager both multinationals and indigenous companies will need in the years to come. The education proposed, founded on understanding and appreciating mediation between the global *and* the local, is appropriate for *both* public and private sector executives.

In the learning age, the local and the global should be in continuous interaction. This can result in creative and vibrant learning communities with a committed sense of place, described by scholars recently with terms such as 'dynamic rootedness'[35] and 'shared spatial dynamics'.[36] Chapter 6 examines why and how cultural and social resources matter in developing creativity and innovation, and uses examples from each to illustrate their potential value. The example in the realm of cultural resources is language, especially in the context of its role in nurturing meaning and identity. The other example is building social resources through developing communities.

Finally, Chapter 7 looks into the future, drawing on the book's theme that integrated policies – developing rooted identity, meaning, distinctiveness, character and the application of scientific methods – are crucial drivers of learning and innovation. A key challenge is to build a multilingual and multicultural society harnessing the energy, enterprise and pioneering spirit of Ireland's new immigrants who are committed to the new place called home. With a coherent national purpose, Ireland can develop as a learning society, competing successfully and sustainably in a globalised world. The book concludes by imagining possible outcomes in the year 2022, the centenary of independence.

Notes

1. Pearce, D.R. (ed.) (2001), *The Senate Speeches of WB Yeats*, London: Prendeville Publishing.
2. Gunnigle, P., Heraty, N. and Morley, M.J. (2006), *Human Resource Management in Ireland*, 3rd edition, Dublin: Gill & Macmillan. This has a review of these concepts in the Irish context.
3. Ketels, C.H.M. (2006), 'Michael Porter's Competitiveness Framework – Recent Learnings and New Research Priorities', *Journal of Industry, Competition and Trade*, 6, pp. 115–36.
4. Porter, M.E. (1998), 'Clusters and the New Economics of Competition', *Harvard Business Review*, November–December, pp. 77–90.
5. See, for example, Dierickx, I. and Cool, K. (1989), 'Asset Stock Accumulation and Sustainability of Competitive Advantage', *Management Science*, 35(12), December, pp. 1504–11; Prahalad, C.K. and Hamel, G. (1990), 'The Core Competence of the Corporation', *Harvard Business Review*, May–June, pp. 79–91.
6. This perspective shares features in common with that advocated by others. For instance, in a visionary book Jonathan Porritt asserts that the different resources that countries possess need to be managed so that the yield from each sustains people now and in the future. See Porritt, J. (2006), *Capitalism as if the World Matters*, London: Earthscan.
7. American Chamber of Commerce in Ireland (2007), *Retuning the Growth Engine*, Dublin, p. 4.
8. American Chamber of Commerce in Ireland (2007), *Retuning the Growth Engine*, Dublin, p. 8.
9. 'Michael Polanyi and Tacit Knowledge', available at <http://www.infed.org/thinkers/polanyi.html>.
10. Viney, M. (1986), 'Woodcock for a Farthing: the Irish Experience of Nature', *The Irish Review*, 1, pp. 58–64.
11. De Paor, L. (1979), 'Ireland's Identities', *The Crane Bag*, 3, pp. 22–9 (see p. 28).
12. Outram, D. (1986), 'Negating the Natural: Or Why Historians Deny Irish Science', *The Irish Review*, 1, pp. 45–9.

13. Ó Riain, S. (2008), 'Competing State Projects in the Contemporary Irish Political Economy', in M. Adshead, P. Kirby and M. Miller (eds.), *Contesting the State*, Manchester: Manchester University Press, pp. 165–85.
14. National Economic and Social Development Office (2006), *Learning Society Foresight Project: Delivery of Consultancy Services – Call for Outline Proposals*, Dublin: NESDO. NESDO is currently undertaking a foresight project on Ireland's future learning society. Details on the project FuturesIreland are available at: <http://www.nesdo.ie/futuresireland/index.html>.
15. For a comprehensive examination of productivity in Ireland from a range of experts, refer to Aylward, C. and O'Toole, R. (eds.) (2007), *Perspectives on Irish Productivity: A Selection of Essays by Irish and International Economists*, Dublin: Forfás.
16. Preston, P. (2005), 'The Cultural Turn versus Economic Returns: The Production of Culture in an Information Age', *The Republic*, 4, June, pp. 60–79.
17. Landes, D. (1998), *The Wealth and Poverty of Nations*, London: Little, Brown and Co., p. 516.
18. Enterprise Strategy Group (2004), *Ahead of the Curve: Ireland's Place in the Global Economy*, Dublin: Forfás.
19. Government of Ireland (2007), *National Development Plan 2007–2013: Transfoming Ireland,* Dublin: The Stationery Office.
20. Mathews, P.J. (2003), *Revival: The Abbey Theatre, Sinn Féin, The Gaelic League and the Co-operative Movement*, Notre Dame, IN: University of Notre Dame Press.
21. For example, both Horace Plunkett and Douglas Hyde were guarantors of the Irish Literary Theatre; George W. Russell (Æ) was not only a leading intellectual in the literary movement, but also a full-time organiser and later editor of the *Irish Homestead*, the organ of the IAOS (the umbrella organisation of Irish co-operatives). Yeats and Lady Gregory lent support to the Irish co-operative movement, while Jesuit Fr Tom Finlay, vice president of the IAOS for many years, was a founder of the Irish Literary Theatre, an editor of various journals

including the *Lyceum*, and a nationalist of impeccable credentials. There were many connections such as these.

22. Fallon, B. (1998), *An Age of Innocence: Irish Culture 1930–1960*, New York: St. Martin's Press, p. 3.
23. The necessity for considering approaches that emphasise shared place rather than cultural difference is becoming urgent if newspaper column inches devoted to potential problems with widespread immigration is any indicator. For example, see 'We Must Begin the Culture Debate', *Sunday Business Post*, 23 December 2007, and 'If you Value your Irish Identity then it's time to Snub Europe', *Irish Independent*, 19 December 2007.
24. Dewey, J. (1897), 'My Pedagogic Creed', *The School Journal*, 54, January, 77–80.
25. Casey, D. and Brugha, C.M. (2005), 'Questioning Cultural Orthodoxy: Policy Implications for Ireland as an Innovative Knowledge-Based Economy', *E:CO*, 7, pp. 2–10.
26. Wenger, E. (1998), 'Communities of Practice: Learning as a Social System', *Systems Thinker*, 9(5), June, available at: <http://www.co-i-l.com/coil/knowledge-garden/cop/lss.shtml>.
27. Hawken, P., Lovins, A.B. and Lovins, L.H. (1999), *Natural Capitalism: The Next Industrial Revolution*, London: Earthscan.
28. Sweeney, G. (2001), 'Introduction: Innovation and Innovation Policy – the Need for Re-Examination' in G. Sweeney (ed.), *Innovation, Economic Progress and the Quality of Life*, Cheltenham, UK: Edward Elgar, p. 19.
29. Sturt, G. (1993, 1923), *The Wheelwright's Shop*, Cambridge, UK: Cambridge University Press.
30. Murphy, S. (1997, 1966), *Stone Mad*, Belfast: Blackstaff Press.
31. O'Sullivan, M. (2006), *Ireland and the Global Question*, Cork: Cork University Press.
32. 'Challenge is to Adopt Innovative Approach to Globalisation', *Irish Times*, 9 August 2006.
33. The Information Society Council (2006), *Report to the Finnish Government – Efficiency and Vitality in Future Finland,* Prime Minister's Office, February.

34. Beathnach, C. (1992), *An Fearann Breac*, Dublin: Coiscéim; quoted in Nic Eoin, M. (2004), '*Idir Dhá Theanga*: Irish Language, Culture and the Challenges of Hybridity' in C. Mac Murchaidh (ed.), *'Who Needs Irish?' Reflections on the Importance of the Irish Language Today*, Dublin: Veritas, pp. 131–2.
35. Kirby, P., Gibbons, L. and Cronin, M. (eds.) (2002), *Reinventing Ireland: Culture, Society and the Global Economy*, London: Pluto Press, p. 206.
36. Mathews, P.J. (2005), 'In Praise of 'Hibernocentricism': Republicanism, Globalisation and Irish Culture', *The Republic,* 4, June, p. 12.

Chapter 2

The Irish Revival – Character, Creativity and Self-Reliance

> Now, at a century's remove from the momentous events of that period, it may be an opportune moment to begin a renewed analysis of a legacy that has been neglected, misrepresented and trivialized .... At a time when the homogenizing pressures of globalization on local cultures have registered as a major concern ... the achievements, as well as the failures, of the Irish Revival may have much to teach us about the cultural dynamics of Ireland in the twenty-first century.
>
> P.J. Matthews, 2003[1]

Introduction

The famous American jurist Oliver Wendell Homes once said, 'Continuity with the past is only a necessity and not a duty.'[2] Prospering in a multicultural world requires that individuals understand their own cultural values. Successful intercultural encounters, in fact, demand such individuals. Only people grounded in their own culture can appreciate diversity and the cultural values of others with whom they must co-operate. If not, they are alienated persons, lacking a sense of identity that, ultimately, retards a real enterprising spirit. Self-reliance is an act of emancipation from harmful forms of dependence, and a way of preserving cultural identity. Belgian development expert Thierry Verhelst says:

> It is not simply a question of undertaking a simple 'return' to one's sources (traditionalism or obsession with the past or some kind of deceptive cultural 'purity') but rather of having 'recourse' to the past, so that each people may draw from its own heritage the reasons and means for living, for reconstructing its identity and, if need be, for evolving. For it may be necessary to change in order to safeguard what is essential.[3]

The Irish Revival took place during the period of roughly three decades between the death of Parnell (1891) and the foundation of the Irish Free State (1922). It was a time of turbulence and creativity, ferment and exploration, which kindled a national spirit and stimulated a sense of economic, social, and political optimism and self-confidence. While the network of organisations and initiatives that defined it drew strength and inspiration from a newly rediscovered past, the Irish Revival was simultaneously a revolutionary enterprise, challenging and sometimes overturning established forms in many cultural, commercial and political arenas. This chapter argues that the Revival, often wrongly perceived as an anti-modern literary or narrow cultural movement, was a far broader and richer enterprise. In reaching back to regain the lost legacy of the Revival in order to apply its thinking to today's learning age, we examine its logic and the elements within it that reflected an emerging ethic of identity, self-reliance, creativity and innovation.

Revival: Contemporary Strands

Defining Characteristics

Often viewed as largely an aesthetic or artistic movement with a political dimension, the Revival was actually far broader. Regrettably, much of the attention paid to the Revival focuses on the petty disputes of its leading intellectuals and artists, and obsesses over the faeries of George Russell (poet Æ) and the mystical meanderings of Yeats rather than engaging with the more grounded elements of the Revival that dramatically affected the material and social circumstances of common people. The 'loose cadre of intellectuals' who spearheaded the Revival did so in a variety of spheres, many of them, such as commerce, sport and science, quite concrete and practical.[4] These same leading lights argued that these elements were intertwined: culture could power commerce, language and sport while creating social capital, which in turn could help develop an efficient competitive economy. A shared national identity, self-confidence and sense of place were all prerequisites to the development of *character* and the imperative to be *creative* and *innovative*. While Standish O'Grady, Lady Gregory, W.B. Yeats and others began to shape a new notion of what it meant to be Irish through recreating Ireland from the epics and sagas of an heroic past, Horace Plunkett, more prosaically and practically, was doing something similar in the economic sphere. According to Plunkett:

> Ireland must be recreated from within. The main work must be done in Ireland and the centre of interest must be Ireland. When Irishmen realize this truth, the splendid human power of their country, so much of which runs now idly or disastrously to waste, will be utilized; and we may then look with confidence for the foundation of a fabric of Irish prosperity, framed in constructive thought and laid enduringly in human character.[5]

The Revival represented an energetic and conscious attempt on the part of a small group of intellectuals, artists, social reformers and practical dreamers to recreate a shared sense of Irish identity, or more properly to *create* a new understanding of what it meant to be Irish. This shared sense of Irishness was, of course, contestable terrain and there was no unanimity on what this meant. D.P. Moran and his 'Irish-Irelanders', at one extreme, saw Irish identity as characterised by the exclusive use of the Irish language membership of the Catholic Church, nationalist political beliefs and a refusal to play 'foreign' games.[6] Others like Yeats, Plunkett and Hyde shared a sense of Irish identity that was more inclusive, pluralistic and expansive, with room in the tent for Irish of both traditions and classes. Interestingly, this identity was generally inclusive, at least before the politicisation of the Gaelic League and to a lesser extent the GAA. Anglo-Irish enthusiasts of the language, like Lady Gregory and J.M. Synge, even created their own style of English language coloured with Irish idioms, a form of Irish-English.

Further, and perhaps ironically, many rediscovered their Irish identity by reaching back to the past to reclaim a language, traditions and cultural pride seemingly lost or obscured in some real or imagined Celtic twilight. It was not a one-dimensional stereotype, but a rich and complex concept, open to negotiation, refinement and change.[7] The movement was simultaneously modern, forward-looking and in a sense global, looking abroad for inspiration and new ideas, and eager to learn from as well as play a role in the larger world. For example, Arthur Griffith, founder of Sinn Féin, studied the Hungarian example of a dual-monarchy system with an eye to its application in the Irish political context. Irish co-operative organisers like Plunkett and his associates travelled on the continent to study best practices in agricultural organisation and technology, and Fr Tom Finlay drew from the ideas and practices of the Raiffeisen credit union movement in Germany. The ideas of Denmark's Nikolaj Grundtvig (1782–1873) were later to resonate in the Irish co-operative movement. Grundtvig's folk high schools, which emphasised continuing education for adults and the importance of the study of natural history, language and literature (the old Norse sagas) for the creation of a national identity, all found expression in Plunkett's co-operative philosophy.[8] Pádraic Pearse, strong proponent of the Irish language movement and later a leader of the 1916 Rebellion, was fascinated by the case of Belgium and the manner in which it accommodated its two national languages.[9] Labour organisers like James Connolly and James Larkin were dabbling in international socialism, and political nationalist leaders were busy building both extensive organisational contacts and effective fundraising apparatus abroad in the United States and elsewhere. Ireland was not to become a fortress, sufficient unto itself, but rather a full sovereign participant in the political and economic world.

The various movements that gave shape and form to the Revival were fiercely independent but intrinsically interrelated, and were no less forward looking for being locally rooted. Each, while reaching back to the past for inspiration, served as an incubator of creativity, invention and entrepreneurship in various aspects of national life. They served as dramatic and powerful forces of change that pointed towards a vision of Ireland as politically independent, self-confident, economically prosperous, and spiritually and culturally fulfilled. That this grand project was to later run aground upon the shoals of issues, events and decisions both within and outside of Ireland, is neither surprising nor of particular significance to our purposes here. Although this vision was never articulated as one seamless manifesto, its strands were distinct and the sense of Irish identity it presented was robust, if not uniform. Still, there existed certain core characteristics that were common to many organisations.

Foremost among these was self-reliance, what Plunkett called *character*: the notion that the responsibility for development resided in Irish, not foreign (at the time, British) hands. The Revival was characterised by a broadly based self-help ethos, a forward-looking orientation, and an ambitious and admittedly sometimes utopian agenda. It was rooted in a distinct sense of place and a native self-confidence that grew naturally out of a robust sense of Irish identity and an intimate connection with the natural, social, cultural and human assets of Ireland. The Revival provided a platform for eminently practical co-operative organisers and their initially sceptical farmer members, idealistic patriots, effervescent language enthusiasts and literati of all stripes who contributed to the democratic, experimental, exciting mosaic of the time.[10] From this platform, a diverse sense of Irish identity began to emerge. These broad characteristics constituted in their essentials an underlying structure for this otherwise diverse movement.

Departing from both parliamentary and physical force politics, those involved were nevertheless radical and revolutionary in their outlook, looking inside at themselves and the Irish nation for the solutions to their problems rather than to an English parliament to attend to its 'Irish problem'. Hence, the co-operative movement harnessed the collaborative efforts of Irish farmers in furthering a common agenda, the Gaelic League spearheaded a 'de-Anglicisation' effort through the medium of the Irish language, the GAA banned 'foreign' games in favour of native Irish (and even newly created) sports, the Sinn Féin party emerged to proclaim a manifesto of 'ourselves' and the Irish Literary Theatre explicitly set out to create a national theatre. P.J. Mathews argues:

> The extent to which the self-help movements transformed the social, economic and cultural practices of turn-of-the-century Ireland in a progressive and democratic fashion has yet to be fully recognized. The manner in which they attempted to lead a progamme of social and cultural change that was not anathema to Irish cultural distinctiveness was, perhaps, their greatest achievement and a vitally important contribution to Irish decolonization.[11]

Although their trajectories were to be increasingly diverse, these elements of the Revival movement incorporated certain core principles that combined to foster a new sense of Irish identity. Declan Kiberd holds that the Revival:

> … achieved nothing less than a renovation of Irish consciousness and a new understanding of politics, economics, philosophy, sport, language and culture in its widest sense … the exponents of the Irish Renaissance shaped and reshaped an ancient past, and duly recalled it, giving rise to an unprecedented surge of creativity and self-confidence among the people.[12]

The following sections describe in more detail how, during the Revival, the various movements in the realms of economic organisation, natural history and science, sport and recreation, and language and education, redefined how the Irish people related to one another and to the rest of the world.

Economic Organisation

Among the economic groups were the Irish co-operative movement and the Irish Agricultural Organisation Society (IAOS). Their founder Horace Plunkett best articulated the aspects of the Revival that focused on the development of a native commercial character and a self-help ethos. Plunkett's movement, which encapsulated the 'great co-operative idea', was in reality an all-encompassing campaign of personal transformation and national revitalisation.[13] The co-operative form of organisation itself was expected to help turn the Irish national character towards commercial habits of efficiency, quality and even entrepreneurship. It would inspire the adoption of new technology in agriculture and industrial production and new methods of business practice. The co-operative movement advocated an absolute change of character, and concerned itself with better living, education and the creation of what is now called social capital, those beneficial interconnections among people, and between people and their various communities, that generate symbiotic and reciprocal bonds of personal responsibility and community support. Æ, Plunkett's assistant, thought of these efforts at co-operative organisation as the pursuit of 'the golden heresy of truth' and urged a synthesis of all co-operative efforts into a 'co-operative commonwealth'.[14] Although Plunkett never reached the same fanciful heights as Æ, he did in fact have a rather luminous vision for Ireland, although grounded in the concrete realities that characterised his crusade to improve the material circumstances of the Irish people.

The substance of this movement was neatly encapsulated in Plunkett's well-known slogan of 'better farming, better business, better living'. Similar in purpose to the 'Three F's' of the Land Leaguers, the 'Three Betters' slogan became the rallying cry for the emerging co-operative movement in Ireland, detailing the necessity of reinvigorating agriculture, developing a practical commercial ethos, and, most importantly, fostering a better quality of life for the majority of people.[15] The 'better business' component would, of course, be fostered through the extension of this co-operative movement throughout Irish agriculture and beyond. But, in another step that was unusual for one of his station and class, Plunkett advocated the involvement of the government in fostering the development of 'better farming'. This would occur, not by subsidies and other welfare payments that he felt would sap the commercial vitality of the farmers, but through a judicious application of funding for technical education, new technologies and other methods for developing an agricultural community that would have the wherewithal to help itself. For Plunkett, state aid should only be dispensed 'in such a manner as to stimulate and strengthen the self-reliance of the People'.[16]

The Department of Agriculture and Technical Instruction (DATI) was founded in 1900 as the first 'Home Rule' Irish ministry, primarily through the efforts of Plunkett and a broad-based coalition he painstakingly assembled. It was composed of unionists and nationalists, Protestants and Catholics, spurred on by Plunkett's colleagues and friends in the Irish co-operative movement. The DATI was a radical departure for Ireland, providing the first home-grown and Irish-controlled indigenous Ministry of State with responsibility for the all-important agricultural sector. It introduced a novel, even revolutionary, form of governance that included a significant voice in decision making for representatives of each county's board of agriculture, as well as representation from the co-operative movement.[17] This whiff of democracy was evident at several levels of the DATI and Dublin Castle was essentially an observer. This was a sea change in the handling of such affairs for the Irish, who were accustomed to being governed from Westminster and the Castle.

The brief of the DATI was substantial. In its early years, with Plunkett as its president (the equivalent of minister today), the DATI focused on assessing the state of Irish agriculture, collecting data and building a base of knowledge, systematically and regularly providing technical advice and instruction to Irish farmers. It also fostered innovation and a business-like approach on the part of farmers, introducing the latest in technology to an industry that was severely handicapped and considerably behind the cutting edge agricultural economies in Denmark, Holland and the UK. One of Plunkett's plans was to create a system of technical institutes throughout the country to engage in what would today be called co-operative extension or adult learning. Indeed, it was the expansion and extension of education to places where heretofore it had never appeared that characterised the Department and its legions of experts in its early years.

The co-operative movement was based on a principle of continuing education for all its members. It advocated the provision of libraries to help better the social lives and intellectual environments of its rural membership, and strenuously lobbied the government for the provision of additional funds for education, especially in rural districts.

Plunkett himself, while simultaneously involved with the co-operative movement, a sitting member of parliament and president of the DATI, was also on the board of the Carnegie Foundation, which spearheaded the building of libraries throughout Ireland. Other organisations, like the Irish Countrywomens Association (ICA) and, much later, Macra na Feirme, were founded as associations for women and young people in rural areas, again with an emphasis on community-based education and the enrichment of rural life generally.

However, within all of this, it was the building of character that was, ultimately, Plunkett's primary objective. In addition to new co-operative organisations and technical improvements in agriculture and education (through the DATI), he argued that a commercial ethos would need to be inculcated into the people, but one that valued not just self-capacity but an internal locus of control, the desire for collaborative endeavour and the self-confidence to effect change. Along with these attributes, a community such as Ireland would need to develop 'the business efficiency, the persistence, the sobriety and punctuality – qualities which are far more conducive to success than mere mechanical skill'.[18] The presence of such attributes in the workforce would act as an incentive for capitalists to invest in the industrial development of Ireland. Moral courage, independence of thought and action, thrift and other similar attributes were also a part of Plunkett's vision of character.

R.A. Anderson, the practical idealist who served as Plunkett's right-hand man for the better part of forty years, summed up the Irish co-operative movement best:

> Its fundamental object was to teach the Irish farmer business methods and habits and to conserve to him the profits of his industry, while at the same time giving him a higher and nobler outlook on life, on citizenship, on fellowship with his neighbours. [The organisers] sought to teach Irish farmers the way by which their foreign competitors had made the most of their opportunities, which were, in many cases, far inferior to ours and who had overtaken and even outstripped us. They promised no El Dorado, no Bonanza. They held out only the prospect of hard, methodical and honest work, to be rewarded by increased and improved production and, by means of co-operation, reduced expenses and, therefore, greater profits from the industry, profits which would be shared by the people, alike in country and town, creating prosperity, encouraging industry, thrift and all those things which go to make a people a nation. Above all, the founders aimed … at the inculcation of charity, the greatest of all virtues, without which neither State nor people can survive and prosper.[19]

This brings to mind the Irish proverb, *'ní neart go cur le chéile'*, which translates to 'no strength without combination.' The co-operative movement put this proverb into practice, leading Irish farmers to organise themselves into co-operative organisations that provided them with market power and some sense of economic independence, inculcated a commercial ethos of self-help and self-discipline, and promoted continuing education, innovation and the adoption of cutting edge technology. It balanced all this with a concern for social capital, that is, 'better living' in the sense of reinvigorating rural life and providing opportunities for culture, fellowship and personal growth.

The co-operative movement was truly a national movement, even if it was not an overtly nationalist one.[20] It recognised the unique conditions attending in Ireland and developed a philosophy that was suited to Irish conditions, well coordinated with other contemporary movements like the GAA and the Gaelic League, and consistent with the history and aspirations of the Irish people. It was a way, aside from the political question, for Irish people to declare their independence from the commercial shackles that had, through the embrace of England, bound them for so long. When Plunkett formed the IAOS in 1894, he was certain that he had just started a peaceful revolution. The movement achieved much, but alas, never fulfilled his highest aspirations.[21]

Natural History and Science

Even during the dark days of the Famine, there was interest in Ireland's resource potential, with some recognising the importance of linking science and local resources to stimulate development. For instance, Robert Kane, in his classic *The Industrial Resources of Ireland*, written in 1844, promoted the necessity for Irish education to unite science and practice.[22] This book was described by nationalist leader Thomas Davis as 'almost all it should be', while Prime Minister Robert Peel regarded it as 'one of the best and ablest, because most practical, works I have ever seen.'[23] It became the bible of Irish technological development until well into the next century. Kane was an unusual individual for that time – an Irish Catholic scientist of

European stature. A world-renowned chemist, he was ahead of his time in insisting on the value of practical industrial education. From 1845 to 1867 he ran the highly innovative Museum of Irish Industry, designed to train applied rather than academic scientists. Clara Cullen points out that Kane wrote little on education except for the last few pages in this book. Yet his views on a range of issues were quite close to those of Plunkett. He wrote that 'temperate habits and … the education which the National system will give to every individual … would render us independent of the wretched political differences on which we waste our strengths.'[24]

Scholars have argued that the architects of the Revival (Yeats is often cited), by virtue of an anti-scientific bias, effectively excluded science from the premise upon which the Revival was based.[25] Plunkett and Æ (particularly in his capacity as editor of *The Irish Homestead*) were among the few who did realise the potential of science for development. Æ celebrated the empirical achievements of scientists like Kelvin and Tyndall, and regarded Anglo-Ireland with its contribution to science as the great modernising vehicle in Irish culture.[26] His multicultural ethic was based on the idea that uniformity of culture was bad for creativity, and that diversity in cultures and ideas fosters intellectual vitality.

Between 1780 and 1880 there was a thriving scientific culture in Ireland, but this was in decline by the period of the Revival.[27] Nevertheless, natural history was prominent in the closing decades of the nineteenth century, especially due to the work of Belfast-born naturalist Robert Lloyd Praeger. His work was stimulated by the same motivation as the Revival: an explosive interest in things Irish and a patriotic urge to provide an identity for Ireland while rejecting models imposed from outside. For that matter, natural history shares common characteristics with folklore collecting, as Seán Lysaght points out in his biography of Praeger:

> There was, first of all, an intense attachment to place as the nursery of biological and cultural identity. Secondly, the fieldworker's investigations were stimulated by the patriotic desire to establish

> an independent identity for Ireland against the hegemony of British models. Finally, from these native arenas of place and integrity, there was a reaching out to a wider European context, which the communities of scientists, folklorists, litterateurs and spiritualists felt was theirs as a validating forum for their projects at home.[28]

Science has been defined as 'the history of the human encounter with the natural world' and an integral component of culture.[29] Natural history, while not given due prominence within the cultural movement of the period, nevertheless includes an obvious local component. It might, if given the opportunity, have perhaps contributed to a broader concept of Irish identity within the Revival. Praeger's substantial body of work is certainly sufficient to warrant his inclusion among the giants of the Revival, yet he enjoys no reputation matching that of Yeats, Hyde, Synge or even Plunkett. The reason for this is best illustrated with a brief anecdote. Poet Séamus Heaney once complained that Praeger, who described the Tyrone countryside as lacking topographical interest, was as a scientist regulated too much by rationality, by 'the laws of aesthetics, of science, and not enough by feeling.'[30] Heaney's relationship with landscape is that of the Catholic/Nationalist tradition, based on *Dinnsheanchas*, the Irish word for the lore of place-names. The Protestant/Unionist landscape of Praeger, on the other hand, was a modernised and socialised one that emphasised labour, education and order, expressed in the ordering of the land through the field sciences. Praeger's relationship came from a tradition that occupied the land for a relatively short period. Still, his sense of place, which was that of the scientist and derived from botany, geology and biology was as authentic and legitimate (even though different) as that of Heaney.

Sport and Recreation

The GAA was founded in 1884 by Michael Cusack, a large, bearded, imposing Irish speaker with a short temper and a passionate (and some might say obsessive) commitment to native Irish games like hurling and football. Its purpose was to protect and nurture these games, in the face of increasing competition from 'foreign' ones. By the later part of the nineteenth century indigenous Irish sport was under an assault not unlike that made upon the Irish language. New sports like soccer and rugby, introduced from England, were catching on in the cities (particularly the capital) and were beginning to capture a following even in the more rural areas. Indeed, some expressed fears that cricket would become the national sport, and observed its growing popularity in urban areas like Cork. While the Irish language had retreated to the western perimeter of the island, the old native Irish sporting games, especially hurling, still enjoyed a fairly robust, if unorganised, existence, strongest in the rural regions. Archbishop Thomas Croke, a popular clergyman and well-known nationalist, is credited along with Cusack for providing the GAA with its initial impetus. His letter of reply to an invitation to join the GAA, widely published in newspapers throughout Ireland, had a massive impact:

> One of the most painful, let me assure you, and, at the same time, one of the most frequently recurring reflections that, as an Irishman, I am compelled to make in connection with the present aspect of things in this country, is derived from the ugly and irritating fact that we are daily importing from England not only her manufactured goods, which we cannot help doing, since she has practically strangled our own manufacturing appliances, but, together with her fashions, her accent, her vicious literature, her music, her dances, and her manifold mannerisms, her games also and her pastimes, to the utter discredit of our own grand national sports, and to the sore humiliation, as I believe, of every genuine son and daughter of the old land.[31]

The GAA set itself at correcting this backsliding by 'reinventing' the old Gaelic games, organising leagues that fostered competition based on the old Irish boundaries of townlands, parishes and counties, and actively boycotting participation in foreign games of any sort. In this they were eminently successful.

From its very beginning, the GAA was tied to nationalist political movements and, in fact, to extreme nationalist political parties; indeed, four of the seven founding members were Fenians. It was no accident that when British troopers wished to exact retribution for the assassination of British agents in Ireland during the War of Independence they did so at the GAA's main venue (modern day Croke Park) in Dublin, in what became known as 'Bloody Sunday'.

While the GAA may have lacked the intellectual underpinnings of some of the other organisations, it served to foster local patriotism and rootedness through creating highly charged, locally rooted and emotional sporting events that captured the attention of all, especially young people, adding colour and excitement to a rural social life that had been largely deprived of it. County competitions became foundational. The GAA took an extreme and less encompassing position on what it meant to be Irish. Certainly, its hostility to foreign games became an article of faith. Its linkages with an anti-British, anti-imperialist, pro-physical force republicanism became increasingly pronounced. Yet this movement was at a more grounded level than that of the intellectuals, and could be viscerally understood by local communities that participated in it with such gusto. In the energy it created, the enthusiasm it generated, and the colour, excitement and passion it presented, it further developed the sense of national identity, a distinctive culture, and the rooted nature of these sports in the cultural fabric of the nation.

This sense of identity, deep attachment to one's native place, and grassroots democracy, has persisted well into the modern era. More than 120 years after its foundation, the GAA has never been stronger. As Seán Kelly, a recent president of the GAA, says, 'The latest edition of the rule book states that the Association shall actively support all our major games and promote them, support the Irish language, support camogie and ladies football and support Irish industry. In other words, the GAA encompasses all aspects of culture in this country …'[32] Yet, for all of its current affluence, the GAA remains a locally rooted, grassroots organisation, dependent on volunteerism and based on democratic principles of governance. As its current rule book says:

> Those who play its games, those who organise its activities and those who control its destinies see in the GAA a means of consolidating our Irish identity. The games to them are more than games – they have a national significance – and the promotion of native pastimes becomes a part of the full national ideal, which envisages the speaking of our own language, music and dances. The primary purpose of the GAA is the organisation of native pastimes and the promotion of athletic fitness as a means to create a disciplined, self-reliant, national-minded manhood. The overall result is the expression of a people's preference for native ways as opposed to imported ones.[33]

Language and Education

As far back as 1596, Elizabethan poet and planter Edmund Spenser, said, 'the speech being Irish, the heart must needs be Irish.' Spenser grasped well that by forcing the Irish to abandon their language, their resistance to colonisation would collapse and their allegiance change.[34] Yet Irish was widely spoken into the nineteenth century. It was dealt a seeming deathblow by the ravages and emigration of the famine years, and was left hanging on by a thread in rural areas and particularly on the far west coast of Ireland. As scholar David Greene says, the rate of change in the case of Irish from English was without parallel anywhere in Europe, possibly the world. Indeed, it is almost inconceivable to imagine the pace at which this occurred or the methods used to end the speaking of Irish.[35] Greene describes what he called the 'linguistic suicide' of the Irish people during the mid-nineteenth century. Parents who knew little or no English were not content that their children should learn English at school. They went even further, insisting the children not speak Irish at all, amazing behaviour since parents usually like to talk to their children in their own language even if they think it best for them to use another in the outside world.

Sir William Wilde (father of Oscar) described this self-policing in detail, after visiting a cottage in Connemara in 1843:

> The children gathered round to have a look at the stranger, and one of them, a little boy about eight years of age, addressed a short sentence in Irish to his sister, but, meeting the father's eye, he immediately cowered back, having, to all appearance, committed some heinous fault. The man called the child to him, said nothing, but drawing forth from its dress a little stick, commonly called a scoreen or tally, which was suspended by a string round the neck, put an additional notch in it with his penknife. Upon our enquiring into the cause of this proceeding, we were told that it was done to prevent the child speaking Irish; for every time he attempted to do so a new nick was put in his tally, and when these amounted to a certain number, summary punishment was inflicted on him by the schoolmaster.

Parents usually shield their children from what is bad. They do not throw away items of value or relinquish them easily; they wish to leave them to their children. In an insightful book *The Great Silence*, which examines the relationships between the loss of the language and national well-being, Seán de Fréine says Irish and all it signified must have been repellent to a child seeing it treated so contemptuously.[36] He describes the impact of this cataclysmic rupture on community values, culture, traditions and, without any doubt, the Irish character, in tones that resonate even today:

> In Ireland, material considerations came to outweigh all others when the institutions on which social life rested were abandoned or undermined for material advantage. Simultaneously with the decline in the language many social occasions – pilgrimages, fairs, gatherings and traditional customs – which hitherto provided

> young people with natural settings and structures for coming together, were suppressed or vanished. And the young, who might have turned a deaf ear to excessive materialism in a society where they could develop their own personalities normally, were left defenceless to its influence in a world of crumbling customs and limited linguistic ability.[37]

During the Revival the Irish language was rediscovered, paralleling developments in recreation and economic organisation. Attempts were made to reinstate it as the language of everyday life and commerce. Yet, by that stage, the language, after a period of steady erosion, was in rapid decline. Worse yet, it was the language of the poverty-stricken, the tongue of ignorance and indigence, and carried the stigma of this. Many who spoke it in everyday life did not wear it as a badge of honour, but rather as a mark of shame. Shortly after the fall of Parnell, a small group of academics and enthusiasts set out to change this. Chief among these promoters of the language was Douglas Hyde, a Protestant minister's son from County Roscommon, who, along with Eoin MacNeill, a Catholic from County Antrim, founded the Gaelic League in 1893.

The League's purpose was to foster the use of the Irish language and support native literature and arts. It was an intellectual, spiritual and even industrial movement. Yet, as the late scholar, writer and poet Seán Ó Tuama argued, in its heyday it was above all else a radical educational organisation.[38] Central to its philosophy was the development of the individual Irish personality. It was radical in its insistence that this personality could not reach its potential except within a community or cultural milieu proper to it. Its notion was that creative, integrated personalities cannot normally be produced without a creative and integrated community having a unique and continuing experience of its own. Again, the imperative was that Ireland needed to travel its own path, retrieving its traditions, customs and language, and building upon it a distinct, modern, forward-looking society, connected to the past but not enslaved by it.

Hyde saw the language as the very embodiment of Irish cultural identity, as being deeply symbolic, and the repository of Irish history and traditions.[39] As historian F.S.L. Lyons notes, this was consistent with the recreation of a distinct Irish identity, separate and unique from the colonial Empire, reflecting 'an interest in the Irish past, in the sagas and annals, the creation of an illustrious history. [With this] the care of the language passed into the keeping of scholars, aficionados, who sought to revive it.'[40] To Hyde, rescuing the language was far more important than politics or the 'Irish Question'. Hyde's only 'Irish Question' dealt with the language, not with the relationship between Ireland and the Empire. A lucid contemporary account of the Gaelic League's ideals, written, ironically, by an English journalist who spent only a matter of months in Ireland, stated:

> [Dr. Hyde] has discovered and proclaimed a great truth – the truth that Ireland is ceasing to be Irish. That is no paradox. The nineteenth century crushed out of the Irish people nearly all the characteristics that made them a distinctive entity. It found them Irish; it left them imitation English. It destroyed their language, their pastimes, their music, their special social atmosphere. One by one the links that bound them to their past were snapped.[41]

In the Gaelic League, and typical of many interactions during the Revival period, there was much cross-over with other cultural and political organisations. Many of the leaders of the 1916 Rebellion, and the subsequent War of Independence, had been inspired by virtue of their involvement with the Gaelic League and in their turn radicalised and politicised the Gaelic League (much to Hyde's dismay). Pádraic Pearse, Thomas McDonagh and Éamon de Valera were among them. This generation was inspired by the retelling and recreation of Irish historical lore, inflamed with a passionate love for the language, possessed of a youthful bias for action, and fiercely committed to the ideal of an independent and sovereign Irish nation.

As an illustration of the image against which the Gaelic League had to fight, Hyde recounted the tale of a woman toff who remarked, when she heard he himself was an Irish-speaker, that 'he cannot be a gentleman if he speaks Irish.'[42] Hyde is remembered for any number of reasons. Among them is his Irish poetry in translation such as *Love Songs of Connaught* and his election as the first president of the Republic of Ireland in 1948. His short speech entitled *The Necessity for De-Anglicising Ireland*, given in late 1892, provides a comprehensive outline of the reasons for and goals of the Gaelic League and the language movement. In this speech, Hyde said:

> When we speak of 'the necessity for de-anglicising the Irish nation', we mean it, not as a protest against imitating what is best in the English people, for that would be absurd, but rather to show the folly of neglecting what is Irish, and hastening to adopt, pell-mell, and indiscriminately, everything that is English, simply because it is English.[43]

This is hardly an indiscriminate trashing of England or foreign influence, but rather attended to Hyde's complaint that the Irish were 'ceasing to be Irish without becoming English' and his criticism that the Irish were aping British fashions, trends, books and entertainments while they were agitating against British rule politically. Of course, the most egregious Irish offence of all was the jettison of Irish and adoption of English. All these, Hyde argued, needed to be rectified.

Hyde suggested that Ireland was in danger of becoming a 'nation of imitators … lost to the power of native initiative and alive only to second-hand assimilation'. He closed his speech by saying:

> I appeal to every one whatever his politics – for this is no political matter – to do his best to help the Irish race to develop in future upon Irish lines, even at the risk of encouraging national

> aspirations, because upon Irish lines alone can the Irish race once more become what it was of yore – one of the most original, artistic, literary and charming peoples of Europe.[44]

To Hyde, the Irish language, if revived, would benefit the character, self-confidence and cultural identity of the Irish people. It would do this by keeping alive the connection with the living tissue of Irish history and traditions, and therefore foster the native creativity and innovation of an independent, proud and self-reliant people. This is a point that historian Tom Garvin downplays perhaps too much when, in describing the consequences of linguistic revival, he argues that the 'smothering capabilities' of Irish as a revived language were great whereas its creative capabilities were relatively limited.[45]

Irish Revival: Legacy

Cultural Identity

During the Revival, there was widespread discussion on how the Irish nation or Irish nationality might be defined or, indeed, if these concepts had any meaning at all. Stephen Brown, in two 1912 articles in the Jesuit journal *Studies*, examined elements of the physical environment, race, language, custom, religion, common interests, history and national governance.[46] He developed a broad definition of identity, which reflected a relatively large body of people living together in a common territory in organised social relations, held together in a kind of spiritual oneness. This 'oneness' was composed of two things, namely memories of historic events shared and suffered in common and actual consent to carry on life as distinct people in charge of their own destiny and shaping their own future. He quoted G.K. Chesterton, who said of the Irish capacity for assimilation: 'Rome conquered nations, but Ireland has conquered races.'[47]

With the political partition of the island in the 1920s, a common or distinctive Irish identity hardly seemed conceivable. Some thirty years ago, before the momentous events of recent years, historian Liam De Paor said of the Republic, 'it is not a sense of identity which sustains the State but the State, for the moment, which sustains a sense of national identity.'[48] De Paor claimed that a broad cultural definition of Irish identity had failed to gain even a 'tenuous verbal hold' on the elites who had governed Irish society since independence. Fintan O'Toole summarises the sentiments of many:

> Many of us may be glad to see the back of holy Ireland, martyred Ireland, and peasant Ireland. Most of us may have wanted nothing so much as to be normal, prosperous Europeans. But what, now that we have arrived, is left to us? What, if anything, is distinctively ours?[49]

Outsiders often have the detachment necessary to offer insights. After a long visit, Australian critic and poet Vincent Buckley wrote in his book *Memory Ireland* about the ambivalence of the Irish.[50] Buckley wrote out of deep cultural and personal links with Ireland and felt the country's loss of national memory intensely. He claimed the Irish, spurred on by politicians, ecclesiastics, media operators and revisionist historians, merely possess a sense of 'corporate identity'. This identity contradicts the one that preceded it, one based on the Easter 1916 Rising and its aftermath. Although that identity had initially proved exhilarating, it became wearying, even to those who had fought to realise it. He blamed this memory loss on a society that is both too rigidly confining and too casually dispersing. Describing the current orthodoxy, he wrote:

> Ireland is not a nation, once again or ever, so the new story runs, but two nations: maybe several; it does not have its characteristic religion – or, if it does, it ought not; it does not have its characteristic language, as anyone can see or hear; it has no particular race or ethnic integrity. Ireland is nothing – a no-thing – an interesting

> nothing, to be sure, composed of colourful parts, a nothing mosaic. It is advertising prose and Musak.[51]

In a more hopeful vein, Michael Mays argues that national identities, far from being extinguished by globalisation, are being reconstituted and renewed in a productive interchange between the global and the local.[52] Mays suggests that Irish identity, which took shape in opposition to Britishness, is being refurbished again, more diversely, but no less vitally. Disconnected from any ancestral or traditional ties to place or landscape, this is an 'uprooted' notion of Irish identity. It represents a sense of 'at-homeness' which many new immigrants, he says, discover for themselves in Ireland. It is the sense of identity that permeates *McCarthy's Bar*, a best-selling account of a British-born journalist's travels in the west of Ireland, defined by hospitality, sociability, acceptance, and a relaxed, good-natured view of the world.[53] Like the ubiquitous Irish pub, now to be found in most decent-sized cities around the world, this Irishness has proven remarkably portable, and represents one of Ireland's most valuable and marketable exports. The Irish pub, ironically called 'the local' by patrons back home, has gone global.

Sense of Place

In Ireland, ironically, a lack of concern for design and aesthetic quality tends to go hand in hand with a preoccupation with place.[54] This affinity with place (it can hardly be called a sense of place) appears to have little to do with tending, cultivating or enhancing the material environment. As Patrick Sheeran argues, there is the paradox of a professed allegiance to places together with an almost total inability to care for them.[55] This nominal sense of place would suggest that it is sufficient merely to name a place to mark one's attachment to it. The place itself is of subsidiary importance; there is little actual need to *care* for it. Sheeran notes the distinction between the terms 'to live' or 'to inhabit', and 'to dwell', which he interprets as 'to be at peace in a protected place.' Historically, he writes, 'the Anglo-Irish dwelt in a land to which they did not belong and the Irish belonged to a land in which they did not dwell.' This remains true today where it appears that the Irish obsession with owning property passes for a more profound sense of place.

The privatisation of the landscape through the seemingly unregulated growth of individualised bungalows, disrespectful of context and community, assertively indicates a denial of any communal sense of Ireland's past.[56] Further evidence of contemporary Ireland's weak links with place can be seen in a country (ironically characterised by its 'green' and wholesome reputation) whose urban streets, motorways and even country boreens are often lined with litter.[57] Granted, the Tidy Towns competition, which started in 1958 and now has 700 competitive entrants annually, is a wonderful attempt at fostering civic pride in places where it did not previously exist. Illegal burning of rubbish is common and a network of giant illegal landfills pockmark the country. This reflects the antithesis of a learning society, which is fundamentally concerned with values, culture, quality, and the historical social, cultural and natural context of a place.

In his book *The Ex-Isle of Erin*, Fintan O'Toole remarks that in Irish the term *sa bhaile,* equivalent to the English 'at home', is never used in the narrow sense of home as a dwelling.[58] It implies instead a wider sense of a place in the world, a feeling of belonging that is buried deep within the word's meaning. This feeling of being 'at home' or 'belonging' represents a deeply rooted sense of place that anchors one's identity. A sense of place anchoring Irish identity, as one scholar put it, should be 'bound up with memory, identity, caring, and articulating the true nature of past experiences so as to creatively engage the present and through that the future.'[59] Joe Lee writes that a sense of place provides a weapon against the levelling principles of economic determinism, arguing there is a clear conflict of interest between:

> …those who worship at the alter of the Tiger, red in tooth and claw, who hold that those in a position to do so should rip off

> whatever they can and the devil take the hindmost, where the individual is the measure of all things, and one's sole duty is to oneself and, on the other hand, those who believe in some idea of society. For the first set of believers, place has no sense whatever, except in a purely functional and opportunistic way. For the second, place has a significant sense, though how it relates to other values needs to be worked out.[60]

Certainly, the notion of a sense of place shapes Irish identity, which in turn has dramatic impact on the relationship of the Irish with the natural world, with their native language and, ultimately, with their international competitiveness. The religion of the ancient Celts was a nature religion.[61] The integrity of all forms of life and interconnectedness with nature were defining elements of this world. It is a pity that, during the Revival, those who re-imagined a new Ireland founded on a Celtic past did not offer more empathy in practice with the non-human.

A major deficiency of the Revival as an important element in defining Irish culture was the exclusion of a more significant role for science, especially natural history which was enjoying great vibrancy at the time, especially among Protestants in the northern part of the island. By not adding this broader scientific dimension to the concept of culture, and not appreciating the powerful contribution that scientific thinking and endeavour could make, the Revival passed up a powerful opportunity to put in train a multi-dimensional or more integrated path to development than the one subsequently pursued by the State.[62] By not appreciating properly Ireland's heritage in natural history, it probably contributed to the erosion of a sense of place, the degradation of the natural environment and the weakening of civic culture in the Republic, as the country underwent industrialisation and became structurally integrated with a global capital and technology infrastructure. If science had played a central role in the Revival, it could conceivably have resulted in a more enlightened attitude to a range of issues such as planning, the environment and rural development. Consequently, Ireland today is not well prepared to face the implications of moving to a more sustainable state; such movement is essential given the EU's emphasis on sustainability as a core objective of national development.

During the Revival, natural history and science played a significant role in nurturing an identity founded on place. Yet such contributions to the development of a distinct Irish identity and sense of place have not been widely recognised despite a number of recent works that examine the socio-cultural history of science and technology in Ireland.[63] John Wilson Foster complains that, in spite of the splendour of Irish literature, he finds the idea of culture promulgated by the Revival thin and unrealistic. The reason is that 'industry, business, science, rationalism, religious Dissenter, the middle class, formal education and democracy – in sum, the bulk of Ulster Protestant culture, were given no important instruments to play'.[64] A broad concept of Irish culture must include an appreciation of this broader heritage of scientific and technological achievement, as well as the potential contribution of immigrants committed to their new home.[65]

E. Estyn Evans, Welsh-born geographer and first director of the Institute for Irish Studies at Queen's University, Belfast, placed Irish identity within the context of the vast time scales of geology. Evans believed that a renewal of a sense of place and the relationship with the land were essential to forge a rich creative spirit throughout the island. He argued that a landscape and people could not be understood except in relation to each other.[66] Evans saw that the clash of native and newcomer, repeated over and over again in Ireland, had struck the sparks for a great blossoming of Irish culture. He held that the solitary farm, a hallmark of rural living in Ireland in a way almost unheard of in other parts of Europe, left a unique mark on Irish character, giving it a certain roughness and independence. At a seminar entitled 'Understanding Ourselves', held in the early 1970s at Benburb, Co. Armagh, he captured how place can determine outlook in the two traditions:

> In Ulster where you find the drumlins you will hear the drums, for the Protestant planters usually chose the most fertile lowland areas, and I suspect that people living in such closed-in lowlands with restricted horizons tend to have limited vision and imagination. I always like to contrast this kind of hidden landscape – Protestant landscape, shall we say? – with the open, naked bogs and hills which are naturally areas of vision and imagination, which are poetic and visionary and which represent the other tradition in Ulster.[67]

Yet Evans maintained that precisely such diversity in heritage and outlook could be a great source of strength in Northern Ireland, when there was acceptance of what he called 'common ground' in the emotions which bind people to a particular place. Evans was convinced that more use of the legends of ancient Ireland in the educational system offered a great opportunity for nurturing understanding, a sense of place and the development of this 'common ground'.

Relevance for Competitiveness

Many involved in the Revival saw Ireland's history (both cultural and natural) and a renewed sense of place as keys to harnessing a spirit of self-discovery or, to use the modern term, *innovation.* Issues of national identity, character development and community were central to economic organisation in the co-operative movement, the development of native industries, and the relationship between business and government. Nevertheless, there is a view even in modern Ireland that equates a preference for the national over the international with being somehow backward or provincial. A recent Irish newspaper editorial illustrates such a mentality. Commenting on the strong domestic demand for the work of Irish artists, the leader writer maintains that this somehow 'reflects a conservatism and a narrowness of artistic taste that seems outdated in this multicultural and globalised world.'[68]

Reclaiming the spirit, effervescence, diversity and creativity of the Revival in order to harness the resources necessary to build a successful society can produce a process of economic development that is socially, environmentally and culturally sustainable. Achieving this vision will not be by virtue of serendipitous chance or a helter-skelter pragmatic adaptation to a dynamic global economy. Rather, it will require a sea change in the Irish conception of sustainable competitive advantage, recognition of the wide range of indigenous resources that can contribute to its creation, and a re-imagining of a successful society, embedded in a global economic network.

In attempting to foster a sustainable competitive advantage, Ireland could study with profit initiatives undertaken during the Revival. For example, Plunkett chose a tack that would make Ireland more self-reliant and economically independent, commercially successful, modern and internationalised. He argued that it could develop economically and socially, thereby achieving its full potential. He believed in the necessity of applying science to development, and advanced modern ideas of social capital, resource efficiency and sustainability. He put great store in practical approaches, while taking particular account of the wider social and cultural context. A spirit of enterprise, personal responsibility, moral courage, self-reliance, national feeling, citizenship and welfare was a driving force in the development vision of Plunkett and Æ. There are lessons to be drawn from this work in the wider Irish economy, not just in agriculture, food and rural development. The concept of well-being and quality of life was also central to their message. The following sentiments by Æ appear to be just as relevant today as when they were written in 1917:

> All these energetic people are conspiring to build factories and mills and to fill them with human labour, and they believe the more they do this the better it will be for Ireland. They talk of Ireland as if it was only admirable as a quantity rather than a quality. They express delight at swelling statistics and increased trade,

> but where do we hear any reflection on the quality of life engendered by this industrial development.[69]

The co-operative vision of Plunkett and Æ to break the vicious circle of low productivity was likely crippled by partition and the land policies of successive Free State governments. There is no doubt but that from the 1920s to the 1940s, the Irish State had a limited understanding of the process of transformation of scientific research into social utility. Ireland was not allowed to develop as did Denmark, for example, where a link between scientific competence and the development of a quality food export market was demonstrated in a domain where science and practice were inseparable.[70]

A sense of self-help characterised all of the strands of the Revival movement. However, even an organisation as overtly practical as the IAOS also paid attention to the quality of life of the rural communities that composed its membership. Along with the self-help dimension came a focus on participation and local democratic governance, and a heightened emphasis on education. Plunkett, for example, held that the Irish education system of the time ill prepared people for industry, turning as he put it 'our youth into a generation of second-rate clerks, with a distinct distaste for any industrial or productive occupation, in which such qualities as initiative, self-reliance, or judgment were called for.'[71] He faulted this system for lacking a national component, for virtually ignoring Ireland and things Irish, and for being excessively theoretical instead of practical.[72] He saw that an emphasis on an Irish identity was essential to encourage pride in place, self-respect and citizenship. Such wisdom could effectively still inform Irish educational policy today.

Common to all Revival movements was a shared sense of place and pride, both at national and local level, characterised by a rootedness of their activities in a rich local cultural, social and physical context. Overriding all else was the sense of being distinctly, uniquely Irish, possessors of a proud history and endowed with a rich culture. The Revival was also thoroughly modern, despite turning its back on certain (primarily English) contemporary fashions and trends. As Declan Kiberd writes:

> The alleged anti-modern element in Irish revivalism, of which revisionist historians have made so much, turns out on inspection to be a prophetic critique of mass-culture and of the vulgarisation of popular taste.[73]

Douglas Hyde and the Gaelic League held that Ireland could reclaim its own distinctive language to the benefit of its sense of cultural identity, national self-confidence and future distinctiveness. The GAA promoted a robust form of Irish identity through sport, teamwork and co-operation, deeply rooted in a hierarchy of local communities and conducive to a more developed sense of cultural self-knowledge and self-reliance. All of the organisations that collectively constituted the Revival advanced some facet of the practical patriotism needed to illustrate a new sense of Irish identity. The Revival provided the germ of a national rebirth, a renaissance, culturally, socially and economically. Most, but not all, connected with the Revival awaited solution to the political question, in the hope that it would provide the Revival with the institutions of State necessary to give more permanent and material effect to its ideals. This, for many reasons, failed to happen. Now, Ireland has another opportunity to develop a national project that could incorporate the ethos, principles and passion of the Revival. The inculcation of this ethos must start with the creation of a learning society that will foster innovation, creativity and, ultimately, competitiveness.

The foundations of the Revival offer a broad set of parameters for contemporary Irish policy-makers in navigating a course that is economically, socially and environmentally sustainable. As Kiberd puts it:

> The need is to reopen ourselves to the cultural philosophy of Hyde, Yeats, Hannah Skeffington and that whole revivalist

> generation, whose project is still incomplete. That generation had awesome cultural self-belief; ours now has the economic acumen. Blended, the two forces might form a constellation to unleash entirely new energies. To do that, however, as President Mary McAleese said, we must make a pact with our past and see in it the very source of our modernity rather than an impediment to further modernisation... If a certain intolerance for our past must become the sign of our current tolerance and modernity, then we will deny ourselves that sense of momentum from the past which points a clear way towards the future, a future which is exhilarating to precisely the extent that it is unknown and unknowable. And if we deprive ourselves of our own past, as some revisionists seem to desire, we would simply be surrendering to the oldest colonial trick of all – the denial of the native's own history.[74]

Contrary to popular impressions, the Revival did not advocate a return to some sort of pre-modern Golden Age or Celtic paradise. Rather, it contributed greatly to a sense of innovation and a spurt of creativity in the arts, culture, sport, nature study and commerce. Experimentation in all of these areas was rife, belying the image of the Revival as a strictly literary affair. Although the sciences were not central to most revival thinking, certainly Plunkett, Æ and others in the co-operative movement advanced a more scientific approach to the understanding and solution of Ireland's development problems. The movement was in many ways international and outward, with many of these groups in touch with the latest thinking in economics, government and politics around the world. The Revival itself was an invention, a creative enterprise in imagining an Irish identity and then retrofitting it onto a glorious past that was also largely a product of the imagination. The Revival 'subscribed to a broad civic nationalism [drawing] on the ideas of co-operation, republicanism, socialism and anti-imperialism.'[75]

Today, a renewed sense of identity need not confine itself to one part of the island. There is a general acceptance, regardless of political persuasion, that the island of Ireland is too small to compete successfully without cross-border co-operation. Since the advent of a power-sharing executive in Northern Ireland, relations between North and South are on a changed footing. In this context, it is surely worth examining how Irish identity might influence the island's overall competitiveness. It is also especially timely given the widespread levels of inward migration over the past decade. A sense of roots (cultural, historical and social) is essential to locate oneself in context, and to appreciate the values and traditions of others. After all, with greater self-confidence there is usually a greater curiosity and openness to the outsider. Yet many immigrants note that the Irish appear to lack a clear sense of themselves and their own culture.[76] This suggests that a redefinition of society will require a great leap in imagination, requiring the Irish to reinvest the mental framework through which they view identity, citizenship, sovereignty and belonging. Exploring a common Irish identity, founded on a profound sense of place and a shared purpose, involving both North-South and 'New Irish' dimensions, is full of exciting promise.

The recent unionist-nationalist power-sharing arrangements in the North and the Green Party's emergence as a Coalition partner in Government in the South make this an especially good time to analyse the issues raised here. To achieve a sustainable and successful learning society, one that is innovative, distinctive and internationally competitive, the country needs to draw on the wisdom of the past and on resources rooted in place, especially those derived by harnessing all the country's scientific, natural and cultural traditions.

The Revival, with initiatives in commerce, agriculture, recreation, education, literature, language and natural science, offers useful lessons today. It is fascinating to consider what a marriage of capability, creativity, innovation, culture, identity, and sense of place might mean for future competitiveness. How Ireland might develop such a sustainable competitive advantage, founded on what we call a New-Revival framework, is the topic of the next chapter.

Notes

1. P.J. Matthews (2003), *Revival: The Abbey Theatre, Sinn Féin, The Gaelic League and the Co-operative Movement*, Notre Dame IN: University of Notre Dame Press, p. 148.
2. Taken from 1899 *Harvard Law Review*, 12 (443), quoted in Posner, E. (ed.) (1997), *The Essential Holmes: Letters, Speeches, Judicial Opinions and Other Writings of Oliver Wendell Holmes, Jr.*, Chicago: University of Chicago Press.
3. Verhelst, T.G. (1990), *No Life without Roots: Culture and Development*, London: Zed Books, p. 159.
4. Matthews, *Revival*, p. 147.
5. Plunkett, H.C. (1904), *Ireland in the New Century*, London: John Murray, pp. 108–9.
6. For a short biographical study of the life and views of D.P. Moran, see Maume, P. (1995), *D.P. Moran*, Life and Times No. 4, Dundalk: Dundalgan Press.
7. Kiberd, D. (1996), *Inventing Ireland: The Literature of the Modern Nation*, London: Random House, p. 1.
8. Plunkett was impressed by the folk high school movement started by Grundtvig, citing it favourably in *Ireland in the New Century* (p. 131). For a review of this movement, refer to Borish, S.M. (1991), *The Land of the Living: The Danish Folk High Schools and Denmark's Non-Violent Path to Modernization*, Nevada City, CA: Blue Dolphin.
9. Ó Buachalla, S. (ed.) (1980), *A Significant Irish Educationist: The Educational Writings of P.H. Pearse*, Cork: Mercier Press.
10. Matthews, *Revival*, p. 146.
11. Matthews, *Revival*, p. 146.
12. Kiberd, D. (1996), *Inventing Ireland*, p. 3 and p. 641.
13. Bolger, P. (1977), *The Irish Co-operative Movement: Its History and Development*, Dublin: Institute of Public Administration, p. 402. Bolger uses the term 'great co-operative idea'.
14. Russell, G.W. (1916), *The National Being*, Dublin: Maunsel and Co.

15. Perhaps not surprisingly, this slogan was later appropriated by US President Theodore Roosevelt as part of his own movement to reinvigorate rural life in the United States through the Country Life Commission.
16. Bolger, *The Irish Co-operative Movement,* p. 85.
17. The Irish county councils had just been instituted through legislation (Local Government of Ireland Act) in 1898.
18. Plunkett, *Ireland in the New Century*, p. 307.
19. Anderson, R.A. (1935), *With Horace Plunkett in Ireland*, London: Macmillan, pp. 285–6.
20. The leaders of the co-operative movement were largely Protestant and many, but not all, were Unionist in their political sympathies. Certainly, Horace Plunkett and R.A. Anderson were unionist, while George Russell (Æ), a Protestant by birth, was nationalist in his orientation. Fr Finlay, the vice president of the IAOS for decades, was a staunch nationalist. Given Ireland at the time, this makes the co-operative movement a fascinating study.
21. See Ó Gráda, C. (1977), 'The Beginnings of the Irish Creamery System 1880–1914', *The Economic History Review*, 30(2), pp. 284–305, for a thorough review of the early days of the co-operative movement and a comparison of co-operative and proprietary creameries. In 1906, the share of creameries which were co-operative was roughly twice as high in Denmark as in Ireland. A recent paper (O'Rourke, K.H. (2007), 'Culture, Conflict and Cooperation: Irish Dairying Before the Great War', *The Economic Journal*, 117(521), October, pp. 1357–79) demonstrates that this was due to political, not cultural or religious, reasons. Denmark was a relatively homogeneous society whereas political divisions in late nineteenth- and early twentieth-century Ireland resulted in less enthusiasm for the co-operative form of enterprise.
22. For a review of Kane's life and work see Wheeler, T.S. (1944), 'Sir Robert Kane: Life and Work; Part I: 1809–1844', *Studies*, 33(130), June, pp. 158–68 and Wheeler, T.S. (1944), 'Sir Robert Kane: Life and Work; Part II: 1844–1890', *Studies*, 33(131), September, pp. 316–20. For a contemporary criticism of Kane's book, see Hancock, W.N.

(1849), 'On the Economic Causes of the Present State of Agriculture in Ireland: Part VI', paper read before The Dublin Statistical Society.

23. Cullen, C. (2007), 'The Museum of Irish Industry, Robert Kane and education for all in the Dublin of the 1850s and 1860s', *History of Education*, July, pp. 1–14.
24. Cullen, 'The Museum of Irish Industry', p. 4.
25. See, for example, Foster, J.W. (1991), 'Natural Science and Irish Culture', *Éire-Ireland*, 26(2), pp. 92–103; Johnston, R. (1983), 'Science and Technology in Irish National Culture', *The Crane Bag*, 7, pp. 58–63; Lysaght, S. (1996), 'Themes in the Irish History of Science', *The Irish Review*, 19(1), pp. 87–97.
26. Allen, N. (2003), *George Russell (Æ) and the New Ireland, 1905–30*, Dublin: Four Courts Press.
27. Davies, G.H. (1985), 'Irish Thought in Science' in R. Kearney (ed.), *The Irish Mind*, Dublin: Wolfhound Press, pp. 294–310.
28. Lysaght, S. (1998), *Robert Lloyd Praeger: The Life of a Naturalist*, Dublin: Four Courts Press.
29. Outram, D. (1986), 'Negating the Natural: Or Why Historians Deny Irish Science', *The Irish Review*, 1, pp. 45–9.
30. Lysaght, S. (1989), 'Heaney vs. Praeger: Contrasting Natures', *The Irish Review*, 7(1), pp. 68–74.
31. Croke, T.W. (1884), 'The Gaelic Athletic Association', letter published in the *Freeman's Journal*, 24 December.
32. Kelly, S. (2006), 'The GAA – Reflecting all that is Good in Irish Culture' in J. Mulholland (ed.), *The Soul of Ireland: Issues of Society, Culture and Identity*, Dublin: Liffey Press.
33. GAA Central Council (2007), *Gaelic Athletic Association Official Guide, Part 1*, Dublin, p. 3.
34. Spenser, E. (1970, 1596), *A View of the Present State of Ireland*, Oxford: Oxford University Press, p. 68.
35. Greene, D. (1972), 'The Founding of the Gaelic League' in S. Ó Tuama (ed.), *The Gaelic League Idea*, Cork: Mercier Press, pp. 9–19 (see p. 10).
36. De Fréine, S. (1978), *The Great Silence*, Cork: Mercier Press.
37. De Fréine, *The Great Silence*, pp. 81–82.

38. Ó Tuama, S. (1972), 'The Gaelic League Idea in the Future' in S. Ó Tuama (ed.), *The Gaelic League Idea*, Cork: Mercier Press, pp. 98–109.
39. Biographies of Douglas Hyde include Dunleavy, J.E. and Dunleavy, G.W. (1991), *Douglas Hyde: A Maker of Modern Ireland*, Berkeley, CA: University of California Press and Ó Lúing, S. (1973), 'Douglas Hyde and the Gaelic League', *Studies*, 62(246), Summer, pp. 123–38.
40. Lyons, F.S.L. (1963), *Ireland Since the Famine*, London: Fontana Press, p. 244.
41. Brooks, S. (1907), *The New Ireland*, Dublin: Maunsel & Co., p. 20.
42. Kiberd, D. (1993), 'Douglas Hyde: A Radical in Tory Clothing?' *Irish Reporter*, 11, pp. 18–20 (see p. 19).
43. Hyde, D. (1894), 'The Necessity for De-Anglicising Ireland' in *The Revival of Irish Literature: Addresses by Sir Charles Gavan Duffy, Dr. George Sigerson and Dr. Douglas Hyde,* London: Fisher Unwin, pp. 117–61.
44. Hyde, 'The Necessity for De-Anglicising Ireland', p. 34.
45. Garvin, T. (2004), *Preventing the Future: Why Ireland was so Poor for so Long*, Dublin: Gill & Macmillan, p. 44.
46. Brown, S.J. (1912), 'What is a Nation?' *Studies*, 1(3), September, pp. 496–510 and Brown, S.J. (1912), 'The Question of Irish Nationality', *Studies*, 1(4), December, pp. 634–54.
47. Brown, 'The Question of Irish Nationality', p. 639.
48. De Paor, L. (1979), 'Ireland's Identities', *The Crane Bag*, 3(1), pp. 22–29 (see p. 29).
49. *Irish Times*, 28 December 1999. Taken from Kirby, P. (2002), 'Contested Pedigrees of the Celtic Tiger' in P. Kirby, L. Gibbons and M. Cronin (eds.), *Reinventing Ireland: Culture Society and the Global Economy*, London: Pluto Press, pp. 109–23 (see p. 23).
50. Buckley, V. (1985), *Memory Ireland: Insights into the Contemporary Irish Condition*, Victoria, Australia: Penguin Books.
51. Buckley, *Memory Ireland*, p. ix.
52. Mays, M. (2005), 'Irish identity in an Age of Globalisation', *Irish Studies Review*, 13(1), February, pp. 3–12.
53. McCarthy, P. (2003), *McCarthy's Bar: A Journey of Discovery in the West of Ireland*, New York: St Martin's Press.

54. Frank McDonald, environment editor of the *Irish Times*, has written many articles and books that catalogue the destruction, contempt for heritage, sloppy thinking, wild speculation, fortunes made, political chicanery, bureaucratic incompetence and pandering to vested interests that characterise many aspects of Irish planning. See, for instance, McDonald, F. (1985), *The Destruction of Dublin*, Dublin: Gill & Macmillan; McDonald, F. (1989), *Saving the City*, Dublin: Tomar Publishing; McDonald, F. (2000), *The Construction of Dublin,* Kinsale, Co. Cork: Gandon Editions; McDonald, F. and Nix, J. (2005), *Chaos at the Crossroads,* Kinsale Co. Cork: Gandon Books.
55. Sheeran, P. (1988), '*Genius Fabulae*: The Irish Sense of Place', *Irish University Review*, 18, pp. 191–206.
56. Whelan, K. (1992), 'The Power of Place', *The Irish Review*, 12, pp. 13–20.
57. Many Irish people and businesses realise the damage done by litter to Ireland's international image. For instance, the organisation Irish Business Against Litter (IBAL) was set up in 1996 as an alliance of companies who believe that litter has a significant impact on Irish economic well-being. IBAL argues that the main sources of Irish prosperity – tourism, foreign investment and food industries – all depend on an image of Ireland as a clean and green island. It realises that Ireland, now a high-cost destination for visitors, has to offer first-class standards of cleanliness. In 2007, IBAL ranked Dublin as the dirtiest city in Europe with Latvian capital Riga as the cleanest ('D is for Dirty as Capital Tops Euro Litter Poll', *Sunday Independent*, 22 October 2007). Given the huge number of Latvians now living in Dublin, maybe their attitude will rub off on the natives.
58. O'Toole, F. (1996), *The Ex-Isle of Erin: Images of a Global Ireland,* Dublin: New Island Books.
59. Smyth, W.J. (1985), 'Explorations of Place' in J.J. Lee (ed.), *Ireland: Towards a Sense of Place*, Cork: Cork University Press, pp. 1–20.
60. Lee, J.J. (1999), 'A Sense of Place in the Celtic Tiger' in H. Bohan and G. Kennedy (eds.), *Are we Forgetting Something? Our Society in the New Millennium*, Dublin: Veritas, pp. 71–93 (see p. 80).

61. Feehan, J. (1997), 'Threat and Conservation: Attitudes to Nature in Ireland' in J.W. Foster and H.C.G. Chesney (eds.), *Nature in Ireland: A Scientific and Cultural History*, Dublin: Lilliput Press, pp. 573–96.
62. The decision to construct the M3 motorway through the Tara/Skryne Valley in Co. Meath typifies a seeming lack of ability in Ireland to balance necessary infrastructural development with preservation of its rich cultural and natural heritage. It must be hard for outsiders to see how one of the richest countries in Europe can justify destroying such a priceless and sensitive landscape.
63. See, for example, Attis, D. (2000), 'Science and Irish Identity: the Relevance of Science Studies for Irish Studies' in P.J. Mathews (ed.), *New Voices in Irish Criticism*, Dublin: Four Courts Press; Bowler, P.J. and Whyte, N. (eds.) (1997), *Science and Society in Ireland: The Social Context of Science and Technology in Ireland 1800–1950*, Belfast: The Institute of Irish Studies; Foster, J.W. (1990), 'Natural History, Science and Irish Culture', *The Irish Review*, 9, pp. 61–9; Whyte, N. (1999), *Science, Colonialism and Ireland*, Cork: Cork University Press.
64. Foster, J.W. (1990), 'Natural History, Science and Irish Culture', *The Irish Review*, 9, pp. 61–9 (see p. 67).
65. A recent Eurobarometer survey of 27 EU states reveals that Irish citizens are the most likely to view the presence of people from minority backgrounds as enriching the cultural life of the nation. Perhaps not unrelated, the flipside of this is that they were well below the EU average when it came to agreeing that young people should stick to their family or cultural traditions ('Most Irish see Cultural Merits of Immigration', *Irish Times*, 25 January 2008).
66. Evans, E.E. (1982), *The Personality of Ireland*, Dublin: Lilliput Press.
67. Evans, E.E. (1984), *Ulster: The Common Ground*, Dublin: Lilliput Pamphlets, p. 2.
68. 'Art Sales in Ireland', *Irish Times*, 15 January 2008. Ciarán MacGonigal and Brian Fallon, two respected figures in the art world, objected strongly in the letters pages in subsequent issues of the newspaper (17 January and 25 January 2008, respectively). They used terms like

'snobbish', 'backward-looking' and 'bizarre' to refute the attack on Irish sales-room values.

69. Russell, *The National Being*, p. 71.
70. Johnston, R.H.W. (2003), *A Century of Endeavour*, Dublin: Tyndall Publications/The Lilliput Press.
71. Johnston, *A Century of Endeavour*, pp. 128–9.
72. O'Neil, D. (1987), 'Explaining Irish Underdevelopment: Plunkett and Connolly Prior to 1916', *Éire-Ireland*, 22(4), Winter, pp. 47–71.
73. Kiberd, *Inventing Ireland*, pp. 144–5.
74. Declan Kiberd (2003), 'Republicanism and Culture in the New Millennium' in R.J. Savage (ed.), *Ireland in the New Century: Politics, Culture, Identity*, Dublin: Four Courts Press, pp. 84–5.
75. Matthews, *Revival*, p. 147.
76. 'We need Vision of who we are and what we want to make Migration Work', *Irish Times*, 27 June 2007.

CHAPTER 3

Creating Sustainable Competitive Advantage

> If we are to maintain our successful momentum, we have to have a competitive advantage somewhere. We do not have it in terms of costs any more, nor in terms of indigenous natural wealth, so we have to develop it through skills and brain power. I don't think we have achieved that.
>
> Peter Sutherland, 2008[1]

INTRODUCTION

Although the Revival represented an approach to development that was uniquely Irish, firmly rooted in place and national identity, in reality many of its ideas had little impact on policy in the years after the formation of the State. While it is important to avoid what Brian Fallon calls the 'demonisation' of this period, there is little sense in sugar coating its failures.[2] After a policy reversal in the late 1950s, the development strategy changed from a reliance on protectionism to an emphasis on FDI. Ireland began to develop a twentieth century economy, which bore fruit only towards the end of the century when it then experienced phenomenal economic growth. It is instructive, therefore, to briefly examine the tortuous path Ireland took to arrive at its present position.

The idea that traditional nationalism is opposed to materialism, the profit motive, technological innovation, secularism, free markets and modernism in all its forms, reflects an unfortunate legacy of the elites who governed the Free State for the first few decades after independence. This is not helpful in disentangling and understanding the various impacts of economic success. A more useful approach is a balanced sorting and evaluation of the evidence, including hard data and 'softer' inferences, to compose a reasonably fair picture of the state of contemporary Ireland.

The varied evidence of Ireland's economic success is compelling, and must offer some inspiration and pride even to sceptics. By most economic measurements, there is much to crow about and, while there are current concerns, most Irish remain optimistic about the future. The key question now is how Ireland will develop a competitive advantage into the future, and how to convert economic achievement into a truly successful Irish society. This chapter examines Ireland's competitive state vis-à-vis those of its international competitors. The modern determinants of competitive advantage are examined, especially the contribution of distinctiveness in culture and place.

The chapter grounds the discussion on current Irish competitive advantage in historical context by reviewing the policies of post-independence Ireland and the narrative and economic and societal implications of the economic boom. It looks at how countries maintain a sustainable competitive advantage, characterised as one that cannot easily be replicated in the long run by competitors. A defining element is the possession of resources that are distinct and valuable. The Revival, by emphasising separateness and distinctiveness, spawned an Irish identity and sense of place that nurtured creativity and innovativeness across a wide gamut of Irish life. Over time, the development of Ireland's economy and society became less rooted in place and more integrated within the international marketplace, a process accelerated during the boom. Ireland is much more vulnerable to competitive threats in an age where imagination and distinctiveness, ironically resources the country potentially possesses in abundance, are increasingly valued. This is precisely what makes the conceptualisation of the Revival so relevant to competitiveness in today's learning society. This chapter lays out a competitiveness or New-Revival framework, based on the core characteristics of the Revival. This has key implications for the development of learning organisations, which are then covered in detail in the next chapter.

Independence to Interdependence

The foundation of the Irish Free State in 1922 provided the opportunity to build a long-dreamed-of nation and society. Yet the 1916 Easter Rising, the War of Independence 1920–1921, and the Civil War 1922–1923 had exhausted the nation. The dispute over partition split the nationalist camp and caused a rift that would fester for decades. Some of the more visionary and dynamic leaders like Michael Collins had already departed the scene. In pursuit of stability and in a remarkable demonstration of continuity, the Free State retained most elements and practices of the outgoing British administration. This fidelity to the colonial heritage, at least regarding government institutions and economic policy, characterised much of the Cumann na nGaedheal administration which came to power in 1923.[3] This administration was right leaning, socially and economically conservative, and a staunch promoter and defender of free trade. Yet, even with its conservative bent, it espoused many of the basic tenets of the Revival. The first decade was characterised by a highly orthodox economic policy, incorporating a laissez-faire approach to regulation of industry and a generally free trade policy. Economic relations with England remained of utmost importance and there was little sense of urgency to change this state of affairs. Cumann na nGaedheal governed for a decade until its defeat by Fianna Fáil in 1932.[4]

With the accession of Éamon de Valera as taoiseach, Ireland steadily moved from a free, open market economy to a policy of import substitution, attempting self-sufficiency in a variety of manufacturing industries. If the first decade demonstrated to other nations that Ireland could govern itself in an austere and financially disciplined manner, the goal of the successive Fianna Fáil governments that governed for most of the following three decades was considerably different. There was a general orientation towards protectionism, import substitution and self-reliance, with Irish ownership of most private industry and a heavy dose of state ownership of major sectors of the economy. Such policies were not necessarily out of step with orthodox economic thought, or with the actions of most other nations during the Depression era. Perhaps a policy of import substitution may have allowed Ireland to weather the turmoil of World War II better and remain neutral.

Nevertheless, from a starting point that was approximate to the European average in 1922, a huge slide in economic performance began. Although Ireland, by the late 1950s, was better off in absolute terms, in relative terms it was worse off than nearly every other country in Europe. Lacking effective, practical policies to give effect to de Valera's ideal Ireland, the country became an island apart, cut off from the global economy. Protectionism succeeded in protecting Irish industries, but not in making them globally competitive.

In 1959, change arrived in the person of Seán Lemass as the new taoiseach. Lemass seemed an unlikely choice to spark any change. It was he who painstakingly crafted Ireland's policy of protectionism, import substitution and native industrialisation, not to mention he had loyally served de Valera, remaining in his shadow for the better part of three decades. But Lemass, a pragmatist, was well aware of the failures and the consequences of Irish economic policy. He was ready to enact a change.

Another favourable occurrence was the accession of T.K. Whitaker, a talented senior staff member at the powerful Department of Finance, to secretaryship of the Department. In 1958 Whitaker wrote a policy document *Economic Development*, which proposed the jettison of protectionist policies and state interference in the economy in favour of a free-trading regime amenable to FDI.[5] This document, given effect by the *First Programme for Economic Expansion*[6] in 1958, proved a blueprint for the transformation of the Irish economy.

The innovative work of a remarkable economist and long-term Chairman of Aer Lingus Patrick Lynch also had a major impact on the revised thinking. Lynch chaired two major surveys sponsored by the Irish Government and conducted in association with the Organisation for Economic Co-operation and Development (OECD) during the 1960s. The first was a survey in respect of scientific research, development and technology, commissioned in 1963. This resulted in the 1965 publication *Science and Irish Economic Development.*[7] The second, also published in 1965, was a scathing analysis of Irish first- and second-level education called *Investment in Education.*[8]

By the early to mid-1960s, the government had done a complete *volte-face*. Trade barriers were dismantled, FDI was not only permitted but aggressively courted, and the nation began to find its economic legs. The 1960s became a 'Golden Age' of Irish economic development during which rates of emigration slowed or stopped. GNP grew at rates in excess of others in Europe and living standards rose by some 40 per cent over the decade.

Of course, the tide of social change in the 1960s managed to reach Ireland as well, leading to an unprecedented questioning of the dominant institutions of the State and the beginning of massive upheaval, most evident in the 1980s and 1990s. Accession to the European Economic Community (EEC), now the European Union (EU), took place in 1973. This had a liberating effect on the economy, accelerating its gradual breaking away from long dependence on the UK. It enabled the country to diversify its trading patterns and integrate more with its continental European partners. Membership of the EEC had other effects. It offered significant support for projects that would increase convergence among member states. Poorer countries like Ireland, and later Portugal and Spain, were allocated structural and convergence funds to enable them to develop infrastructure, education and training. Additionally, Irish farmers reaped considerable benefits from the guaranteed prices offered by the CAP (Common Agricultural Policy) and their new access to the European market.

If the first thirty-five years of the State were characterised by a failed policy of economic nationalism and protectionism, the thirty years after the overthrow of that policy must count as a further disappointment. Although the period began with a great lift in the 1960s, with revived optimism and the sense that things had changed irrevocably, the 1970s and 1980s represented a slap in the face. This was due both to external conditions and internal political choices. The double oil shocks of the 1970s had a sharp and deleterious effect on economic fortunes, and a global recession deeply affected Ireland's growing export-led, FDI dependent economy. In order to prop up the economy by maintaining spending, the government increased borrowing.

By 1987, three decades after the change in Irish economic development policy, and despite the significant economic growth experienced since the 1960s, Ireland found itself once again mired in the economic doldrums, with prospects arguably as bleak as any time during the history of the State. There were four changes of government since 1981, culminating in a Fianna Fáil administration governing with the slimmest of margins, which added an element of political instability to an already uncertain environment. In January 1988 *The Economist* captured the condition of the country in an article that smugly described Ireland as 'poorest of the rich'. Ireland's national debt, which had grown by nearly 600% over the past ten years, totalled over €27 billion, or 122 per cent of GNP (the largest in the then EEC) in 1986.[9] Public debt service consumed nearly 90 per cent of income tax revenue and one third of tax revenues, and there was little room to increase already high personal tax rates. Unemployment was nearly 20 per cent during the first half of 1987, a rate that tends to minimise the extent of the problem since emigration in the mid-1980s had reached epidemic proportions. The Irish, yet again, were voting with their feet. In 1986 alone, net outward migration totalled 40,000 people, most of whom were well educated and just out of university.

James Joyce, in discussing the stories in his book *Dubliners*, described them as 'epiphanies', that is, moments of insight, clarity or intuition that revealed the essential reality of some phenomenon. Such epiphanies were also unexpected and generally unsought, as turned out to be the case with Ireland in 1987. As the country stared into an economic abyss, a collective epiphany seemed to emerge as a consensus among the various powers in the political and economic firmament. The minority Fianna Fáil government not only proposed but also followed through on a programme of fiscal austerity, with government reducing its spending from 1986 to 1987. This behaviour, which would be totally out of character for Fianna Fáil governments of recent vintage, was unexpected.[10] Proving the proposition that nothing drives co-operative behaviour like the prospect of being hung in the morning, the crisis inspired an accommodation with opposition party Fine Gael, who agreed to support the minority government as long as it was moving 'in the right overall direction'. This departure from the normal workings of Irish politics and the bipartisan commitment to gaining control over public finances led to a sequence of further initiatives. Reductions in personal income taxes were linked to moderation in wage demands, a key element in the succession of 'social partnership' agreements that were to continue over the next two decades.

If it is true that success has many fathers while failure is an orphan, it is hardly surprising that many have stepped forward to take credit for Irish economic growth since 1987. There appears to be a consensus on the combination of factors that fuelled the Celtic Tiger boom. Chief among these are membership of the EU, the lowest corporate tax rates in Europe, success in garnering FDI in the high-tech sectors, and the succession of social partnership agreements that kept inflation under control. Other factors such as favourable demographics, a reduced dependency rate as more women entered the workforce, and the generally buoyant global economy of the 1990s also contributed. Of course, many public policy decisions were implemented pragmatically, if not haphazardly, in response to specific circumstances, rather than as part of a concerted and focused programme of national development. Nor are these purely discrete factors, for they overlap with each other in various ways.

The Irish economic success of the fifteen years up to 2007 was little short of phenomenal. Even during the 2001 recession prompted by the collapse of the hi-tech sector, to which the Irish economy was particularly exposed, and the trauma of 9/11, the economy only briefly faltered before continuing on a robust course. By 2008, with a slowing economy and projections of slower growth (with higher unemployment and government deficits), anything short of a complete bust seems a success. Delegations from small nations such as Estonia, Slovenia and Slovakia, recently admitted to the enlarged EU, continue to beat a path to Ireland's door to discover the 'secret' of Ireland's economic *Wirtschaftswunder*, hoping to apply it to their own development model and expecting similar results.[11]

Even more telling is the statistical evidence of Ireland's population growth and the abrupt reversal of the entrenched Irish pattern of emigration. Ireland has the fastest growing population in the EU; in the year ending April 2007, its population grew by 2.5 per cent to just under 4.34 million, the third year in a row the population increased by over 2 per cent per annum.[12] The population is the highest recorded since the post-famine census of 1861 when it was approximately 4.4 million.[13] From losing an average of 27,000 people annually through net outward migration in the period 1986–1991, Ireland experienced average annual inbound migration of 46,000 during the period 2002–2006. Although many of these were 'returned' Irish, increasing numbers hailed from the newly admitted EU states of Eastern Europe.

A vivid example of how far the Irish have come from their history of immigration is the latest Irish pastime of travelling to the United States for weekend shopping in New York. The Irish represent one of the largest and biggest spending groups of tourists in New York; reportedly, as many as 100,000 of them did their Christmas shopping in New York in 2006. David McWilliams writes, 'Where once the Irish pilgrims went to Lourdes, the new holy of holies is midtown Manhattan.'[14] It is a world apart from the age when economic necessity drove the Irish abroad, on journeys that were, of necessity, usually one-way.

The vision of modern Ireland expressed today by government, opposition and various interest groups generally coalesces around a consensus view. The current social partnership agreement *Towards 2016*[15] and the *National Development Plan 2007–2013*[16] supply blueprints for what public policy-makers, and indeed the Irish population at large, say they want. The former presents a vision of Ireland as a dynamic, internationalised and participatory society and economy. The latter, with its catchphrase *Transforming Ireland: A Better Quality of Life for All*, assumes the country will have a total population of five million by 2021, and aims to spend €184 billion in the broad categories of infrastructure, enterprise, human capital and social inclusion.

A key question is: do the policy initiatives that will give effect to these broad goals actually support aspirations for a sustainable and successful learning society?[17]

Ireland After the Boom

Societal Impact

Robust economic statistics present a story so seemingly compelling that many argue the Irish have never had it so good. However, real life is rarely black and white. Economic statistics present, at best, only a partial picture of the health of Irish society. Certainly, the changes that accompanied Ireland's meteoric economic success are little short of cathartic. In the space of one generation, Ireland advanced from an agrarian, pre-modern society, to a post-industrial, post-modern one. Yet in the headlong pursuit of continued economic prosperity, and with all eyes focused on the global economy, there tended to be, at least in the early years of the boom, less focus on the social and environmental impacts of prosperity. There are concerns over the equitable distribution of income, wealth and opportunities, and the alleged exclusion of a significant segment of the population from participation in the economy. There has been a decline of religion and a spectacular fall in the influence of the Catholic Church. Family life appears to have eroded as materialism and consumerism accompanied economic success. Development pressures abound and the natural environment is under increasing threat. Self-searching questions have emerged about the nature of Irish identity and the values that drive Irish society.

A common criticism is that the boom did not disperse its benefits equally.[18] This calls into question the very nature of progress and the value systems inherent in Irish society. Critics claim that the well-off got richer while the poor were left behind, and the numbers of those living at the margins of society have continued to grow. Others take a different tack, arguing that there has been a profound structural shift in the nation, as an affluent middle class has grown larger and more prosperous, and social mobility between classes has radically improved.[19] Given the two opposing views, what does the evidence suggest?

The standard measure of income disparity is the Gini coefficient. This measures equality in disposable household income – wages, pensions, social security, and property such as rent or dividends – reduced by taxes and other contributions. Using the Gini coefficient, Ireland did become somewhat more unequal after 2000.[20] However, it is fair to say that this does not represent a 'smoking gun' with regard to income distribution. Although not a leader by any means, Ireland appears to be only marginally more unequal than the EU average. While similar to other OECD countries, it is on the border between the European social welfare model (such as Scandinavia, Germany, the Netherlands or Austria) and the Anglo-American model (such as the US, UK, Australia or New Zealand) in the distribution of gains from the economic boom.[21]

More telling are the trends for those living in both absolute and relative poverty. If there was some level of equity in the distribution of gains, then relief should at least filter down to those most in need. The statistics are stark. According to the CSO, 7 per cent of the Irish population is living in persistent poverty (approximately 285,000 people), and 20 per cent (or over 800,000 people) are either living in poverty or are in real danger of sliding into poverty.[22] Although there may be some debate concerning the trend, there is a general acknowledgement that such numbers in poverty, or near-poverty, are far too high, particularly for what is now one of the wealthiest nations in the world.

The *2006 World Development Report* presents other sobering data. On its 'Human Poverty Index', Ireland ranks next to last of the eighteen selected OECD countries, with 16.5 per cent of the Irish population living below the income poverty line (that is, living on less than 50 per cent of the median national income).[23] Admittedly, this is a relative measure, but it does show Ireland tilting away from the Scandinavian or European social welfare model and closer to the Anglo-American model.

Given the available evidence, it is reasonable to conclude that while economic development in Ireland during the boom has not served to 'raise all boats', neither does it appear to have excessively polarised the population. On an absolute basis, most Irish people of every economic class are better off than they were before. On a relative basis, however, significant differences that existed before the boom appear to have grown during it.

Quality of Life

Ireland was selected by the Economist Intelligence Unit (EIU) in November 2004 as the 'Best Place to Live in the World'. The EIU highlighted what it called Ireland's 'combination of increasing wealth and traditional values [that] gives it the conditions most likely to make its people happy.'[24] Ireland ranked ahead of Switzerland, Norway, Luxembourg, Sweden and other European countries. The survey assessed a range of factors, including income, health, relative freedom, employment, political stability, physical security, and issues of equality, family and community.

The EIU said that Ireland 'successfully combines the most desirable elements of the new – material well-being, low unemployment rates, political liberties – with the preservation of certain life satisfaction-enhancing or modernity-cushioning elements of the old, such as stable family life and the avoidance of the breakdown of community.'[25] Dan O'Brien, senior editor at the EIU, comments that Irish society had managed modernity's arrival very well.[26] He writes that Ireland enjoys social calm combined with civil and political liberties that are not bettered anywhere in the world. The key to life satisfaction, according to O'Brien, is to have the best of both worlds: the good of the modern and the best of tradition. This is a trick notoriously difficult to pull off because, as he puts it, 'when the old stifling stuff is ditched (think dictatorial clergyman, arranged marriages and excessive deference) many good things seem to get lost as well.'[27]

In the words of Tom Inglis, 'The Irish seem to be riding two happy horses, a spiritual religious one and a secular materialist one.'[28] What makes Ireland attractive and exciting, Inglis maintains, is that it manages to combine the old with the new; a commitment to traditional ways of bonding and belonging mixed with a new freedom and ability for people to explore, express and indulge themselves. In his view, this combination of the old with new ways of being in the world means the Irish still have the best of both worlds. They began to experience this when they combined a mature sense of belonging and emotional well-being with the newly realised pleasures and comforts of consumer capitalism.

The United Nations Human Development Index (HDI) gives Ireland high marks, ranking the country fifth highest in the world after Iceland, Norway, Australia and Canada. This index reflects a broad definition of well-being that provides a composite measure of three dimensions of human development: living a long and healthy life (measured by life expectancy), being educated (measured by adult literacy and enrolment at the primary, secondary and tertiary level) and having a decent standard of living (measured by income).[29] Yet the HDI, while it is a broader measure than GDP and provides some idea of quality of life in its most important components, is by no means an all-encompassing measure.

It is therefore useful to review other facets of Ireland's non-economic structure, particularly key elements of the country's social and environmental spheres, to discern the impact of the boom on quality of life or national well-being.

Education

Ireland has made considerable strides since the days when compulsory education ended at age fourteen and most of the population had only a national school education. Ireland's total spending on education, however, is the second lowest of the EU-25 countries. Ireland spent 4.4 per cent of GDP on education in 2003, compared to an average of 5.2 per cent in the EU-25. Ireland is spending €5,312 per pupil, roughly 7 per cent below the EU average and exceeding only Greece within the EU-15. As children of the baby boomers move through the educational system, there has been a shift in the number of students. Numbers in first- and second-level education are declining from the levels in the mid-1990s, while those in third-level education continue to increase annually. Irish student/teacher ratios and average class sizes, particularly at primary level, are among the highest in the EU. In terms of educational attainment, however, Ireland is the fourth highest in the EU in the number of persons aged 25–34 with a third-level education. Some 39.2 per cent of the population in Ireland had a third-level education in 2005, compared to an EU average of 28.5 per cent. Early school leavers (that is, those leaving school with only a lower-secondary education or without achieving the Leaving Certificate) totalled 12.3 per cent in 2005, lower than the EU average of 14.9 per cent.

A recent summary of research on the social impact of the boom by the ESRI noted that the story of contemporary Irish education is more one of continuity than change.[30] Even as society has undergone drastic and dramatic change, the educational system has largely remained hierarchical and rigid. Children in Ireland 'are caught between two worlds, increasingly treated as adults outside the school context but as children within it.'[31]

Health Care

Few in Ireland can be unaware of a rash of high profile cases where the Irish health care system appears often to have broken down. There are press reports of large numbers of people in hospital on trolleys in hallways for long periods due to a shortage of acute hospital beds, and lengthy waiting lists for elective surgery. There have also been a host of hospital-acquired infections, serious labour disputes with the nurses union, and a controversial move towards a privatised or a two-tier health care system. Yet it is important to peer behind anecdotal evidence to gain a balanced appreciation of the state of the health care system in Ireland.

Ireland's public and private spending on health care in 2002 was 7.3 per cent of GDP, less than the EU-25 average of 8.7 per cent. Some argue that this measure may be less appropriate due to the peculiarities of the Irish case where the repatriation of corporate profits strongly affects total GDP. Using GNP as a base, Irish health care spending is 9.0 per cent of GNP, just below the OECD average of 9.3 per cent.[32] In both absolute and relative terms, Ireland has devoted an increasing amount of resources to national health services in attempts to improve its quality and accessibility. It is highly questionable, however, whether Ireland has received appropriate value from such increased expenditure. Although Ireland operates a system of essentially socialised medicine, with guaranteed access for all and payments based on a needs test, the country is moving increasingly towards privatising elements of the system. Nearly 50 per cent of the Irish population now carries some sort of private health insurance. This, presumably, assures quick access to quality health care and better treatment than what one would receive through the publicly funded health care 'entitlement'.[33] This trend, combined with the creeping privatisation of the health care system, again suggests some turning away from the

European or Scandinavian social welfare model and towards the more free-market Anglo-American model.

Crime and Security

The days of the key left in the front door lock are well and truly gone. Anyone watching news on RTÉ confronts new levels of violence, crime and socially offensive behaviour. Homicides and gang violence, in particular, dominate the headlines. For a country that experienced annual national murder rates in the single digits in the 1970s, this is a profound shock. Many analysts suggest that the problem is still 'manageable'.[34]

There is no doubt that the crime rate is increasing. Yet, in an international context, rates of crime in Ireland are comparatively low. According to the National Crime Council's major study of crime in Ireland, covering the period 1950–1998:

> The Republic of Ireland belongs to a group of countries, which also includes Spain, Russia and Japan, which have low rates of crime. Indeed, in 1998 the rate of recorded crime fell here and in Denmark by six per cent, representing the largest drop in Europe. In terms of violent crime the Republic of Ireland is situated at the lower end of the scale; only Switzerland, Greece, Russia and Japan have lower rates.[35]

Ian O'Donnell argues that focusing on the psychological make-up of individual perpetrators of crime will not take us far in the search for an explanation for the increase in violence.[36] He says that to understand this properly, it is necessary to take into account the wider changes in Irish society, with current trends including a sharp rise in wealth and an increase in migration. Writing in 2007, he asks:

> Is it the best of times or the worst of times? Is it the spring of hope or the winter of despair? On balance it seems fair to

> suggest that Ireland has a modest overall crime problem … there is no escalation in recent times … the crime rate appears low compared with other EU countries.[37]

Clearly, this is not the Ireland of old where violent crime was almost unknown and firearms only known through watching American westerns and gangster films. From a low base, Ireland now experiences a level of crime commensurate with its status as a modern, affluent nation. In a comparative international context, there is perhaps little cause for concern if one believes crime to be an unpleasant but necessary by-product of prosperity and development. If globalisation teaches us anything it is the necessity of trade-offs. Still, one must ponder whether the absolute change from what had been is more important than a comparison with other nations. In assessing the seriousness of crime in Ireland, the evaluative lens that is used calls the tune.

Social Capital

If de Valera thought of Ireland as a society and not an economy, then surely it is far more common these days in Ireland to engage in discussion of the economy rather than the nation. Anecdotal evidence supports this subjective impression, but harder, empirical data is difficult to come by. Just how robust is community life in Ireland? What is the condition of Ireland's stock of social capital? The National Economic and Social Forum (NESF) defines the term 'social capital' as follows:

> Important social processes and relationships – informal social support networks, friendship, neighbourhood generosity, interpersonal trust and volunteering activity – but also aspects of local and community development, public private – voluntary partnerships and civic spirit. Although the term is relatively new in Ireland, the underlying concepts are not. Social capital draws on processes which are crucial in community development and the

> functioning of a democratic, inclusive and cohesive society. Likewise, community development helps generate higher levels of trust and social participation. Effective democracies rest on two essential foundations: civic attitudes of inclusion, tolerance and regard for the rights of others, and civic behaviour.[38]

To critics, social capital in Ireland is eroding precipitously, with ties that once bound individuals to distinct localities unravelling as populations become more mobile and affluent. They point to the proliferation of 'soulless' suburbs emanating further and further afield from urban centres, particularly in Dublin, as evidence of destruction rather than creation of social capital. In this view, rural areas, repositories of the ideal Ireland envisioned by de Valera, diminish in importance as society is increasingly urbanised. The new suburbs are viewed as devoid of personal interaction, neighbourliness and collective community action.

Yet this view is contested. A study found that such critical views are exaggerated. In a survey of four suburban localities on the periphery of Dublin, it discovered:

> …a picture that is much less bleak than that which fuels the popular imagination. Generally speaking, our respondents 'electively belonged' to their communities – they felt attached to the place where they lived.[39]

The study concluded that Ireland's new residential spaces 'did not register a fundamentally deficient social fabric'.[40] Yet it acknowledged that intense development was spawning further pressures that could destroy or at least compromise the high quality of life that Ireland's young and affluent are seeking. The study linked social capital in the suburbs with a 'pattern of demographic homogeneity that marginalises those at different family stages'.[41] In other words, members of the demographic majority build networks and connections, while those 'outsiders' who are old, economically deprived, or otherwise demographically different are left to their own devices. In assessing the health of community and the stock of social capital in Ireland, as with other assessments of contemporary Ireland, a certain level of ambivalence seems justified.

Cultural Capital: Music and Performing Arts

Most definitions of culture centre upon the set of shared beliefs and customs, traditions and values that any group uses to make sense of its world.[42] Taken together, these create a complex system for understanding the world, making value judgements as to what is right and wrong, valuable or not, and making decisions accordingly. It is the very basis for the identity of a people. Understood as a marketable commodity, Irish culture seems at a zenith. The world seems not to get enough Riverdance-type spectacles, Celtic Women, Irish Tenors, or other contemporary packaging of traditional Irish music and dance. The days when Irish performers appeared in blackface for the opportunity to perform on American vaudeville stages are gone. Within the international pop culture scene an Irish label is cool so, at this level at least, Irish culture is enjoying robust health. However, like much else in Ireland, this represents contestable terrain. Critics suggest this culture is often superficial, contrived pandering to audiences who want a whiff of the 'auld sod'. Perhaps it represents a hankering after a mythical Ireland that never was, or an updated 'stage Irishness' for the twenty-first century. Some critics fear a steamrollering of the core of traditional Irish music so it becomes commercialised beyond recognition and is rendered inauthentic. Noted ethnomusicologist Mick Moloney offers a different perspective. He observes:

> Irish music and dance traditions are among the most visible global symbols of Irishness in the world today, defining and articulating a cultural center at a time of unprecedented social change at home and abroad. Most performing artists, enthusiasts, and cultural commentators would probably agree that Irish music

> and dance are enjoying the best of times in an extraordinary cultural renaissance.[43]

Irish music has always altered, adjusted, adapted and changed itself within the contexts in which it has been performed. Like the notion of culture itself, it has been a dynamic process, not a museum artefact to be placed upon a shelf, dusted off and admired from time to time.[44] In a larger sense, Irish culture as represented by its performing arts represents a living, changing, adapting complex whole, a vital touchstone for the Diaspora and 'at home' Irish, of particular importance at this time of rapid globalisation.

Cultural Capital: Irish Language

In addition to music and the performing arts, a distinct aspect of Irish culture and identity is the language. While there are still pockets of native Irish speakers in the Gaeltacht (mostly on the western seaboard), the hotbeds of interest in the Irish language are urban centres like Dublin and Cork, and in Northern Ireland, as well as far-flung outposts throughout North America and beyond. The Irish have an attachment to the language, yet largely refuse to use it in everyday life. Learned in school by many, it is lost soon after leaving by most. It has been under pressure for centuries, driven to the edge of extinction, yet still clings stubbornly to life as a living language. Perhaps it is beginning to thin, losing some of its quality, texture and richness in the face of twenty-first century complexity. Yet even the English of Dublin today is hardly reminiscent of the quality heard during the time of Joyce or even Behan.

Statistics tell one story but simple observation suggests another. According to the 2006 Census, Ireland had about 1.7 million Irish speakers or roughly 42 per cent of the population. On the face of it, this would suggest that the Irish language is in a robust state. Yet, of those who claim to speak the language, 27 per cent speak it only within the Irish educational system and not at all outside. A further 25 per cent of those who claim to be able to speak Irish never, in fact, speak it. Of those who do speak Irish, only 3 per cent speak it on a daily basis, while others use it more sparingly.[45] Even these statistics are suspect. Firstly, they are self-reported and there are serious doubts about whether those who claim a working knowledge of the language actually are fluent. Secondly, even for those who claim to speak the language 'weekly' or more rarely, one wonders at what level they speak it. Is it merely to quote a phrase in Irish, offer a toast, or say 'hello' or 'goodbye'?

A Government report states that within two decades, Irish will die out as the primary spoken language in the Gaeltacht. Brian O'Connell writes:

> It's a bleak assessment and, unless radical measures are taken, the premise seems to be that Irish as a living language may soon be *marbh* [translation: 'dead']. Yet, such dire predictions have been a feature of government reports and media commentary for the past half-century, with the Gaeltacht areas coming under particular scrutiny. Coupled with this, Irish-language policy has often been criticised for narrowly focusing on resuscitating the language in the Gaeltachts instead of imaginatively tackling the national reality.[46]

Casual observation would seem to bear this out. Walking through many Gaeltacht areas, one hears little Irish spoken and signs in English are common. English is clearly the language of commerce, and it would be difficult to transact even simple business in many shops through the medium of Irish. The 2006 Census indicates that some 46 per cent of students within the Gaeltacht speak little or no Irish at all.

Yet, while it seems paradoxical, there is a clear and continuing enthusiasm for the language. As one young woman quoted recently said:

> I think the language is getting more popular again. In college when people learn I am a fluent speaker they are nearly always

> impressed. It used to be that people weren't really proud to speak it in bars in front of people, but now anyone I meet with a bit of Irish is mad keen to have a conversation.[47]

The main Irish-medium radio station Raidió na Gaeltachta has a reputation for quality broadcasting and for creative, trendy and innovative programming, as has the television station TG4. Gaelscoileanna, primary and secondary schools where instruction is exclusively through the medium of Irish, are among the most elite schools and in great demand. Students are flocking to them (at least their parents are flocking to send them there). These parents are often very modern, cosmopolitan and upwardly mobile.

Natural Environment

Ireland's economic success has put the natural environment under serious threat. Ireland, as an EU member, endorsed the Kyoto Treaty to reduce carbon dioxide and other forms of greenhouse gas emissions. It committed to constrain greenhouse gas emissions by 2012 to an amount no greater than 13 per cent over 1990 emissions. Yet emissions in 2006 were already more than 25 per cent higher than 1990 levels. As things stand, Ireland will overshoot its Kyoto targets by almost 100 per cent.[48] The country faces whopping fines if it fails to reduce emissions to the Kyoto limits by then. Relative to other EU countries, Ireland's greenhouse gas emissions are very high. Ireland's level of acid rain precursor emissions (sulphur dioxide, nitrogen oxide and ammonia) are also some 20 per cent higher than that agreed in the Gothenburg Protocol 2010. These facts speak volumes concerning Ireland's spirit of environmental stewardship.

The Government must undertake additional policies and measures sent to it by the EU. These measures include reductions in energy consumption and emissions, accompanied by significantly increased use of renewable energy. Yet the Government will still have to buy its way out of trouble in meeting the agreed target by buying carbon credits in an international trading system. However, while the Government has set aside €270 million to foot the bill for this, the cost could rise significantly if the price of a tonne of carbon rises. In theory this system permits the world to reduce its carbon emissions at the lowest possible cost, by lowering emissions where it is most practicable. Since Ireland has the financial ability to do this, it will probably be able to comply with the letter of the law.

Much, but not all, of Ireland's rate of emissions is related to the country's love affair with the automobile. The Environmental Protection Agency (EPA) report, *The Environment in Focus 2006*, points out that emissions in the transport sector alone are double what they were in 1990; emissions of nitrous oxide, produced primarily by motor vehicles and another component of acid rain, continue to increase in tandem with the number of road vehicles.[49] Even so, Ireland still has fewer automobiles per person over fifteen years and older than any other country in the EU-15 except Denmark and Portugal, a fact that does not bode well for future attempts to lower greenhouse gas emissions. Yet there are positive signs. Concentrations of 'black smoke' for example, usually emitted by use of bituminous coal, have shown significant reductions, and the air in many Irish cities has shown measurable improvements over the past decade.

Perhaps one advantage that Ireland has is that it has not had the opportunity to abuse its environment with any great effect until the recent economic boom. As a late starter, the environment remains relatively unspoiled compared to other nations. Yet the vaunted Irish landscape, which surveys say is the nation's premier tourist attraction, is under threat from bad planning. County councils often overturn the recommendations of their own professional planners and give approval to contentious development projects, often for politically expedient reasons. Wildlife is also under threat. At least 150 species of native Irish wildlife, including the red squirrel, birds, owls, bats and others are in danger. An Taisce (The National Trust) claims that coastland habitats have been spoiled due to inveterate approvals of aquaculture activities, while wetland habitats were being filled with construction waste.

Even with massive government investment in recycling facilities, the country is generating more rubbish than ever, with a rising amount going to landfill. A recent Department of Transport report says that, by 2016, traffic in Dublin in the morning peak hour is set to slow to an average of 8 kilometres per hour (from its current 13 kilometres). Greenhouse gas emissions from transport could increase to 19 million tonnes of CO_2, a whopping 265 per cent increase over 1990 levels. The report says, by 2016, car ownership in Ireland is expected to exceed average EU levels as car use increases and the proportion of those commuting by walking and cycling continues to decline. Increased car exhaust pollution will cause alarming levels of obesity and a variety of other respiratory illnesses while the increased congestion will lead to a decline in the country's competitiveness.[50] At a time of accelerating pressures on the natural environment, the country will find itself hard pressed to maintain the relatively high standard of natural services it currently enjoys. Serious change is clearly required, but there seems little will to effect it.

Ireland's Competitiveness

The *Annual Competitiveness Report 2007* of the National Competitiveness Council (NCC) defines competitiveness as the ability of Irish-based firms to achieve success in international markets in order to provide Irish people with the opportunity to improve their living standards and quality of life.[51] The NCC says improving living standards depends, among other things, on raising incomes through strong productivity growth and providing high quality employment opportunities for all. Given Ireland's small domestic market, this requires a healthy export sector. The NCC says an internationally competitive economy must be embedded in a business environment and a broader socio-political climate that encourages high levels of investment in enterprise, public infrastructure, skills and knowledge, and provides the appropriate incentives and flexibility for economic actors to respond to change.

Measured by costs, Ireland's competitiveness has eroded since joining the Euro in 1999. According to the *OECD Economic Outlook*, the cumulative rise in the Irish consumer price level amounted to 31.4 per cent in the eight years to 2007, a faster rise than in all of the major countries with which Ireland trades.[52] By comparison, in the Euro area as a whole, prices rose by 18.8 per cent, in Britain by 13.2 per cent and in the US by 24.3 per cent. Ireland, although still among the most competitive economies in the world, has seen its ranking decline sharply since 2000. Of fifty-five countries benchmarked by the Institute of Management Development (IMD) in its *World Competitiveness Yearbook*, Ireland was ranked fourteenth overall in 2007, a fall of ten places since 2000.[53] In the *Global Competitive Report* published by the World Economic Forum (WEF), Ireland was ranked in the top quartile (twenty-second of 131 countries) in 2007, but this was a fall of seventeen places since 2000 (the UK at ninth is now well ahead of Ireland).[54] The country's infrastructure also ranked poorly, a sticking point for those conducting business in Ireland. Irish ports were sixty-fourth best, roads sixtieth best and railway infrastructure fifty-fifth best in the world. The NCC concluded that Ireland's strengths included the macroeconomy, fiscal policy, the labour market, the market and regulatory framework, and the attitudes and values in Irish society to globalisation and competitiveness.[55] Its weaknesses were in prices, infrastructure, innovation, R&D and environmental sustainability.

Generally, Ireland's rankings are boosted by strong current measures of competitiveness, such as productivity levels and employment indicators, rather than likely drivers of future competitiveness, such as infrastructure and a culture of innovation. Of the drivers of future competitiveness, Ireland's weaknesses are in areas that require long-term attention, rather than those aspects more easily remedied. Yet Ireland's overall deterioration in competitiveness may not yet be reflected in changes in living standards. Its ranking on the latter has actually gone up since 2000: in GNP per capita, Ireland is fifteenth of twenty-eight OECD countries (up four places since 2000).[56]

There were really two phases to Ireland's remarkable economic growth from the early 1990s to almost a decade and a half later. Multinational companies set the first phase in motion by their high levels of investment. High value-added export-led growth drove the economy during this period. This lasted until about the year 2000 when the second phase, driven by domestic growth, kicked in. This recent phase saw export success combine with rising national confidence and low interest rates to stimulate household and government spending. Domestic sectors, in particular consumption and construction, supported by high levels of overseas borrowing, have been the engine of growth for the economy in recent years. However, this domestically driven boom is currently decelerating as increasing Eurozone interest rates and an international credit crunch combine with high household debt levels to reduce domestic demand. The contrast between the two phases could not be starker, with the external economy, the main contributor to growth in the first phase, now negatively impacting the second phase.

The NCC Report asserts that the domestic boom has overshadowed the evidence of weakening in the country's international competitiveness. Irish households now spend more than they earn, while the current account balance (the balance between Ireland's foreign earnings and expenditure) has developed a large and growing deficit, projected to be around €10 billion by the end of 2008. Ireland's debt per capita has increased rapidly in recent years so that today, apart from Luxembourg, Ireland is the most indebted Eurozone member, both relative to national income and on a per capita basis. With house prices increasing dramatically from 2000 until 2007, household borrowing increased, more than doubling between 2003 and 2007, so the average Irish person was almost €35,000 in debt in 2007.

Ireland's labour productivity since 1990 has been strong. From the mid-1990s until recent years, Ireland achieved faster growth in overall factory productivity than other EU countries and the US. Recently, however, the country's productivity growth rate has slowed considerably, going from an average of 5 per cent per annum between 1995 and 2003 to 1.3 per cent per annum between 2003 and 2006. This is below the OECD average of 1.7 per cent during this period and well below the Irish average of 3.3 per cent achieved between 2000 and 2003. In the late 1990s, it grew at almost twice the OECD average whereas, from 2003 to 2006, the average annual growth rate was below the OECD average. By 2007, according to NCC reports, Irish productivity levels had converged with the OECD average.

As in other advanced economies, Ireland's productivity is strongest in the private high technology sector and in a small number of export-oriented manufacturing and services sectors. Yet productivity growth has also now slowed in these, while the large and growing domestic services sectors continue to perform poorly. Unlike the boom years where jobs growth was often in high-productivity modern manufacturing, high-technology or export services run by multinational companies, much of the recent jobs growth has been in locally traded services and construction where the rate of productivity growth is much lower. Since 2000, strong employment growth in Ireland has occurred in precisely those sectors with poor productivity performances, such as domestic services, construction and the public sector. In services, which now account for about two of every three people in the Irish workforce, productivity is only about half that of manufacturing. Public services now employ more than one in five Irish workers, a figure higher than either manufacturing or construction. These services, especially health and education, have very weak productivity growth rates. This in turn has reduced overall national labour productivity growth rates.

Yet, while Irish productivity growth rates have been slowing, the cost base has been rising. The cost of living is now some 20 per cent above the EU average and the gap is widening. Although unit labour costs in manufacturing, which constitute one-eighth of the workforce, have not increased significantly since 2003, costs in sheltered sectors of the economy, including utilities, catering and communications, are rising at a rate of at least twice the Eurozone average. The NCC urges that Ireland enter a new phase of economic growth where it regains international competitiveness. It says the country must display a singular commitment to promoting a competitive business environment to ensure it can sustain improvements in the standard of living and quality of life.

Ireland displayed a great ability over the past decade to generate large numbers of jobs, virtually solving its long-term unemployment problem. Ireland created many thousands of new jobs in recent years, attracting labour from elsewhere in the EU in the process. However, since 2000, the bulk of these new jobs have come from the non-trading sectors, in particular public services and construction. Manufacturing and agriculture lost jobs over this same period. Of the 166,000 new jobs created between February 2005 and February 2007, almost half were in construction and a further fifth each in financial services and retail services.[57] In 2007 construction accounted for an astounding one in seven Irish workers, compared to one in seventeen in the US, which itself is more dependent on construction than other OECD economies. However, since the end of 2007 construction growth has also slowed.

In Ireland, employment in services increased by 58 per cent in the decade to 2004. This compares with growth of only 5.6 per cent in manufacturing over the same period.[58] Employment growth in internationally trading services has been significant, albeit starting from a low base. Its distribution has also changed over the decade. Growth has been particularly strong in software and ICT related services (e.g. data processing), financial services and other non-ICT related services (dominated by legal, accounting, consultancy, market research and education services). While employment levels in the pharmaceuticals/chemicals and medical technologies sectors have grown, employment in ICT hardware and engineering has declined significantly since 2000.

Ireland's growth in exports during 2000–2003 was well above the OECD average, but Ireland's relative position worsened in 2003–2006. Consequently, Ireland is losing its overall share in world markets. The country's share was 1.2 per cent in 2006, down from 1.4 per cent in 2002, with the share of goods trade dropping from 1.3 per cent to 0.8 per cent. Ireland's share of services trade, a smaller but growing component of overall trade, increased from 1.9 per cent to 2.5 per cent over the same period.[59]

The composition of Irish exports, worth over €154 billion in 2007 (following €138 billion in 2006), is changing rapidly. An increase in exports of chemicals, in particular medicinal and pharmaceutical products, has been offset by a fall in a range of other manufacturing sectors, particularly ICT hardware. Almost 90 per cent of Irish exports derive from foreign-owned firms operating from Ireland. Exports from the food and drink sector, where Ireland has distinctive competitive advantages, continue to account for the largest share of indigenous exports (54 per cent). In 2007, the country produced an exceptional increase in exports from this sector to Asia. A further one-fifth of indigenous exports worth come from software development and other internationally traded services. Sectors not traditionally drivers of export earnings, including environmental services and construction such as prefabricated buildings, have increased their export values since 2000.

Overlooked in the past is the importance of services, a sector where Ireland potentially has significant competitive advantages. Services exports are growing at two to three times the rate of goods exports, increasing their share of overall exports.[60] While goods exports grew by just 1 per cent in 2007 (following 0.8 per cent in 2006), services exports increased by 18 per cent (following 14 per cent in 2006), a rate 50 per cent faster than the global market. In 2000, the export of services from Ireland accounted for as little as 22 per cent of total exports. By 2007, this had increased to 42 per cent of total exports (forecast by the ESRI to rise to 45 per cent by 2008) with high value-added knowledge-intensive exports in computer services, financial and insurance services, business services (including consulting), operational leasing and tourism. Ireland is now the fifth most important exporter of commercial services exports in the world, with 4 per cent of all global commercial services exports sourced in Ireland (compared to less than 1 per cent of global goods trade). The country is on track to export more services than goods by 2010.

The above summarises the current state of Irish competitiveness. While many aspects are quite positive, it is clear the country can no longer depend on low costs to attract large-scale international projects in manufacturing. Other countries are now duplicating many of the features used in the past, such as an educated workforce and low taxes, to attract mobile investment. A new approach is urgently needed.

New-Revival Framework

Inimitable Resources

The word 'resources' means different things to different people at different times and in different places. A feature of the concept of a resource is that it involves both evaluation and purpose.[61] Erich Zimmermann famously said, 'resources are not, they become; they are not static but expand and contract in response to human wants and actions.'[62] Natural capital comes from the beneficence of nature while human capital is identified by individual knowledge, skills, competencies, capabilities, behaviour, expertise and creativity. Social capital is captured by the relationships between people while cultural capital is identified by inherited attitudes and values. There are many parallels conceptually between these different forms of capital. For instance, cultural capital and natural capital are inherited from the past. Both impose a duty of care on each generation, which is the essence of sustainability.[63] They are also similar in that the function of natural ecosystems is to support and maintain the natural balance while cultural ecosystems support the vitality of a society. A fundamental principle of sustainability is that no part of the system exists independently of any other part. Cultural capital contributes in a manner similar to that of natural capital. Just as neglect, overuse or underinvestment of natural capital can lead to an ecosystem breakdown, a similar argument can be made with regard to cultural capital. It is reasonable to suggest that a failure to sustain the cultural values that provide individuals with a sense of identity and meaning in their lives might also lead to a loss of welfare and economic output.

Scholars nowadays hold that certain resources, particularly those that are knowledge-driven, play a critical role in value creation by providing the fundamental source of competitive advantage. A *Harvard Business Review* paper, for instance, asserts that the 'only true source of competitive advantage is the ability to conceive the entire value creating system and make it work.'[64] Twenty years ago, Michael Porter, in his influential book *The Competitive Advantage of Nations*, introduced a conceptual framework for a country's competitiveness. He regarded its linchpin as the productivity that companies located in a country possess.[65] Nations create their most important factors of production or resources and they succeed in industries where they are particularly good at this. However, nowadays, basic factors, such as a pool of labour or a local raw-material source, do not constitute an advantage in knowledge-intensive industries. Porter argued that today a nation's competitiveness depends on the capacity of its industry to innovate and envisaged that in a world of increasingly global competition, the nation had in fact become more, not less, important. His analytical tool, a 'diamond' comprising four elements, namely demand conditions, factor inputs, context for firm strategy and related and supporting industries, captured the determinants of national competitive advantage. This advantage is created and sustained through a highly localised process, with differences in national values, cultures and histories all making key contributions.

Porter addresses this issue with his notion of the stages of economic development, arguing that countries compete on distinctly different sets of underlying qualities as they develop.[66] Ultimately, a country must upgrade constantly to sustain its competitive advantage and can only create sophisticated levels of value through continuous innovation.

A related perspective is the so-called resource-based view of a firm. According to this, a firm tries to link its internal capabilities (what it does well) and its external environment (what the market demands or values and what competitors offer).[67] It achieves and sustains a competitive advantage by possessing certain key resources, called capabilities, which produce value for the organisation, doing it in way that competitors cannot easily replicate. A competency is an internal capability that a firm performs better than other internal capabilities and this produces a sustainable competitive advantage if it improves the firm's efficiency and effectiveness, if it is rare, tacit, and not easily imitable, substitutable or exploitable. A crucial task of managers is to identify, develop, deploy and protect such key competencies or resources in order to create value. It follows that the less visible a resource is, and the more difficult its impact on value is to understand, the greater the likelihood that it may represent a source of sustainable competitive advantage.[68]

Rooted Irish-Global Competitiveness

It is worth comparing our Neo-Revival framework to current official thinking. Figure 2 shows the 'competitiveness pyramid' the NCC presently uses to conceptualise Ireland's competitiveness.[69] At the apex, it places *sustainable growth* in living standards, what NCC regards as the ultimate *goal* or *outcome* of competitiveness. Below this are the *essential conditions* to achieve competitiveness, namely (1) *business performance*, (2) *productivity*, (3) *prices* and *costs,* and (4) *labour supply*. Below these again are *policy inputs* covering three pillars of future competitiveness: (1) *business environment* (including *taxation*, *regulation* and

Figure 2: Competitiveness Pyramid

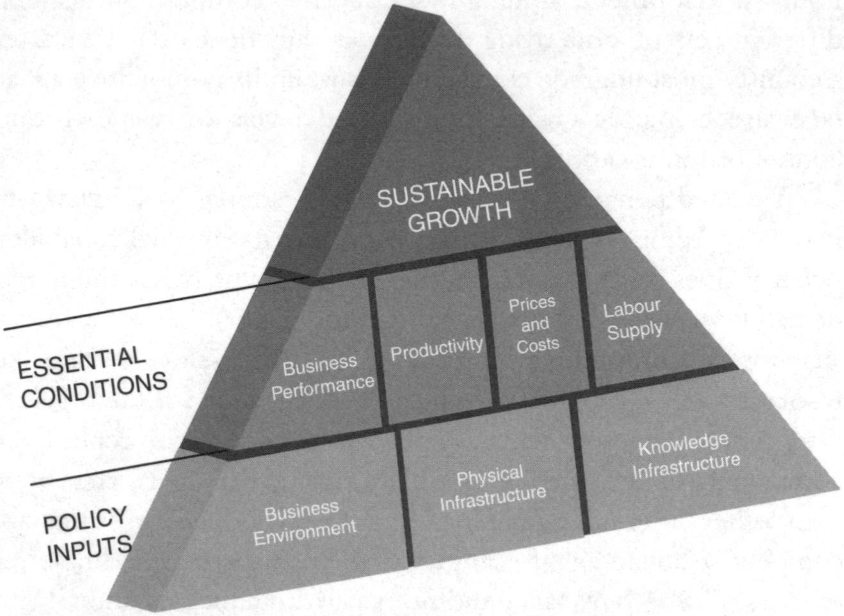

Source: NCC (2007), Annual Competitiveness Report, Dublin: Forfás.

competition, and *social capital*), (2) *physical infrastructure* and (3) *knowledge infrastructure*.

Our alternative to the above, the New-Revival framework, is presented in Figure 3. The outer ring depicts the three *policy inputs*: (1) *distinct, inimitable, rooted resources*, (2) *systems thinking*, and (3) *meaning, identity, sense of place* and *tacit knowledge*. The inner ring, or the *essential conditions* to achieve competitiveness, are: (1) *high total productivity*, (2) *dynamic learning organisations, communities* and *regions*, and (3) *sustainable interdisciplinary innovations*. The *goal* or *outcome* now is to achieve a *sustainable* and *successful learning society*.

The NCC's goal of setting sustainable growth (defined by material living standards, an economic metric measured by GNP per capita) rather than a sustainable and successful learning society (similar to quality of life) as the primary goal of competitiveness differs from the approach used in the New-Revival framework.[70] While the NCC accepts that a high quality of life should be an objective, its overriding

Figure 3: New Revival Framework

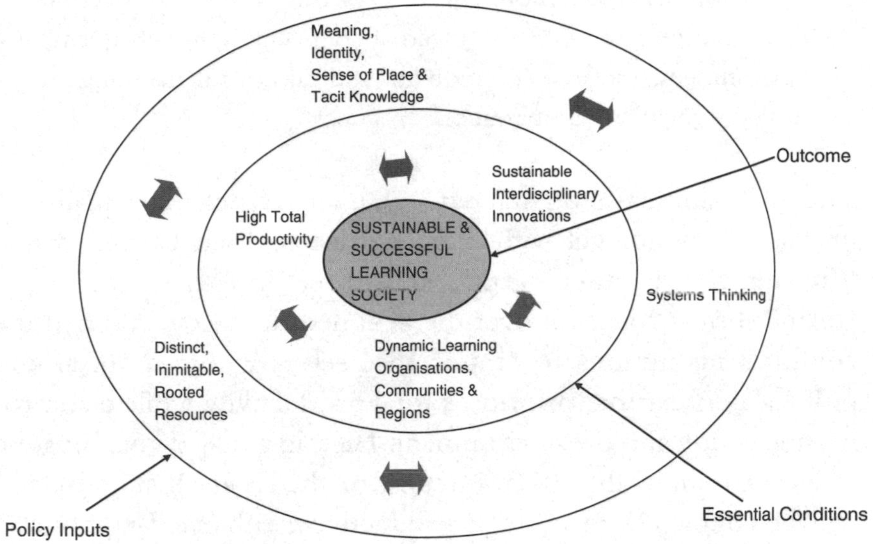

emphasis on living standards runs counter to the thinking in the latest NESC Strategy Document, *People, Productivity and Purpose.*[71] In the past there was a perspective that economic reality set limits to Ireland's social and environmental possibilities. Today NESC accepts that the future strength of the economy depends on intangibles such as social capital. This represents an attempt to enrich how Irish economic, social and environmental factors relate to what NESC terms the 'successful society'.[72] NESC defines the latter as a society in which individuals, families, enterprises, associations and communities flourish and in which the public system enables them to achieve their changing goals. It argues that Ireland's low-quality social cohesion and environmental standards could limit the country's ability to achieve a dynamic knowledge-based economy and thereby international competitiveness. As NESC puts it:

> Now, the medium and long-term strength of the economy depends not only on increased investment in physical infrastructure and

> scientific research, but also on deepening of capabilities, even greater participation, more effective systems of social protection and care, internal as well as external connectivity, a high quality environment, more social mobility and successful handling of diversity, including immigration.[73]

The NCC emphasis on standard of living rather than quality of life also does not gel with how Taoiseach Brian Cowen, when Minister for Finance, articulated three integrated priorities Ireland should focus on over the next decade.[74] Cowen urged the country's institutions to embed themselves within a social and political context that prioritises total productivity while also promoting equity and the environment. He said a major goal must be to ensure that, by the 2016 centenary of the Easter Rising, Ireland will be characterised by high productivity, enhanced equity and the promotion and safeguarding of the environment. It is clear that sustainability or quality of life, not an economic measure like standard of living, is becoming the goal of Irish development policy, forming the bedrock of the country's international competitiveness.

The sustainable and successful society goals, advanced by NESC and recently the Taoiseach, are consistent with the New-Revival framework. In other words, future prosperity depends on the productivity of *all* resources, especially unique intangible capabilities and competencies. The New-Revival framework also differs from the NCC approach in that it based on systems thinking, the essence of sustainable development, rather than linear thinking. It recognises that social capital is not a component of the business environment but ultimately a societal factor driving productivity and competitiveness. Family, social and other factors are central to national competitiveness, and are not merely supportive of economic growth by feeding into higher standards of living, which is clearly out of line with an ethic of sustainable development.

Policy Implications

Official thinking as articulated by Government organisations like Forfás and NCC differ in fundamental ways from what is proposed here. The New-Revival framework also seems to run counter to conventional policies on Irish competitiveness, innovation and learning. Specifically, Irish public policy-makers pay little if any attention to considerations of culture, identity, emotions, instinct, intuition, meaning or sense of place as issues in development.[75] Nor do they seem to accept the enormous potential of sustainability as a solid foundation upon which to build international competitiveness through innovation and learning.

The New-Revival framework is somewhat akin to the direction in which the Irish Business and Employers Confederation (IBEC) appears now to be moving. IBEC Director of Policy Danny McCoy recently argued that cost-curtailment is a necessary but not sufficient condition to drive Irish competitiveness.[76] He says the country must also enhance the building blocks of the economy, namely its physical, human, social and natural capital. Indeed, sustainability as a process could be a perfect match given Ireland's natural and non-natural resources, and represents an enormous competitive opportunity.

The dominant development logic, however, generally paints a different scenario. This suggests that if economic growth can be maximised and massive infrastructure projects completed, Ireland will 'arrive' and then have the luxury to address non-economic or quality of life concerns that emerge as a by-product of growth. Economists Patrick Honohan and Brendan Walsh, speaking at the 2007 Dublin Economics Workshop in Kenmare, questioned whether it was plausible for the future to continue like the past:

> What evident capacity limits are being neared that cannot be addressed through increased infrastructure investment? If we

> can pursue this strategy – as we have up to now – without a worsening of income inequalities, will it not provide a greater concentration of collective resources that can be brought to bear on social problems? Might a scaled up economy generate its own productivity dynamic, through what enthusiasts for large cities call economies of agglomeration? On the other hand, can a prolongation of rapid population and economic growth be managed in an environmentally sustainable manner?[77]

The strategy of maximising economic growth in order to generate resources to promote social (and environmental) well-being begs several questions: What if the reverse is true? What if future competitiveness and vitality can only be assured by simultaneously addressing economic, social and environmental concerns? Are non-economic issues only addressed as an afterthought, a nuisance or a corrective measure to be 'managed' once maximum economic growth is pursued? Can social and environmental goals that are central to quality of life and well-being be disconnected from economic goals? Can they only be tackled properly when, and if, resources become available? Perhaps those who drive public policies, often economists, and those who implement them, such as engineers and planners, are too far removed from each others' ways of thinking to achieve a coherent approach to improving both international competitiveness *and* the quality of life in Ireland.

Several initiatives have been announced in recent years to enhance Ireland's competitiveness, including the *National Development Plan 2007–2013*, *Transport 21*, the *Strategy for Science, Technology and Innovation*, the *National Skills Strategy* and a cross-departmental implementation of the Enterprise Strategy Group Action Plan. There is general acceptance that the factors that underpin Ireland's competitiveness and prosperity will be different in the future. Perhaps the working paradigm used for defining competitiveness also requires radical change. To get the ball rolling in this direction, a conference organised by Forfás/NCC in January 2008 entitled *Re-conceptualising Ireland's Competitiveness*, was branded as a 'conversation between business, policy-makers and academia', designed to 'look at emerging opportunities and changes and help identify the key success factors for sustaining Ireland's competitiveness.'[78] In promoting the conference, no mention was made that cultural and social capital might also represent key building blocks in developing Ireland's innovative capabilities and international competitiveness. The range of speakers, admittedly illustrious business executives, policy-makers, trade unionists and academics, was quite narrow. Their backgrounds suggest they do not place major significance on issues of identity, sense of place, meaning, rootedness or sustainability in competitiveness. Perhaps the views of psychologists, sociologists, geographers, historians, poets, linguists, artists, and those with experience of spiritual and community development would have added a rich dimension to the conversation, and possibly provided a more likely spur to re-conceptualising national competitive advantage.

NESC notes that Ireland's experience since independence displays the positive relationship between economic dynamism and cultural vitality.[79] A rooted Irish-global identity, through its impact on emotions and feelings, has the potential to make a special contribution to stimulating creativity, innovation and competitiveness. Contemporary Ireland can be considered a laboratory to determine whether a small, island economy can follow a development path that is economically, environmentally, socially and culturally sustainable, while being consistent with the hopes and aspirations of the Irish people. In the past, there was a sense that economic reality set limits to Ireland's social and environmental possibilities. It is now generally accepted that the medium and long-term strength of the economy itself will depend on intangibles such as social capital, knowledge and resources founded on social relationships. A grand vision of a sustainable and successful society, based on New-Revival thinking, could become a galvanising national project driving Ireland's innovation and competitiveness agenda.

Implementing the Framework

Distinctive Qualities

According to John Bradley, former research professor of Economics at the ESRI, because the process of global competition is organised today by multinationals, not governments, a small country like Ireland has little power to influence its destiny other than by focusing its economic policies on identifying and developing local factors, especially relatively immobile ones.[80] It should therefore concentrate on greater complexity in products and services where its special capabilities can add the most value. Bradley argues that in an increasingly interdependent world, Ireland must learn to mediate connections between the local and the global, and influence how its own specific assets are mobilised within the range of opportunities available globally.

With Ireland almost addicted to foreign (especially US) investment and technology, it will continue to lose economic and other forms of autonomy if it fails to develop an indigenous entrepreneurial culture – ironic for a country that fought so hard for independence. Yet, if it continues to rely extensively on international companies, the enormous challenge it faces is to identify the specific contribution it can make to worldwide innovation within companies' operations. IBM Chairman and CEO Sam Palmisano recently called the new model of international business a 'global' rather than a 'multinational' one.[81] What he classified as 'globally integrated enterprises' now dominate the international business scene. Rather than duplicate operations across different national and international regions, a globally integrated enterprise structures an array of centres, each specialising in a different area such as procurement, manufacturing, research, sales or distribution. The company then fashions its strategies, management and operations worldwide to pursue a goal of worldwide integration of production and value delivery. Since country boundaries define less and less the limits of these companies' thinking or practices, Ireland must identify what unique resources and value propositions it can place within such globally harmonised business operations if it is to compete successfully.

Ireland's distinctive resources have the potential to develop a culture full of innovative, creative and entrepreneurial vitality. Take IT, for instance. Software development draws on intangibles such as a creative mindset and human relationships. This seems ideal for Ireland since it has enormous potential for growth, with competitive success depending on intangible resources founded largely on human and social capital. As a 2004 McIver consulting report for FÁS (National Training and Employment Authority) points out, software differs from many other industries in that most of its key productive resources require judgement and significant intellectual competencies or capabilities.[82] The quality and nature of the learning undergone by software developers is crucial to the business performance of companies. In addition, communities of practice form an important vehicle for learning in the sector. Yet, to-date, especially compared to the US, such communities are not well developed in Ireland. The report advocates an interdisciplinary higher education approach as the way to stimulate this sector. This would involve setting up IT industry institutes with strong technology, business, software engineering, electronic engineering and computer science credentials. Technology journalist John Sterne, author of the book *Adventures in Code*, which describes the role former start-ups like Norkom, Iona and Fineos played in the development of the indigenous software industry, agrees this industry has a profile ideal for Ireland.[83] Sterne says software development is naturally conducted by small teams, which suits Ireland since these companies thrive in an environment where there are hundreds of others rather than a few large ones. Yet he feels there is now an unhealthy emphasis by state agency Enterprise Ireland (EI) on creating a few large players instead of developing a vibrant but large pool of smaller software companies that suit the Irish character better.[84]

Another sector where Ireland appears to have distinct advantages is internationally traded services. Services are best thought of as complex systems of value co-production built on relationships featuring strongly negotiated meaning. The Services, Science, Management and Engineering (SSME) research and teaching programme at the University of California, Berkeley typifies many characteristics required in a unified approach to the kind of services education needed in Ireland.[85] It is an inherently interdisciplinary way of studying how to create, capture and re-invest in order to create value through services innovation. The disciplines of economics, computer science, engineering, law and organisational psychology all participate in the programme, each providing important perspectives on the evolution of the information and services economy. Yet this approach is extremely difficult to develop in Ireland given the structures, operations and mission of the country's third-level sector. For services innovation, the role of science needs to be complemented by a better understanding of diverse sources of innovation, including insights from disciplines such as psychology, the social sciences and humanities.[86] Yet taking advantage of Ireland's distinctive competencies will require a fundamental change in public policies on education and the missions and operations of institutions. In particular, this will involve a revamp of learning and teaching methods, and a reassessment of the definitions of scholarship and research.

A competitive advantage based on distinctive characteristics is likely to be more sustainable than alternative propositions, like the one espoused by IBEC that Irish competitive advantage is based on what it calls the Irish 'can do' attitude.[87] In a report aimed at foreign corporate decision-makers, and with the objective of securing further direct investment, IBEC identifies a skilled workforce, a favourable tax regime, and an enterprise-focused business environment as major reasons for investing in Ireland. A problem with relying on these selling points in the future, however, is that they may be duplicated or even surpassed by other countries. For instance, the Foreign Policy Globalisation Index 2007 (conducted in partnership with A.T. Kearney) ranks Ireland fifth among seventy-two counties while Estonia is tenth.[88] To all practical purposes, Estonia has no corporate income tax and its bureaucracy is benign: when a problem arises, 'the government just steps in to let investors do their thing.'[89]

Cultural Identity

A distinctive point-of-view or cultural perspective plays an increasingly important role in the music people hear, the clothes they wear or the food they eat. Personal tastes emerge from knowledge rooted in the values and experiences of specific cultures and shared places.[90] Italy offers some fascinating examples to illuminate the importance of culture, experienced feelings and meaning in innovation. For example, Roberto Verganti attributes the 'edginess' and creativity of Italian design to 'radical design-driven innovation'. Apart from its functionality and styling, what matters to the user is a product's emotional and symbolic value, or meaning. This proposes to the user a system of values, a personality and identity that goes beyond style. Italian design is invisible, a heritage that cannot be shared; the country's arts and crafts resources have been developed over generations and successful manufacturers have developed a superior capability to understand, anticipate and influence new product meanings. Verganti puts it:

> [Italian manufacturers] search for radically new design languages by looking at socio-cultural phenomena that are not so visible now but that will be trends tomorrow and reality in the future. They do not look at the phenomenon of the 'bandwagon'. Instead they *detect* the whispers of the current socio-cultural models, *identify* those feeble voices that are likely to get louder in the future, *select* from among them those whispers that best meet their own values, and *help* those voices become understandable and meaningful in a new product offering [author emphasis].[91]

There is increasing interest in protecting and developing local identity; this is very different from the days when Theodore Levitt in a famous *Harvard Business Review* article proclaimed, 'Different cultural preferences, national tastes and standards, and business institutions are vestiges of the past.'[92] Nowadays, opposite arguments are likely to be made. John Fanning, chairman of McConnells Advertising, a prominent mainstream Irish communications company, holds that there is an increasing determination by Irish consumers to resist excessive homogenisation by the 'global juggernaut'.[93] He says that while language, art, music, literature and the environment are the usual weapons of choice, local branding or 'buying local' is also playing a key role in this resistance.

The potential of tradition and distinctiveness for business is being driven internationally by a reaction against a bland consumer culture. This in turn has enhanced the value of those aspects that make a country different or make it stand out due to distinctive characteristics. This is a real opportunity for Ireland. In the years ahead, David McWilliams argues that tradition, competence, uniqueness, lineage and nostalgia are likely to become important selling points for many Irish products.[94] He cites the example of Jameson, Ireland's leading whiskey brand, which actively trades on its Irishness in markets as far away as South America. With Ireland's economic blueprint now looking a bit 'shabby', he urges a new core brand fusing the traditions of the old Ireland with the demands of the new. As McWilliams sees it, a national or 'Irish' factor is critically important in stimulating an enterprise ethic. In his book *The Pope's Children* he says that Irish traditions should now be viewed as a precious resource, offering a 'brimming and inspirational font'.[95] The characteristic of a successful Irish personality type, McWilliams' Hibernian Cosmopolitans (HiCos), is exactly this effortless ability to fuse the local with the international:

> Far from drowning that which makes you different in a sea of bland, fake, generic consumerist product, globalisation allows difference to thrive. The difference is the key: this is where the value is and it is what people are striving for. The reaction to rampant consumerism has been a 'keeping it real' backlash.

> Hibernian culture fits this 'real' bill ... When everything is accessible, the inaccessible becomes valuable.[96]

McWilliams regards the HiCos as leaders of the 'new Ireland' of the twenty-first century. The HiCos, he says, blend an attachment to traditional Irish customs, language and sport with the global sophistication, discrimination and competencies of cosmopolitans.[97] They are, in effect, another blending of the best of the old and the new. They characterise the first professional elite to celebrate the traditional culture from which the GAA springs as well as the international business culture, which pays for corporate boxes at the new Hogan Stand at Croke Park. Traditionally, McWilliams says a love of the GAA went hand-in-hand with a suite of other more greener, narrower views including support for economic isolationism. Not anymore.

The connection between Revival thinking and present international trends is clear in the role played by identity, culture and place in productivity, psychological well-being and the innovation process. Even though Seán Lemass was the politician most responsible for opening Ireland up to international trade and investment, he understood very well the importance of maintaining national distinctiveness. He believed that national characteristics had the potential to either drive or retard Irish development. He saw nationalism as the most dynamic element in Irish development and the key motive that inspires people to work for the country's advancement. In a speech in 1961, he said:

> I do not believe we can build our country by abandoning any of the characteristics of our nationhood. A policy of retreat in this respect would herald the defeat of all of our national purposes. The people of the world will respect us only to the extent that we respect ourselves, our history, our traditions, our culture and our language. If Ireland is going into the EC it is all the more important that we should preserve and develop every characteristic and value which distinguishes us from other nations. The movement

> of the Irish people which brought us so far on the road to independent nationhood was never inspired by materialistic motives alone. If it had, it would have failed, and we in our day will fail also unless we recognise and utilise the spiritual forces which activate both men and nations. Of these, nationalism, the desire to see the advancement of one's own country, is very potent, and it is by harnessing that force behind a comprehensive plan, which embraces not only economic affairs but also every aspect of national endeavour, that we can make this country secure.[98]

A difficult challenge for Ireland is to recognise and exploit the potential in linking national identity, distinctiveness and innovation. In 1961, Córas Tráchtála (Irish Export Board) turned to Scandinavian industrial designers for advice on improving the standards of Irish industrial design. The Report of the Scandinavian Design Group had an enormous impact on the subsequent development of Irish design.[99] The Group were struck by the manner in which Irish culture had developed a distinct leaning towards literature, theatre, the spoken word and abstract thinking, rather than the other side of human activity, namely creation by hand or machine and, more generally, the visual arts. The report cautioned against a national propensity for the shallow utilisation of foreign models, and urged that particular attention be paid to national characteristics that would enable Ireland to market something out of the ordinary, something with a distinctive Irish quality. In textiles, for instance, the Group found Irish firms imitating foreign styles and production techniques, which they regarded as a disastrous approach. They argued that a preferable policy would have been to experiment with new ideas and production methods, to concentrate on a few excellent lines and endeavour to produce something of unique design and quality. Nor was the Group suggesting the simple unqualified transplantation of Scandinavian design to Ireland. This would simply kill what might be saved of the original Irish values and culture, and would stifle the development of true Irish traditions, thereby scuttling whatever international opportunities may have been possible.

Today's society is a network one where intangibles such as relationships, interactivity, flexibility and trust are the dominant features. It is interesting to note the role of national identity in the development of the network society in Finland, a country Ireland is often urged to emulate. The evidence suggests that cultural identity and a strong national sentiment represent important sources of meaning and value, essential components of the network society there.[100] The Finns see no inconsistency in aiming for a dynamic integration in the global economy while also strongly affirming their culture, unique language and national identity. They have a close affinity to nature (not the usual Irish idea of subjugating it) and do not view technology in contradiction to culture, but as a tool to create a new culture. Perhaps Irish policy-makers do not fully appreciate how cultural and social factors might represent similar drivers of innovation.

Brendan Tuohy, former secretary-general of the Department of Communications, Marine and Natural Resources, has vast experience in analysing the factors responsible for Ireland's international competitiveness. He considers a sense of identity crucially important in Irish innovation and competitiveness. Forging connections between the local and the global is essential, as he told graduates at a recent conferring in University College Cork:

> As we tackle global issues and play on the world stage, it is that strong sense of our own identity that will support us. And that comes not just from us as individuals but also from the communities in which we grew up and in which we now live. It is nowhere more visible than on the hurling and football pitch where the sense of commitment to local, county or national team can be so strong.[101]

Tuohy urged graduates to reflect on the long tradition of the Irish in engaging with and influencing the world. Going back to the early monks who travelled Europe leaving a huge legacy in education, he urged Irish people to draw lessons from their ancestors – 'their sense of adventure, their sense of going into uncharted waters and bringing their culture and love of learning with them.'[102] In developing social networks, the love of chat and communication means the Irish have natural advantages, but Tuohy argues that this is enhanced by a strong sense of cultural identity.

People with confidence in their own culture absorb many different ideas, yet are not dominated by external or globalised cultural influences, a great help in innovation. Sweeney puts it well:

> Being distinctive, thinking differently and having different information enable a community to be creative and innovative. Being the same, having the same information or thinking the same way make it difficult to be creative and build a competitive advantage. Homogenisation into one globalised culture is a massive barrier to innovative development, whereas the local homogeneity and cohesion are the basis of the trust in which members are held and differentiate it.[103]

Efforts to improve innovation are more likely to be successful if innovations are appropriate to the needs and resources of the country and aligned to a strategy for enhancing national reputation. A powerful and positive national brand can provide a crucial competitive advantage in a globalised economy.[104] Traditional strategies and concepts such as brand equity, image, positioning and identity now feature in efforts at national branding. Keith Dinnie points out, however, that a national brand is not a simple process. Northern Ireland, for instance, markets itself as 'Irish' in Irish-friendly markets and as 'British' in British-friendly markets.[105] He shows that the best way to underpin a national brand is with a strong national identity, by ensuring the brand remains an encapsulation and expression of the nation's true essence. This is resulting in many countries capitalising on the power of branding in order to compete by promoting values indigenous to their heritages, cultures, economies, environments, ethnicities and histories. For a country to 'live the brand' it must be reflective of the people and the culture in that place. Particularly valuable characteristics, which Dinnie called innate or nurtured assets, are enduring elements of national identity. Such distinctive attributes are unique and impossible to copy.[106]

Advantage of Place

A territory is smaller than a region and larger than the locality. A territorial production system innovates by enhancing its special resources, using these to adjust to changes occurring in the technological and market environment it faces. There are two types of logic driving these production systems.[107] The first, the norm in Ireland, is where the territory relies on large foreign firms with hierarchical structures whose subsidiaries do not fully integrate in the host country; this places the territory in a position of dependence. In the second, there is a strong link between the firm and the host country; either a foreign subsidiary or indigenous firm integrates into various relationships within the territory. The firm helps build a *milieu* or functioning system that governs the practices, norms, rules, values and behaviour of various actors and the relationships between them.

A characteristic of an innovating milieu is that it anchors its global competitive advantage in knowledge unlikely to exist elsewhere. Since innovation is a collective process, an innovating milieu implies a host of formal and informal relationships based on co-operation, non-hierarchical links and trust. A milieu can only be preserved in the long run if specific resources are identified and fostered and social capital built up over time. This is why it is crucial a milieu does not lose cohesion. Individual interests cannot take precedence over those of the community or short-term profit given priority over long-term development. The link with Plunkett's co-operative movement is clear: a trusting milieu improves creativity while reducing the risks and costs inherent in innovation. This happens when an individual or firm knows that others are also committed to a process in which the costs and benefits are not assessed in advance and success is not assured. A milieu offers opportunities for the dissemination of know-how, without the risk of one side gaining it all; various partners share a similar work ethic and a common desire to co-operate. In contrast, a culture of suspicion can prevent development of innovation networks since it nurtures opportunistic behaviour that threatens the stability of the relationships.

The real strength of local economic development efforts comes from social capital. Competitive advantage arises when locals recognise their common identity, concentrating efforts so that belonging to a specific place becomes a strength. The basis for success comes from the willingness and capacity of locals to co-operate to achieve shared objectives. As one study showed, local stakeholders know the value and use of local resources and can coordinate themselves thanks to familiarity, reciprocity and the sharing of common needs and objectives.[108] A good example of this is territorial marketing. While everybody knows that parmesan cheese comes from Parma, nobody knows the individual entrepreneurs who produce it. Similarly, people don't worry about the producer but about the origin when buying Champagne, Swiss watches or Sri Lankan tea.

There are hopeful signs that the spirit of the Revival survives in relation to links between place and enterprise. Worker co-operatives often find it challenging to be fully accepted by Irish accountants, bankers, legal professionals and state agencies as a suitable mainstream structure for persons who wish to form a limited trading company. However, a recent Forfás commissioned report on the co-operative enterprise sector suggests there may now be more potential for a greater role for the co-operative approach in Ireland. As the Minister for Trade and Commerce said at its launch:

> Co-operatives are the expression of the idea that people can agree to work together on an equal basis and share equally in the results of their work. This concept fits well with wider societal objectives, such as those of social cohesion and of increasing the stock of social capital. The continued development of the

> co-operative model could be valuable in providing an additional dimension to social partnership in Ireland. For example, co-operatives may have the potential to play a role in addressing social policy and quality of life issues such as those arising from long working days, commuting, isolation and lack of community facilities, by filling market gaps, providing public and community services, and developing community assets.[109]

A comprehensive study of the worker co-operative concept in Ireland points out that the co-operative can be an ideal twenty-first century business model, an inclusive form of business entity, tightly controlled by those who work in it.[110] With a flexible and responsive structure, harnessing employee involvement, empowerment and partnership, a co-operative has a visible built-in social conscience.

A 2008 report by the Futures Academy of the Dublin Institute of Technology, written for the Urban Forum, points out that the future for Irish cities is to capitalise on their distinctiveness and unique assets.[111] A city like Cork, for instance, should exploit its distinctiveness as a 'city of water' with amenities and resources such as the River Lee, Cork harbour and its docklands. Innovative projects that maintain the integrity of a place, are sensitive to identity, and are tolerant of diversity and different cultures, represent critical ways of developing sustainable and inimitable competitive advantage. As one speaker said at a 2005 conference, cities should have 'the ability to value and build up an inheritance of knowledge, culture and institutions without being trapped by the past.'[112] They need to be open to external ideas and have the ability to synthesise knowledge from outside as well as inside. They must act wisely on the basis of knowledge of themselves, accompanied by an ethic of social and environmental responsibility.[113]

Richard Florida suggests that because of the advancement of social partnership, Ireland is well placed to capitalise on the creative age and become a truly sustainable society.[114] Wealth is no longer about big factories but the ability to create new ideas, not just around products, but in culture, entertainment and the arts. The challenge is to build social cohesion based on creativity while also involving immigrants. In his view, the most successful cities will be based on 'ordered chaos' rather than social compliance. Evidence from other sources is consistent with this view; it is softer issues, such as culture and the environment, encapsulated in the term 'quality of life', which will determine the most successful cities and regions in the future.[115]

Recent research by Tourism Ireland confirms the economic value of harnessing Irish identity, distinctiveness, sense of place and a sustainable ethos.[116] The organisation's proposed new country brand, encapsulated in the slogan, 'Ireland – An Island of Unique Character and Characters', will ring hollow if the place is like everywhere else. Character is about mental and moral qualities such as courage, and it is here, in the Horace Plunkett sense, that Ireland's reputation is vulnerable. A strong competitive advantage, what makes the country stand out as a destination, lies in its image of a beautiful, green land populated by friendly, welcoming people. Visitor surveys show time and again that it is people, the culture and the country's natural heritage that brings them to the country. In 2007, first-time visitors to Ireland were asked to rate their expectations at the start of their holiday; at the end, they were asked whether these expectations had been met. Place and people were predominant. Tourists look for an experience that is different or unique to them; until now at least, Ireland appears to have largely delivered on this. Nevertheless, the results also indicate that those from the European mainland feel Ireland is falling short of delivering on a promised green pristine environment.[117] Tourism Ireland's chief executive says that if the country claims greenness, it has to be able to deliver at that most fundamental base level.

It is no surprise then that, at its 2007 annual conference, Fáilte Ireland (National Tourism Development Authority) concentrated on the Irish environment and recommended new policies to fight off the potential mismatch between the clean green image used to lure visitors to Ireland and the actual reality. Clearly, the Irish tourism industry now realises it has to collectively act to safeguard its market. This €6.1 billion industry accounts for 3.8 per cent of Ireland's GNP and depends on Ireland's unique environment for its very survival. Fáilte Ireland Chairperson Gillian Bowler urged the tourism industry to take responsibility and consider how it can contribute to bringing about more enlightened and sustainable policies and procedures. Its CEO Shaun Quinn said that 85 per cent of the 7.5 million people who come to Ireland every year claim a very important factor in making their decision to visit is the quality of the landscape and its unspoiled environment. He noted that these fragile resources are now under pressure; tourism more than any other sector has everything to lose from damage to the natural environment. Quinn said the industry should embrace environmental good practice such as better water, energy use and waste management. It should exploit the very real growth opportunity with ageing populations in the US and continental Europe looking for nature-based tourism. His message was clear: the tourism industry must stand fast against those actions and policies that are perhaps inadvertently undermining the quality of Ireland's environmental product.

The following three chapters delve further into some critical aspects of the New-Revival framework. Chapter 4 covers the development of learning communities and organisations in both the private and public sector. The emphasis is on the central role of learning organisations in creating value from tangible and intangible resources. Since human capital is a crucial element of the intangible resources of an organisation, Chapter 5 concentrates on its development within educational institutions, both at school and higher education levels. The chapter maintains there is a need for radical change in both the missions and operating principles of Irish educational institutions. Particular attention is paid to business education in view of its importance for Irish managers who must increasingly learn to mediate between the local and global. Since competitiveness depends so much on the development of cultural and social resources, the focus in Chapter 6 is on the special contribution of these two. Language and communities are used, in particular, to illustrate how such resources can contribute to value creation and sustainable competitiveness.

Notes

1. Sutherland, P. (2008), 'So how did we get here?' *Innovation* (*Irish Times* Business Magazine), February, p. 18. From interview with the former EU Commissioner, currently chairman of BP and the London School of Economics in Sweeney, P. (ed.) (2007), *Ireland's Economic Success: Reasons and Lessons,* Dublin: New Island Books.
2. Fallon, B. (1998), *An Age of Innocence: Irish Culture 1930–1960*, New York: St. Martin's Press, p. 3.
3. Cumann na nGaedheal ('Party of the Irish') was comprised of the pro-treaty elements of the Sinn Féin party and came to power in 1923 as the first elected government of the Irish Free State. During 1922 Ireland had been governed by a provisional government. Cumann na nGaedheal subsequently evolved to become the present day Fine Gael party.
4. Fianna Fáil split off from the 'anti-treaty' Sinn Féin party in 1926 and was led by Éamon de Valera.
5. Government of Ireland (1958), *Economic Development*, Dublin: The Stationery Office.
6. Government of Ireland (1958), *Programme for Economic Expansion*, Dublin: The Stationery Office.
7. Government of Ireland (in association with OECD) (1965), *Science and Irish Economic Development: Report of the Research and Technology Survey Team appointed by the Minister for Industry and Commerce in 1963*, Dublin: The Stationery Office.
8. Government of Ireland (in association with OECD) (1965), *Investment in Education: Report of the Survey Team appointed by the Minister of Education in 1962*, Dublin: The Stationery Office.
9. Department of Finance, '2004 Budget, Table 9: Trends in National Debt and General Government Debt', Dublin, available at: <http://www.budget.gov.ie/2004/table9.asp>. These accounts have been restated in Euro.
10. Such austerity, however, did not extend to Taoiseach Charlie Haughey, whose personal spending habits appeared to accelerate in

direct proportion to the diminishment of public spending in other spheres.

11. A National Irish Bank study in 2008 estimated that, excluding owner-occupied housing, the average household in Ireland has wealth of €352,000 but is servicing average debt of €127,000. According to the same study, Irish people are buying more luxury jets, fast cars and leisure boats than any other Europeans, see 'Champagne Nation', *Irish Examiner*, 13 February 2008.
12. 'State has the Fastest-Growing Population of EU States', *Irish Independent*, 18 December 2007.
13. Central Statistics Office (2006), *Census 2006: Preliminary Report*, Dublin: The Stationery Office.
14. 'New York is our new Lourdes as we shop till we drop in the Big Apple', *Irish Independent*, 6 December 2006.
15. Government of Ireland (2006), *Towards 2016: Ten-Year Framework Social Partnership Agreement 2006–2015*, Dublin: The Stationery Office.
16. Government of Ireland (2007), *National Development Plan 2007–2013: Transforming Ireland*, Dublin: The Stationery Office.
17. Comhar (Sustainable Development Council) held a national conference in October 2006 to contribute to the NDP preparatory process by discussing the links between, for instance, sustainability, productivity and competitiveness. A key recommendation was the establishment of a 'Sustainability Fund' to invest in enterprise and community activity that achieve demonstrated improvement in environmental performance, while also advancing competitiveness and social cohesion. This was not, however, taken into account in the NDP (conference proceedings available at: <http://www.comharsdc.ie/_files/comhar0704.pdf>).
18. For example, Kirby, P. (1997), *Poverty Amid Plenty*, Dublin: Trócaire/Gill & Macmillan; Conference of Religious in Ireland (1996), *Progress, Values and Public Policy*, Dublin: CORI; and (2007), *Planning for Progress*, Dublin: CORI.

19. See, for example, McWilliams, D. (2006), *The Pope's Children*, Dublin: Gill & Macmillan; Fahey, T., Russell, H. and Whelan, C.T. (eds.) (2007), *Best of Times? The Social Impact of the Celtic Tiger,* Dublin: Institute of Public Administration.
20. National Competitiveness Council (2007), *Annual Competitiveness Report 2007, Volume 2: Ireland's Competitiveness Challenge*, Dublin: Forfás, p. 19.
21. While this statement is true about income distribution, a different picture emerges when it comes to wealth. Here there is far more inequality: ignoring the value of housing, the top 1 per cent of the Irish population owns 34 per cent of the country's financial wealth, at least 300 people have net assets of over €30 million and as many as 100,000 or 2.5 per cent of the population are possibly millionaires (Bank of Ireland (2007), *The Wealth of the Nation*, Dublin: Bank of Ireland Private Banking).
22. Central Statistics Office (2007), *Measuring Ireland's Progress 2006*, Dublin: The Stationery Office, pp. 42–3.
23. United Nations Development Program (2006), *Human Development Report 2006*, New York.
24. Economist Intelligence Unit (2004), *Quality-of-life Index: The World in 2005*, London: EIU.
25. *Quality-of-life Index: The World in 2005,* p. 3.
26. 'Civic Virtues Survive amid Wealth', *Irish Times*, 17 November 2004.
27. 'Civic Virtues Survive amid Wealth', *Irish Times*, 17 November 2004.
28. Inglis, T. (2008), *Global Ireland: Same Difference*, Routledge: New York, p. 189.
29. United Nations Development Program (2007), *Human Development Report 2007*, New York.
30. Smyth, E., McCoy, S., Darmody, M. and Dunne, A. (2007), 'Changing times, Changing Schools? Quality of Life for Students' in T. Fahey, H. Russell and C.T. Whelan (eds.), *Best of Times? The Social Impact of the Celtic Tiger*, Dublin: Institute of Public Administration, p. 139.
31. Smyth and McCoy *et al.* 'Changing times, Changing Schools? Quality of Life for Students', p. 3.

32. Layte, R., Nolan, A. and Nolan, B. (2007), 'Health and Health Care' in T. Fahey, H. Russell and C.T. Whelan (eds.), *Best of Times? The Social Impact of the Celtic Tiger*, Dublin: Institute of Public Administration, p. 114.
33. Layte and Nolan *et al.* 'Health and Health Care', p. 114.
34. O'Donnell, I. (2007), 'Crime and its Consequences' in T. Fahey, H. Russell and C.T. Whelan (eds.), *Best of Times? The Social Impact of the Celtic Tiger*, Dublin: Institute of Public Administration, pp. 245–64.
35. Young, P., O'Donnell, I. and Clare, E. (2001), *Crime in Ireland: Trends and Patterns, 1950–1998*, Dublin: The Stationery Office, p. vi.
36. 'The New Murder Machine', *Sunday Business Post*, 6 January 2008.
37. O'Donnell, I. (2007), 'Crime and its Consequences', p. 262.
38. National Economic and Social Forum (2003), *The Policy Implications of Social Capital: Forum Report Number* 28, Dublin: NESF.
39. Corcoran, M., Gray, J. and Peillon, M. (2007), 'Ties that Bind?: The Social Fabric of Daily Life in New Suburbs' in T. Fahey, H. Russell and C.T. Whelan (eds.), *Best of Times? The Social Impact of the Celtic Tiger*, Dublin: Institute of Public Administration, p. 196.
40. Corcoran and Gray *et al.*, 'Ties that Bind?' p. 196.
41. Corcoran and Gray *et al.*, 'Ties that Bind? p. 196.
42. See, for example, Hofstede, G. (1997), *Cultures and Organizations: Software of the Mind*, McGraw-Hill: New York.
43. Moloney, M. (2006), 'Re-Imagining Irish Music and Dance' in A.H. Wyndham (ed.), *Re-Imagining Ireland*, Charlottesville, VA: University of Virginia Press, p. 123.
44. Musician and academic Micheál Ó Súilleabháin practices this type of innovation in Irish music, reworking and absorbing outside influences in a positive manner.
45. Central Statistics Office (2006), *Census, Principle Demographic Results*, Dublin.
46. 'The Last Word?' *Irish Times*, 21 July 2007.
47. 'The Last Word?' *Irish Times*, 21 July 2007.

48. 'Taxpayer to Foot Bill if Kyoto Target not Reached', *Irish Independent*, 28 November 2007.
49. Environmental Protection Agency (2006), *Environment in Focus 2006: Environmental Indicators for Ireland*, Johnstown Castle Estate, Wexford: EPA.
50. 'City Traffic to Crawl at 8kmh', *Irish Independent*, 27 December 2007.
51. National Competitiveness Council (2007), *Annual Competitiveness Report 2007, Volume 1: Benchmarking Ireland's Performance/Volume 2: Ireland Competitiveness Challenge*, Dublin: Forfás.
52. 'Currency Risk to Exports here to Stay', *Irish Times*, 18 January 2008.
53. Institute of Management Development (2007), *World Competitiveness Yearbook*, IMD, Lausanne, Switzerland.
54. World Economic Forum (2007), *Global Competitiveness Report 2006–2007*, Cologny/Geneva: WEF.
55. National Competitiveness Council (2007), *Review of International Assessments of Ireland's Competitiveness*, Dublin: Forfás. The international assessments are: the World Economic Forum's *Global Competitiveness Report*, the Institute for Management Development's *World Competitiveness Yearbook*, the EU's Growth and Jobs Strategy, including the Centre for European Reforms' *Lisbon Scorecard* and Huggins Associates' *European Competitiveness Index*.
56. Forfás Press Release (2007), *Council Highlights Areas Vital to Enhancing Ireland's Competitiveness*, 29 November, p. 6, available at: <http://www.competitiveness.ie>.
57. Coleman, M. (2007), *The Best is Yet to Come*, Dublin: Blackhall Publishing.
58. Forfás (2006), 'Services Innovation in Ireland – Options for Innovation Policy', Dublin, September, p. 1.
59. National Competitiveness Council (2007), *Annual Competitiveness Reports 2007*.
60. The bad news is that Ireland still runs a substantial services trade deficit, importing more than exporting, for instance in tourism, communications and business services. As in manufacturing, service exports are dominated by international companies.

Anthony Foley points out that Ireland has a tough task if it is to build up its indigenous service export capability ('Service Export Performance', *Business & Finance*, 15 February 2008, pp. 56–7).

61. Gilmor, D.A. (ed.) (1979), *Irish Resources and Land Use*, Dublin: Institute of Public Administration, p. 6.
62. Zimmermann, E.W. (1933), *World Resources and Industries: A Functional Appraisal of the Availability of Agricultural and Industrial Resources*, New York: Harper and Brothers.
63. Throsby, D. (2001), *Economics and Culture*, Cambridge, UK: Cambridge University Press.
64. Norman, R. and Ramirez, R. (1993), 'From Value Chain to Value Constellation: Designing Interactive Strategy', *Harvard Business Review*, 71, July–August, pp. 65–77.
65. Porter, M.E. (1990), *The Competitive Advantage of Nations,* New York: Free Press. A shorter version of Porter's ideas are in Porter, M.E. (1990), 'The Competitive Advantage of Nations', *Harvard Business Review*, March–April, pp. 73–93.
66. Porter, *The Competitive Advantage of Nations.*
67. See, for example, Barney, J.B. (1991), 'Firm Resources and Sustained Competitive Advantage', *Journal of Management*, 17(1), pp. 99–120; Collis, D.J. and Montgomery, C.A. (1995), 'Competing on Resources', *Harvard Business Review*, July–August, pp. 118–28; Grant, R.M. (1991), 'The Resource-Based Theory of Competitive Advantage: Implications for Strategy Formulation', *California Management Review*, 33, pp. 114–35; Wernerfelt, B. (1984), 'A Resource-based View of the Firm', *Strategic Management Journal*, 5, pp. 171–80.
68. Fahy, J. (2000), 'The Resource-Based View of the Firm: Some Stumbling Blocks on the Road to Understanding Sustainable Competitive Advantage', *Journal of European Industrial Training*, 24, pp. 94–104.
69. National Competitiveness Council (2007), *Annual Competitiveness Report 2007, Volume 1: Benchmarking Ireland's Performance/Volume 2: Ireland Competitiveness Challenge*, Dublin: Forfás.

70. Attention is increasingly devoted by Irish economists and academics from other disciplines to the distinction between standard of living and other subjective concerns characterised by personal well-being, quality of life and sustainability. For example, refer to McCoy, D. and McGuirk, G. (2002), 'Matching our Standards of Living with Quality of Life Concerns', paper presented at the Heterodox Economics Annual Conference, Dublin, 9–10 July; Brereton, F., Clinch, J.P. and Ferriera, S. (2006), 'Quality of Life and Environmental Amenities: A Subjective Well-Being Approach', Working Paper, School of Geography, Planning and Environmental Policy, UCD.
71. National Economic and Social Council (2005), *NESC Strategy 2006: People, Productivity & Purpose*, Dublin: NESC.
72. NESC, *Strategy 2006*, p. xiv.
73. NESC, *Strategy 2006*, p. ix.
74. 'Achieving the Fastest Rate of Productivity Growth of any EU Country – A Roadmap for the Next Phases of Irish Economic Policy', keynote address by (then) Tánaiste and Minister for Finance Brian Cowen, Indecon Public Policy Lecture, Royal Irish Academy, Dublin, 19 November 2007.
75. For a good example of how issues facing Ireland are officially conceptualised, see the following by former Chief Executive of Forfás John Travers, available at: <http://www.forfas.ie/news.asp?page_id=218>.
76. McCoy, D. (2007), '2008 will be a Springboard', *Business & Finance*, 21 December 2007, pp. 80–1.
77. 'Irish Economy at the Crossroads', *Sunday Business Post*, 14 Ocober 2007.
78. Available at: <http://www.competitiveness.ie>.
79. NESC, *Strategy 2006*, p. 108.
80. Bradley, J. (2007), 'Small State, Big World: Reflections on Irish Economic Development', *Dublin Review of Books*, 3, Autumn, available at: <http://www.drb.ie>.
81. Palmisano, S.J. (2006), 'Globally Integrated Enterprise', *Foreign Affairs* 85(3), May/June, pp. 127–36.

82. McIver Consulting (2004), *Software Industry Training Study*, prepared for FÁS, Dublin.
83. Sterne, J. (2004), *Adventures in Code*, Dublin: Liffey Press.
84. Kennedy, J. (2004), 'Code Warrior', *Silcon Republic.com*, 15 December 2004, available at: <http://www.siliconrepublic.com/news/news.nv?storyid=single4192>.
85. Details on this innovative programme available at: <http://ssme.berkeley.edu>. Also refer to Chesbrough, H. *et al.* (2006), 'Designing a "Services Science, Management and Engineering" Discipline and Curriculum', position paper for workshop: 'Education for Services Innovation', Washington, DC, 18 April.
86. National Competitiveness Council (2006), *Annual Competitiveness Report 2006, Volume 1: Benchmarking Ireland's Performance/Volume 2: Ireland Competitiveness Challenge*, Dublin: Forfás.
87. 'Irish "Can Do" Attitude Fuels Investment by Foreign Companies', *Irish Independent*, 6 November 2007.
88. 'The Globalization Index 2007' (2007), *Foreign Policy*, November/December, available at: <http://www.foreignpolicy.com>.
89. 'The Globalization Index 2007', *Foreign Policy*.
90. OECD (1996), *Territorial Development and Human Capital in the Knowledge Economy: Towards a Policy Framework*, LEED Notebook No. 23, Paris: OECD.
91. Verganti, R. (2003), 'Design as Brokering of Languages: Innovation Strategies in Italian Firms', *Design Management Journal*, Summer, pp. 34–42.
92. Levitt, T. (1983), 'The Globalization of Markets', *Harvard Business Review*, May/June, pp. 92–102 (see p. 96).
93. Fanning, J. (2007), 'Local Branding', *Innovation* (*Irish Times* Business Magazine), December, pp. 54–5.
94. 'Tradition, Nostalgia and Lineage are the Way Forward', *Sunday Business Post* , 28 October 2007.
95. McWilliams, D. (2005), *The Pope's Children: Ireland's New Elite*, Dublin: Gill & Macmillan, p. 224.
96. McWilliams, *The Pope's Children*, p. 228.

97. McWilliams, *The Pope's Children*, p. 222.
98. Speech, Dublin, 20 September 1961, quoted in Horgan, J. (1997), *Seán Lemass: The Enigmatic Patriot*, Dublin: Gill & Macmillan, p. 305.
99. Córas Trachtála (1961), *Design in Ireland*, Dublin: Córas Trachtála.
100. Castells, M. and Himanen, P. (2002), *The Information Society and the Welfare State: The Finnish Model*, Oxford: Oxford University Press.
101. Brendan Tuohy, address at conferring at University College Cork, 10 September 2007.
102. Brendan Tuohy, address at conferring at University College Cork, 10 September 2007.
103. Sweeney, G. (2001), 'Social Capital: The Core Factor in Economic Resurgence' in G. Sweeney (ed.), *Innovation, Economic Progress and the Quality of Life*, Cheltenham, UK: Edward Elgar, p. 157.
104. A good example of how lucrative an Irish brand can prove to be is illustrated by the scam perpetuated by the bogus Irish International University (IIU). Until exposed by an undercover BBC report, hundreds of overseas students were given educational visas to enter Britain. IIU offered worthless degrees but maintained the illusion of a valid education through an elaborate but highly misleading website. It has thousands of graduates, and held 'graduating' ceremonies in rented facilities in the Divinity School in the heart of Oxford University, available at: <http://news.bbc.co.uk/2/hi/uk_news/education/7175730.stm>.
105. Dinnie, K. (2007), *Nation Branding: Concepts, Issues, Practice*, Oxford: Butterworth-Heinemann.
106. The same logic applies to a 'personal brand', which, according to one expert, is about character and saying something unique, compelling, authentic and consistent about the individual ('Rebranding Yourself', *TimesOnline*, February 2008, available at: <http://women.timesonline.co.uk/tol/life_and_style/women/body_and_soul/article3416498.ece>).

107. Maillat, D. (2001), 'Territory and Innovation: the Role of the Milieu' in G. Sweeney (ed.), *Innovation, Economic Progress and the Quality of Life*, Cheltenham, UK: Edward Elgar, pp. 137–43.
108. Canzanelli, G. (2001), 'Overview and Learned Lessons on Local Economic Development, Human Development, and Decent Work', Working Paper, Universitas, ILO, Geneva, October.
109. Forfás (2007), *Ireland's Co-operative Sector*, Dublin: Forfás.
110. Hughes, C. (2000), *The Evolution of the Worker Co-operative Concept in Ireland*, MSc Thesis, NUI Cork, unpublished.
111. Futures Academy (2008), *Twice the Size? Imagineering the Future of Irish Gateways*, Dublin Institute of Technology, report for the Urban Forum. The Urban Forum consists of Engineers Ireland, the Irish Landscape Institute, the Irish Planning Institute, the Royal Institute of the Architects of Ireland and the Society of Chartered Surveyors.
112. Charles, D. (2005), 'CRITICAL: City Regions as Intelligent Territories: Inclusion, Competitiveness and Learning', conference on 'Intelligent Territories', Employment Research Centre, Trinity College Dublin, 2 December.
113. There is increasing recognition that the competition for investment capital and the most talented workers will not be between countries but between city regions. A recent report for the Dublin Chamber of Commerce, therefore, called for Dublin to brand itself as a 'knowledge city' by 2012 with internationally recognised infrastructure, skills, productivity and competitiveness ('State must get behind drive to make Dublin a World-Class Knowledge City', *Irish Times*, 25 January 2008). A 2004 report also by the Chamber, *Imagine Dublin 2020*, also called for a 'knowledge city' with its own 'distinct cultural identity'.
114. 'Ireland on Cusp of "Creative Age", says Culture Guru', *Irish Times*, 19 October 2007.
115. 'Winning Cities have Technology – and Culture', *Irish Times*, 11 June 2003.
116. 'Ireland Gets a Makeover', *Irish Independent*, 14 January 2008. Tourism Ireland works with the two tourist boards on the island of Ireland,

Fáilte Ireland in the Republic and the Northern Ireland Tourist Board. Tourism Ireland was established under the framework of the 1998 Good Friday Agreement.

117. In 2008, Dublin ranked seventh in a league table of the most popular city destinations in Europe, down from third a year earlier. Customer satisfaction has dwindled with a survey revealing the number of visitors satisfied with the value for money they get dropping from 52 per cent to 41 per cent between 2000 and 2006. In order to sell the city better, Dublin tourism chiefs plan to spend more than €110 million over three years to eradicate litter in the capital ('Dirty Dublin to shell out €116m on Tidy-up and Tourism Drive', *Irish Independent*, 15 January 2008).

CHAPTER 4

Developing Learning Organisations

Qu'est ce que fait la difference entre l'Angleterre riche et florissante, et l'Irlande pauvre et imbecile? Le savoir industriel.

What has produced the difference between the rich and flourishing condition of England, and the poverty and weakness of Ireland? Industrial knowledge.

Robert Kane, 1844[1]

INTRODUCTION

The previous chapter maintained that value creation, derived from both tangible and intangible rooted resources, should be the core of learning and innovation to sustain Ireland's competitiveness. It also argued for the necessity of increased productivity in Ireland, especially of indigenous industry. In a learning society, value creation through enhanced productivity is achieved through innovation in networked organisations and communities, which, in addition to 'rational' approaches, emphasises values, personal growth, empowerment and emotional intelligence. A key element is meaningfulness created through goal-oriented applications at the personal, community, local and national level. Generating relationships of trust, community, imagination, purpose, motivation and meaning is as crucial as science and technology for developing a learning society. The challenge in developing a culture of learning and innovation is to create rich social relationships or networks. Emphasis is placed on action, application, problem-solving skills and practice, rather than on academic science or theory.[2]

A critical problem with the current public policy that assumes scientific research alone can build a learning culture is that such an approach tends to be mostly concerned with the question: why are things the way they are? This does not address a question crucial to learning and innovation: how do things change?[3] The best way to create value in Ireland through learning organisations is to link the rationality of science, the formation of individual character through practice, and the development of culture through identity and rootedness. This coherent theme is close in spirit to the links Horace Plunkett made between character, co-operation, discipline, identity, commercial capability and scientific practice.

As a recent survey of human resource managers indicates, developing learning organisations is a key challenge for Irish industry. The managers believe their companies possess low capability in this area.[4] While many policy-makers regard scientific research as its centrepiece, innovation has more to do with a state of mind, attitude and commitment, and the ability to turn resources into value. This holds true whether learning organisations are in the private, public or community sectors. This chapter looks at each sector, identifying central elements in value creation. Productivity, competitiveness and sustainable development are best founded on people working and learning together; caring for and developing resources rather than over-exploiting them. As discussed in the last chapter, Ireland's potential is best achieved through developing learning organisations where the country has distinctive competencies. This is especially so in the case of sustainable innovation, a subject also covered in this chapter.

LEARNING, MEANING AND VALUE

In essence, a number of streams of thought converge in the word 'value', such as:

- 'value' in the economic sense or the degree to which objects are desired and measured by how much people are willing to pay for them.
- 'values' in the sociological sense or a conception of what is ultimately good, proper or desirable in life.
- 'value' in the linguistic sense or the meaning or importance people associate with a word.[5]

The three interpretations are related. For instance, money and language are related in that communities share meanings by means of markets and conversation, in other words, through both objective and subjective exchange.[6] Just as money tends to escape from control by state-made regulations, modern communications is leading to English becoming a sort of international *lingua franca*. Meaning, short-hand for the inner world of reflective consciousness, is defined by the human ability to hold mental images of material objects and events, develop ideas and concepts, make choices and formulate values, intentions, goals, strategies and power relations.[7] Value and meaning, individual or shared, are linked in that if something conveys meaning the more valuable it tends to be or the more a person or society is willing to pay for it. Since culture is a determinant of meaning, culture and value are related. Values in the sociological sense have a moral dimension, defining what some prescribe others *ought* to want in order to make the world a good place in which to live. Richard Bawden expresses this kind of view, stating that values:

> ...reflect a focused concern for the well-being of the relationships between people and their environment, as evaluated as

much by ethical, aesthetic, spiritual and ecological concerns, as by technical, economic, practical, social and political ones.[8]

What he saw as a narrow conceptualisation of value sparked Irish supermarket supremo Senator Feargal Quinn to write in his book *Crowning the Customer* that he heaves a sigh of despair whenever he reads that an accountant has reached the top in any organisation.[9] Quinn, who advocates giving employees meaningful responsibility in customer service, says a customer-driven focus is long term, encompassing factors that are intangible and unpredictable. In contrast, the accountant is driven by the short term, the tangible and the predictable. While he accepts that it is possible for an accountant to become customer-driven, Quinn says all their training rebels against it.

Yet the way in which investment decisions are often made illustrates that the accountant's concept of value often dominates decision making.[10] This can be illustrated as follows: suppose a company is deciding whether to invest in a new project. An individual manager, who knows exactly what the company wants and whether a project will achieve it, can easily compute the value created by using so-called discounted cash flow analysis. Such a technique, covered in basic finance courses, essentially compares monetary benefits generated during the project's life with monetary outlays.[11] If the former exceed the latter, then the project is understood to create value and the decision on whether to proceed is trivial. Yet within one organisation there can be many different perceptions of risk or uncertainty held by individuals involved in the project.[12] One possibility is that the person doing the analysis may be uncertain about whether the project will succeed or not in generating benefits. This means there is risk present and evaluation involves looking at possible scenarios based on what-if or sensitivity-type analysis. The interest rate used to discount future benefits must be increased to reflect the presence of this risk. How much risk exists is a subjective call, so no simple answer exists and the decision requires judgement.

Another possibility might be that, even when there is no uncertainty about the outcome, various individuals involved in the project might disagree about what each wishes to achieve from it. In this case, agreement and consensus can only emerge through a process of discussion, conversation, negotiation or bargaining. Individual values and commitment obviously play a part in how this decision is made. A final possibility is that there may be both uncertainty about the outcome and the objective (in other words, both situations described above might hold). In such a case, inspiration and intuition are the best ways to make the project decision.

When organisations see value only through the lens of the accountant, evaluation is simply a matter of discounting monetary values from the future to the present. The future is seen to exist and individuals are asked, using evaluation tools, if the company wishes to be in that future. However, the future does not exist: these individuals must make it! Narrow evaluation procedures cannot create this future. When individuals use the accountant's lens exclusively, this in itself influences whether the future will ever even be created. To satisfy the accountant, individuals may distance themselves from the project, thereby reducing the probability that the future will be one they themselves ultimately create. The actual future needs to be forged out of the active generation of ideas, commitment and enthusiasm; in other words, it must be created through a combination of objective and subjective or human-centred decision making.

This example, although simple and contrived, illustrates that the best learning environment to create value often requires a culture of shared purpose, conversation, relationships, reflection and negotiated meaning. Grappling with value within an environment that stresses conversation and action can foster an innovative climate. Developing such a climate is usually more important than learning rational or quantitative techniques. In fact, the process of investment appraisal itself may be the real source of the value ultimately achieved. In other words, there may often be more return on the learning environment created than on the investment itself.[13] This means it is more important to develop learning environments where individuals can explore various possibilities through discussion, questioning and reflection than trying to find 'the right' answer themselves.

Creating Public Value

While conceptually similar to private value discussed above, the creation of public or common goods value is different in that many others in society jointly share ownership. Therefore, public sector executives can be best viewed as explorers commissioned by society to discover, define and produce public value. This is the perspective that a seminal figure in public management, Harvard academic Mark Moore, pursued in a classic text *Creating Public Value*.[14] While the worldview of those working in public services is similar to that in private services organisations, society often has much different expectations of each. Imagination and initiative exhibited by public servants are often viewed as dangerous to the public interest, while the same qualities among private sector executives are seen as conducive to welfare.

In undertaking to search for and discover public value, Moore says managers should be responsive to constant political guidance and feedback. However, their role is not simply one of devising the means for achieving mandated purposes; they must themselves become agents in helping to discover and define what might be valuable. In effect, they become important innovators in changing what public organisations do and how they do it. This raises the managerial role to one of ethical responsibility. In other words, they must be willing to openly state their views about what they regard as valuable and be willing to subject these views both to political commentary and to operational tests of effectiveness. They should not hide their views or frustrate efforts to test their operational or administrative theories, reporting honestly on what their organisations are seeking, doing and accomplishing. Moore's contention is that public sector managers must exhibit a certain kind of consciousness, and be imaginative, purposeful, enterprising and calculating, thereby increasing value for the organisations they lead and the broader society. This passage illustrates the intricate links between dispassionate or objective decision making and inspiration:

> In search of value, their minds range freely across the concrete circumstances of today seeking opportunities for tomorrow. Based on the potential they see, they calculate what to do: how to define their purposes, engage their political overseers and coproducers, and guide their organizations' operations. Then, most remarkably of all, they go ahead and do what their calculations suggest they should.[15]

Cool, inner concentration, Moore says, should guide the calculations of those leading public organisations. A 'managerial temperament' should combine two qualities often thought opposed. Firstly, there is the psychological strength and energy that comes from being committed to a cause. Secondly, there is the capacity for diagnosis, reflection and objectivity associated with disinterestedness. The overriding goal for a public services executive, therefore, is akin to that of his or her counterpart in, for example, an international trading services company: to work in partnership with various stakeholders to co-create and sustain value from resources, especially intangible specialised skills or competencies. Of course, a public services organisation has potentially a huge advantage: its purpose is to create public rather than private value. This can have positive implications for individual commitment and the possible relationships managers have with their customers, the public.

Value creation, therefore, should be a driving imperative for all Irish public sector managerial behaviour, rather than operating, as former GAA President Peter Quinn puts it, on an old administrative model.[16] Quinn is a director of the Quinn Group, an Irish multi-business empire run by his brother Seán, which spans insurance, stockbroking, cement manufacturing, hotels and pubs, and made profits of €433 million (on a turnover of €1.45 billion) in 2006.[17] In Quinn's view, Irish universities, their business schools, most of the training organisations, funding bodies and statutory agencies operate within the old administrative mindset. As a result, Quinn says, this does damage to Ireland's future development potential.

Yet, even where there is a consensus about value creation as the goal, a major conceptual problem arises due to the widespread monetisation of values in Irish society. The standard methodology for assessing the value of infrastructure projects, for instance, is cost-benefit analysis. Derived conceptually from economics, this technique treats human behaviour as individualistic, rational, utility maximising, and shorn of all cultural or social context.[18] In such a world, society is made up of self-interested individuals rather than the dynamic, interactive and complex social relationships that exist among people in real communities. Conventional economics, which focuses on factors amenable to monetary valuation, can assist policy-makers in assessing how value for money can be achieved when choosing between alternative investments similar in nature. However, investment decisions that have so profound an impact on the quality of life of current and future generations should not be based solely on factors that can only be estimated in money terms.

The experience of Luas, Dublin's light rail system run by the Railway Procurement Agency (RPA), provides an instructive example. Since service on Luas began in 2004 its positive spin-offs have been so substantial that they call into question the adequacy of cost-benefit analysis to evaluate any transportation project or indeed any project with a definite social dimension.[19] A feature of Luas is the popularity of the service at times of day traditionally regarded as off-peak. By offering a high-frequency service, with high reliability, people within the catchment area of Luas have embraced the service to a greater extent than suggested by economic modelling. The unanticipated benefits of Luas have included, for instance, additional off-peak passengers for shopping and entertainment, improved access for the disabled, increased volume of inbound visitors, and more travel to inner-city neighbourhoods. Yet the cost-benefit analysis originally used in analysing public investment in Luas was based only on estimating the direct monetary effects of investment in infrastructure. It focused largely on savings in journey time relative to other modes of transport. This neglected many critically important social benefits, which, along with a quality service for passengers, resulted in high capacity utilisation at all times of the day.

The challenge for policy-makers is to recognise the limits of economics and that the valuation of intangible qualities requires a broader approach if dynamic, innovative and healthy communities are to be achieved. A community that nurtures creativity is likely to be based on local relationships, not one characterised by commuting long distances for employment, education and recreation. A decision-making methodology has to reflect the changing aspirations for such communities. A rail project like Luas not only contributes to the economic development of the communities it serves but is itself an instrument of wider social change. The conventional approach is therefore not appropriate for considering infrastructure that has a significant social impact. Decisions on infrastructure projects should also address how the project will affect shared values such as a sense of community, neighbourliness or the potential for nurturing integrated manageable communities. It is these qualities that in turn determine the capacity of a locality for enhanced creativity, innovation and sustainability.

Value through Partnerships

Particular attention is now being given to achieving value for money through effective management of public sector investment. Yet value creation is not simply about minimising the financial or non-financial resources devoted to a public service. Nor is the lowest cost the same as value for money, defined as an optimum combination of cost, quality, efficiency and effectiveness. This is why in the past few years there has been much new thinking about the respective roles of the State and private interests in the provision of public services. For instance, many public-private partnerships

(PPPs) between public sector organisations and private sector investors and businesses have been set up to design, plan, finance, construct and/or operate Irish infrastructure projects.[20] Until now, such projects were normally provided through traditional state procurement mechanisms. In a PPP, while the public sector retains ultimate responsibility for providing a service, the actual delivery becomes the responsibility of a private party under a long-term agreement or 'concession'. The concessionaire builds a project for the State and is paid by means of performance payments over a lengthy period. Incentives are created that lead to greater efficiency, since payment is tied to performance through the life of the contract. Emphasis switches to measuring and rewarding superior performance rather than the ownership of assets. When they offer increased value for money, PPPs can be a viable option for public infrastructure projects and delivery of public services over traditional procurement methods. The perceived benefits of PPPs are that the private sector, guided by the profit motive, is more innovative and cost-effective in providing public services. By transferring risk and, correspondingly, reward to the private sector, PPPs ensure that issues like design and construction take the 'whole life' of the asset into account. The public therefore gain access to private sector skills that can lead to more flexibility, responsibility and higher quality public services.

Another area with potential for innovative value creation approaches is State support for the delivery of critical social services. The roles of the public and voluntary sectors are complementary and both parties would benefit if new forms of partnership were created that would permit a longer-term perspective than at present. While ultimate responsibility for social services rests with the State, the critical role of voluntary organisations is rarely recognised in terms of State support. These organisations often lack funding security, and rely on voluntary subscriptions and special promotional campaigns to bolster resources. From the State's perspective, by funding voluntary groups in this haphazard manner, it does not get the degree of oversight that would be reasonable considering the level of funding provided. There is seldom a direct link between the operations of a voluntary group and the mission of the funding State social services agency. Rather than seeing voluntary groups as strategic allies or partners in tackling issues of public need, the State itself sometimes duplicates the same service. It is clear that a new vision is needed so the State and the voluntary sector can work together as partners to enhance the concept of civil society. A fresh approach to partnership with the voluntary sector could offer an infusion of new blood, perspectives and operating methods.

Drawing from the experience of PPPs to-date, a new form of partnership called public-voluntary partnerships (PVPs) has recently been suggested.[21] Just as PPPs provide physical infrastructure and are designed to encourage innovative design, reward performance according to the results achieved, and adopt a long-term perspective, PVPs might be similarly structured to encourage innovative solutions to social problems provided by people who have the most relevant grassroots experience. PVPs would recognise the existing long-term commitments to individuals and communities. The ethos of voluntary agencies is to show dedication to the people being served that goes far beyond what could reasonably be expected from paid employees. Nevertheless, the conceptual framework underlying PPPs and their development to-date offers hope for those engaged in social ventures; they may learn and apply the same thinking in the case of PVP structures.

PVPs would obviously face a different set of circumstances, reflected in their remit, operational needs, public demand and indicators of performance. A PVP would be founded on the principle that a project consistent with the mission of a State agency be identified and an output specification determined. Then, to achieve value for money, a competitive process perhaps involving a number of voluntary groups would be set up. Some groups might even co-operate, build consortia or involve private sector partners with special expertise in particular aspects of the work. Once negotiations are completed and the winning bid is determined, a detailed partnership process would be put in place, embedded in a legal contract containing such items as performance indicators and payment terms. Just as in PPPs, the winning bid may not necessarily be the lowest cost, but the proposal that offers the best value in meeting the State's objectives over the long term. The use of PVPs offers hope that the manner in which different aspects of work in the social arena might be conducted in the future will change in fundamental ways. The proper design of PVPs could lead to the development of clearly defined, agreed and shared policy objectives, resulting in a dynamic and performance-related culture in voluntary organisations. The real challenge is to develop appropriate structures such as PVPs to provide guidance to voluntary agencies so they can concentrate on their underlying mission and achieve results. The State in turn can provide the type of financial incentives and regulatory framework it uses to stimulate private initiative in other activities.

The emphasis in the next section is to refute a common suggestion that the commercialision of research, especially scientific research within higher education institutions, is what primarily leads to innovation. While R&D can indeed be a valuable component, the most important element in stimulating an innovation culture is the development of learning communities and organisations.

Research and Innovation

Rationality, Intuition and Interpretation

Some of the most exciting research in politics and economics is based on the realisation that humans are motivated by more than material or individual self-interest. Many researchers have pointed out that an assumption that human behaviour is driven exclusively by rational, self-interested calculations is false.[22] Activities such as charity, altruism and volunteerism illustrate the role that emotions and commitment play in communities. Mainstream economics joins a simple model of human behaviour with complicated mathematical models that often dazzle non-specialists. Yet its premise is straightforward: society is composed of individuals, each of whom has a clear idea of what he or she wants out of life, and tries to get as much as possible for the least amount of sacrifice and effort. Society is simply the outcome of all this self-interested activity.

Many sociologists, whose subject is society itself, proceed in a somewhat similar manner. However, a society, like an organism, is distinct from the individuals that comprise it. By focusing on human beings as the component units of societies, some sociologists try to show that we can understand a society in terms of its individual parts. Yet the behaviour of interdependent human beings cannot be fully explained by studying them singly.[23] In fact, the opposite is more likely true: many aspects of individual behaviour can only be understood if one sets out to study interdependence and the relationships among individuals within communities. This is why the social and cultural context is such a crucial factor in learning and innovation.

Economists accept that imagination and emotion play little or no role in their models. Many accept that economic value systems are narrow and simplistic, leaving little room for the mysteries of individual behaviour or indeed of inspiration and personal insight.[24] Yet much public policy seems driven by the assumption that these economic models still work well. The founding fathers of economics were aware of this problem. The intellectual foundations for rational self-interest or market-led models are books like Adam Smith's *The Wealth of Nations*[25] and Charles Darwin's *The Origin of the Species.*[26] Yet much less attention seems to be paid to other works by the same authors in which the emotions figure prominently. Smith's *The Theory of Moral Sentiments*[27] and Darwin's *The Expression of the Emotions in Man and Animals*[28] describe how moods and feelings, and 'sympathy' for one's fellows, are essential in understanding economic behaviour and survival.

Austrian economist Joseph Schumpeter expressed the dynamic nature of innovation with his term 'creative destruction'.[29] Schumpeter recognised that the risk taker – the entrepreneur or innovator – by destroying, transforming and creating, produces an economy in a constant state of change. However, innovation is very difficult to incorporate within mainstream economics because this implies change, disequilibrium, complexity and continuous adjustment. Conventional economics, while good at describing the operation of established markets, does not do a good job when it comes to people's creativity, motivation or the rationale they use when interacting with each other.[30] Innovation is especially hard to capture when it is assumed a general theory can explain everything.[31] Some modern economic theories that incorporate knowledge – so-called new growth (or endogenous) and evolutionary theories – are limited in how they conceptualise the essence of what it is to be human. These models feature socially isolated and rational individuals, essentially simple stimulus-response machines, and allow for only marginal changes, rather than the more complicated properties of dynamic systems, peopled by individuals driven by emotional and psychological needs. Such models are especially unsuited to a learning society that is systematic, quality driven, inclusive, outward looking and value conscious. Without a moral or ethical dimension offering a theory of value, economic models cannot properly handle the complex relationships in economic, natural and social environments. This issue is central to the development of a sustainable development and successful learning society.[32]

One of Albert Einstein's famous quotes goes, 'The intuitive mind is a sacred gift and the rational mind is a faithful servant. We have created a society that honors the servant and has forgotten the gift.'[33] A sense of place, associated with human emotions and feelings, is a key element of innovation. Yet public policy-makers often assume innovation is really about scientific research or rational ways of knowing. The Austrian philosopher of science Karl Popper held that science should not exclude passion, imagination or creative intuition. He argued against the assumption that two cultures exist, one scientific or rational and the other aesthetic or irrational. The scientist and the artist are not engaged in incompatible activities but both try to extend people's understanding of experience by the use of creative imagination. In other words, they each use rational as well as irrational faculties. Popper argued that it is wrong to see science as a craving to be right. He said ignorance grows with knowledge; there will always be more questions than answers. He emphasised problem solving and gave tradition importance. As Bryan Magee writes in a lucid guide to this thinker, 'in everything we are, and everything we do, we inherit the *whole* past, and however much we might want to make ourselves independent of it there is no way in which we possibly can.'[34] Magee adds:

> Popper does not say, though he might have done, that our very existence itself is the direct result of a social act performed by two other people whom we are powerless to choose or prevent, and whose genetic legacy is built into our body and personality. We are social creatures to the utmost centre of our being. The notion that one can begin anything at all from scratch, free from the past, or unindebted to others, could not conceivably be more wrong.[35]

Conversation and Relationships

In essence, two fundamental processes lie at the heart of learning organisations, and indeed of entire economies. One, called analysis, problem solving or rational decision making, dominates industrial management thinking, engineering practice and economic policy making. Companies focus constantly on it, treating an innovative concept as a problem to be solved as efficiently as possible, often reducing innovation to merely a set of engineering requirements. It is also the ethos that dominates many business programmes (especially MBA degrees), as well as thinking that drives much innovation policy in Ireland.

The other process, what might be called irrational, inspirational or intuitive thinking, is close to what Richard Lester and Michael Piore call 'interpretation'. This is more about orchestrated structured conversations that emerge from a community that conceives and discusses new products and services.[36] Drawing on research at the MIT Industrial Performance Center on innovations in a range of dynamic sectors like mobile phones, medical devices and fashion, Lester and Piore show how the pressures of globalisation lead many companies to try to get new products to market as quickly as possible. This drives them to favour project-driven analysis, closure rather than long internal conversations, certainty over ambiguity and the exclusion of troublesome stakeholders. What is required is balance between the analytical and interpretive processes. However, the current emphasis on expanding market competition risks choking off the vital interpretative spaces required for innovation.

Embracing and exploiting ambiguity and confusion among stakeholders such as designers, engineers, marketers and customers illustrates that learning and innovation is largely a social enterprise. Interpretation is not just about 'listening to the customer', but about redefining the product concept by observing people and anticipating what they never imagine they might actually want. This is why many corporations now include ethnographic interpretations in consumer research to get better insights into issues of identity, lifestyle and meaning.[37] Providing ideas that resonate deeply with consumers, they look for less obvious patterns to inspire and inform thinking. Quite often, these sorts of enterprises actively tackle sustainability issues and are most sensitive to looking deeply into economic and social interdependencies. They are most receptive to new approaches to discovery and to creating various networked partnerships that deliver meaningful value.

Research Policy

The EU Commission, through its Lisbon Agenda, is aiming to make Europe the most competitive knowledge economy in the world. Research in the generation and application of scientific knowledge, especially in information technology and the biosciences, is regarded as critically important to achieve this goal. Until recently, little attention was devoted to ensuring that science and technology became drivers of Irish development.[38] Now a key policy objective is to develop a knowledge-driven or learning society to generate high productivity and sustainable competitiveness. To do so, recent Irish Government reports such as the 2004 *Enterprise Strategy Report*[39] and the 2006 *Strategy for Science, Technology and Innovation, 2006–2013* (STI Report)[40] strongly advocate moving the country up the value chain. The STI Report contains a commitment to relatively massive (by Irish standards) spending on R&D over the next seven years of some €3.8 billion in public and private funds. State agency Science Foundation Ireland (SFI) is spending enormous resources on the development of R&D centres in third-level institutions in order 'to promote innovation' and 'become a more knowledge-driven economy'. Under the *National Development Plan 2007–2013*, the State will invest a staggering €8.2 billion in science, technology and innovation.[41] To boost R&D, third-level institutions plan to double the number of Ph.D. graduates.[42]

This increase in spending on R&D in higher education is certainly impressive. Overall R&D expenditure in this sector has almost quadrupled over the period 1996–2006 in current spending terms, rising from €238 million in 2000 to over €600 million in 2006, now about average as a percentage of GDP among twenty-five EU countries.[43] Higher education researchers per thousand workers in the labour force rose from 1.2 in 2000 to 2.2 in 2006, with Ireland going from twenty-fourth to thirteenth place among twenty-nine OECD countries during this period.[44] Yet this huge financial commitment to research, especially in universities, may not necessarily result in increasing levels of innovation.[45] Such investment, in the hope it will spur innovation through academic spin-offs and interaction with commercial enterprises, might not even represent good value for money. As UCC economists Declan Jordan and Eoin

O'Leary demonstrate, the greater the frequency of direct interaction between Irish businesses and higher education institutions, the lower the probability of both product and process innovations in these businesses.[46] They conclude that substantial public investment in research at Irish universities might possibly have a negative effect on the innovative output of Irish business, undermining future prosperity. This means that the centrepiece of Ireland's policy to promote innovation, namely interaction between business and academia, might have a limited effect. Promoting innovation by clustering suppliers, customers, competitors, third-level colleges, support agencies and high-technology companies on a local or regional basis may not even be the most viable option. They suggest that the extent to which a region can benefit from academic research depends on factors such as the relevance of the research to business, the absorptive capacity of the business, and the strength of local knowledge dissemination networks.

Such criticism has not been accepted lightly. A Government spokesperson argues that these findings derive from a 'false premise that the Government policy is static and unresponsive to emerging trends.'[47] The comments by Frank Gannon, director general of SFI, are worthy of note. He claims that others, and 'not just the Irish', are following this same policy and Ireland has no choice since there is no plan B.[48] The Advisory Science Council (ARC), the Government's high-level advisory body on science, technology and innovation policy issues, argues that the onus is on business to move fast to exploit the output of academic research many may not have wanted in the first place. Recent comments by Mary Cryan, ARC chairwoman, suggest a re-think in approach to innovation may be necessary:

> Research is of limited use if its results end up on a shelf, or end up being exploited elsewhere. Great strides have been made in investment in higher education; now we need to ensure we can exploit the research results that come from that investment.[49]

Official thinking is that research spending will lead to commercial enterprises, but how and when? Éamon Ryan, now a government minister (but a Green Party TD when the STI Report was published), wrote at the time that Government spending on R&D was unlikely to bear fruit in developing an innovation society if investment was to be confined to science and technology.[50]

Science media researcher Brian Trench maintains the media is unwilling to engage critically with this central aspect of science policy in Ireland.[51] He argues that the concept of knowledge encapsulated in formal scientific research and its translation into technical innovation is too narrow:

> The knowledge at issue is neither the intuitive knowledge that the arts bring nor the critical knowledge of history, philosophy, and social sciences. Rather, the knowledge economy privileges scientific knowledge. In so doing, it takes a restricted view of the possible contributions of science. In concentrating on wealth generation and national competitiveness, it downplays the possible contribution of science to improving the quality of life.[52]

Trench says there is little public engagement with the priorities and purposes of research or with its social, philosophical and ethical implications. He points out that although former Taoiseach Bertie Ahern's foreword to the STI Report claims 'people are at the heart of the knowledge society', in fact the roles that people can actually play are limited. Effectively, the social and cultural context for scientific innovation is ignored. By focusing on science merely as a means to an economic end, Trench argues that policy-makers are missing the contribution a greater awareness of science can make to a more active citizenship.

It has been demonstrated repeatedly that there is no relationship between the money spent on R&D and the prosperity of a country or region. The success of an innovation policy has far more to do with qualitative, social and attitudinal factors, such as trust and cohesion, than expenditures on scientific research per se.

The same is true at firm level. There is almost no correlation between increased R&D spending or idea generation and company improvements in sales, profitability or share prices unless there is an accompanying change in processes, systems, structures or capabilities. For instance, two recent reports from international consultants Booz Allen Hamilton suggest that non-monetary factors may be the most important drivers of a company's return on innovation investment (the reports call this ROI^2).[53] In order to increase ROI^2, a company needs to focus on ways that increase the effectiveness of innovation expenditures. These studies suggest that superior results derive from the quality of the organisation's innovation process, and the bets it makes and how it pursues them, rather than the magnitude of the spending itself. It is clear that innovation is not a discrete activity but a multifunctional capability that requires several kinds of competencies.

Two other studies, one from the IBM Institute for Business Value and another from an IDA Ireland-sponsored Economist Intelligence Unit (EIU) survey, conclude that companies are transforming the way they carry out R&D.[54] Relationships and trust seem to matter most. A growing number of companies are looking beyond their own internal R&D teams for ideas and innovation. Outsourcing and offshoring are increasingly common in a global innovation network model, so-called 'research without walls'. The EIU Study reports that the proportion of companies with at least some overseas R&D activity is now at 65 per cent, rising to a predicted 84 per cent in three years time. Similarly, 64 per cent currently outsource part of their innovation process to external organisations, rising over the next three years to 75 per cent. As the trend towards global innovation networks rises, the role of human capabilities and skills is becoming increasingly important. Richard Straub, keynote speaker at the third International Conference on Services and Innovation, held in Dublin, pointed out that such innovation happens not within the four walls of a lab but in partnership with others.[55] The shift away from knowledge creation towards its trading and usage means that generating new ideas is no longer as important as a talent for accessing the global pool of knowledge, networking and making *connections*.[56] In other words, knowledge workers in an innovation-led services economy need flexibility, openness and multiple skill sets, characteristics far different than those coming from a research-driven academic environment or those traditionally sought in a product economy. Yet many Irish students still graduate from an academic system shaped by the structure designed by an industrial mindset and the traditional research-led culture.

To respond to these global challenges, and consistent with the basis of our New-Revival framework, Ireland should aim to create the kind of innovation environment that, by developing learning organisations, is adept at identifying distinctive and inimitable resources with potential to add the greatest value. This does not necessarily mean spending enormous resources on R&D, although state-of-the art research would certainly remain an important element of the country's innovation strategy.

Seeing knowledge conceptualised in narrow terms by policy-makers possibly led Seán Ó Riain to use the expression 'nurturing many knowledges' in the title of a paper he presented on innovation.[57] He cites the 2005 Fáilte Ireland Visitor Attitudes Survey that found that:

> …around seven in every ten holidaymakers visited historical and cultural attractions during their stay and around two in every three toured by car, highlighting the importance to Ireland of the sightseeing and culture oriented holidaymaker.

Ó Riain asks, what impact do expenditures on R&D have on tourism when it is culture, history, archaeology and the Irish language that are keys to innovation in this industry sector? Spending on the latter would undoubtedly lead to a higher ROI^2, yet innovation policy in Ireland tends to treat society as synonymous with the economy and assumes that the laboratory is the only place where research can take place. What is needed instead is an innovation policy that supports the diverse ways in which people come to know, understand and value.

Knowing and Feeling

The heart of an innovative culture is a frame of mind, a way of thinking, of identifying and using resources to create value, rather than the discovery of new objective knowledge per se. Indeed, a 2005 report commissioned by Forfás points out that new knowledge is often not very important in stimulating business innovation.[58] The report stressed that existing knowledge usually constitutes the vast majority of knowledge used in any innovation. Ireland's innovative capabilities and self-reliance in economic activities depend most of all on a strong cultural base. This, in turn, depends on the development of vital cultural and social capital. Some notion of a common identity, solidarity or a high level of social capital in a community or society is crucial to innovation, since these are critical to the formation of productive relationships. A country's wisdom, values, traditions and self-knowledge give it breadth, purpose and confidence, and these are the critical components in generating a prosperous and successful learning society.

Different forms of knowledge play a crucial role in stimulating innovation and there is a complex relationship between research, knowledge and innovation. Michael Polanyi illustrates that strong personal feelings and commitments permeate creative acts, especially acts of discovery.[59] Polanyi (not surprisingly, two of his famous works are called *Personal Knowledge* and *Meaning*) argues that informed guesses, hunches, inspiration, intuition and imaginings cannot necessarily be stated in propositional or formal terms.[60] Polanyi was aware that often people know more than they can tell, or they cannot state what they know in formal or codified terms. Yet tacit forms of knowledge are as legitimate as R&D in the processes of exploration and discovery. They play an especially central role in services innovation and the outsourcing of R&D, where competencies such as the ability to foster relationships are central to sustainable competitive advantage.

Knowledge is more than facts, theories or codified information. It is *constructed* rather than *received.* Its most valuable characteristics are these tacit elements, feelings, meaning, human interactions and intangible processes embodied in relationships. *Know-what* and *know-why* constitutes codified knowledge while *know-how* and *know-who* constitutes tacit knowledge.[61] Simply put, innovation is more about what we *do* with knowledge than the knowledge itself.[62] Doing and valuing are at the heart of innovation and distinguish it from scientific research, which centres on thinking and reflection.

Assumptions must change about what constitutes research, how knowledge is conceptualised and current approaches to scholarship. The traditional definition of research centres on the discovery of true and objective knowledge, a scientific perspective that sees 'real research' requiring quantification. Yet, as Stanford University art educator Elliot Eisner holds, rather than research being a species of science, in fact 'science is one, and only one, species of research'.[63] It would help if institutions gave more recognition to other approaches for discovering new knowledge and understanding, as embodied in action research for example. The scientific form of research has no monopoly on the ways in which humans inquire. Where once the aim of research was to discover knowledge that was true and 'objective', the way it 'really is', it is now recognised that there may be infinite ways in which something may become known. A view increasingly under challenge is that only through research do we find out what works; once this is known, it will tell us what to do and how. The idea that research conclusions can be applied like prescriptions for action independent of context, Eisner suggests, 'underestimates the inevitable gap between theoretical knowledge and practical action'.[64]

Harry Boyte writes, 'science asks "how" questions, but it neglects questions of meaning, purpose and value.'[65] Because of the authority of science, the focus is often on efficiency and technology rather than on the meaning and significance of what is created, the work process itself or the definition of 'wealth'. Teaching is often seen merely as 'instruction', accompanied by the disappearance of a sense of community and public purpose, especially within third-level institutions. Many faculty members have disengaged from public life and this ethos of disengagement is fed by an uncritical celebration of science. Even though discredited intellectually, the philosophy of positivism structures research, disciplines, teaching and institutions. Its proponents argue that science rests on the discovery of permanent standards of rationality that are waiting to be discovered and applied. This slights 'ordinary knowledge' and depreciates the capacities, talents and interests of the non-expert and the amateur. It is also often antagonistic to common sense, tradition, craft and practical knowledge mediated through everyday experience.

Higher Education Role

While the Irish higher education sector tends to focus on technology transfer as its main contribution to industry, international evidence shows that often the most important contribution is the quality of the learning offered to students, local communities and enterprises.[66] Colleges should attempt to serve as a public space for local conversations about the future direction of technologies, markets, products, services and the myriad of social issues affecting a community. The close ties between university research and commercial entities have been criticised since these often tend to crowd out the university's role in cultivating and preserving quasi-public 'spaces for interpretation' that are supportive of innovation within the communities in which they are located.[67] The importance of this public role seems in general underappreciated by Irish higher education institutions.[68]

The innovative idea and its development have many inputs; scientific research is only one. An innovative process, led by learning organisations, would see academic research acting as a window on the world, identifying and acquiring knowledge from elsewhere as well as internally. For innovation to prosper, Roy Johnston argues, it is not necessary for educational institutions to make 'great discoveries' but to be part of the global network of science in order to know when a discovery is significant and be able to organise locally to profit by it.[69] Clearly this requires a scientific understanding of the properties of materials and the production process, especially the ways in which human and organisational factors impact value creation.

Public policies in the higher education sector should champion links with indigenous industry, promoting a radically different approach to research and innovation that is more appropriate for small and medium-sized enterprises (SMEs). Colleges could contribute far more to society by adapting knowledge originating elsewhere to local conditions, thereby aligning their contribution to the realities of the local economy. This might also unlock and redirect knowledge that already exists in a region but has yet to be put to productive use. It might involve clusters of related projects. Such a commitment to the local would require a paradigmatic shift by the Irish universities involving a new appreciation of the value of place beyond its function as a space in which to learn.[70]

The current approach to higher education research is unlikely to lead to a learning society. The manner in which SFI disburses its massive allocation of funds has, as Seán Ó Riain puts it, 'transposed the logic of FDI attraction into the world of science and technology'.[71] The Irish higher education model of innovation is largely conceptualised as a linear one comprising basic research leading to commercialisation through technology transfer. A recent Government report recognises that the present model is not working properly. It states, 'higher education-enterprise collaboration operates at a very low level in Ireland and … structures in place to encourage and support the process have failed to achieve significant results.'[72] It suggests consideration of an Applied Research Foundation as an analogue to SFI to remedy the situation. Another recent study examined the potential of so-called 'competence centres' which now operate in some countries.[73] These are typically based in academic institutions and deliver industry-driven research programmes.

The following section looks at learning organisations guided by the New-Revival framework developed in the last chapter. Because enhanced productivity and a culture of innovation in the public sector plays an especially important role in determining national competitiveness, the potential of Irish public learning organisations is described in detail.

IRISH LEARNING ORGANISATIONS

Private Sector

For decades, there have been calls for indigenous companies to play a more central role in Irish development. Yet the multinational sector remains dominant. Ireland still finds it difficult to reach its true potential through native entrepreneurial enterprise – as outlined in 1992 by the Government-appointed Culliton Commission. The Commission recommended strengthening the capabilities of indigenous companies and nurturing a strong entrepreneurial spirit, demonstrating the importance of such a spirit by placing the following on the front cover of its report:

> We need a spirit of self-reliance – a determination to take charge of our future – to build an economy of real strength and permanence which will give jobs and wealth sufficient to our needs.[74]

Some fifteen years later, Frank Ryan, chief executive of Enterprise Ireland (EI), the state agency responsible for the development of Irish manufacturing and services companies, continues to stress the need for growing a strong indigenous sector. He writes the following in EI's current strategy document *Transforming Irish Industry, 2008–2010*:

> We must now become the architects of our own economic future. This means we must focus our energies and resources on growing a cohort of Irish companies with the ambition, leadership and innovation necessary to achieve global scale.[75]

To give EI its due, the organisation has been quite successful in achieving its targets over the three-year period 2005–2007. For instance, the total level of new exports from the indigenous sector was just short of €4 billion against EI's three-year target of €3 billion. Also, high potential start-ups at 221 exceeded its target of 210 firms while over 619 companies were engaged in meaningful R&D (that is, investing at least €100,000 per year), which was just above its target for the period.[76] Innovation, with particular emphasis on international services, is now at the core of EI's strategy. Its key elements are to consolidate existing growth in overseas markets, capitalise on emerging opportunities and stimulate the emergence and development of global companies of scale. Yet the danger is that, as Ireland's attractiveness as a location for FDI wanes, policy-makers may depend on strategies for indigenous industry not grounded in unique or inimitable competitive advantages that ensure long-term sustainability.

EI does not appear to recognise a distinct Irish advantage: rooted Irish-global identity as the key resource for stimulating innovation. This is a weakness in general in official thinking on innovation, whether at individual, enterprise or regional level. Government reports rarely seem to consider a rooted-resource identity as a factor in fostering productivity and competitiveness. For example, the 2007 Forfás report *Towards Developing an Entrepreneurial Policy for Ireland* calls for a world-class entrepreneurial environment, suggesting Ireland needs an approach similar to the drive that attracted FDI.[77] It identifies key areas for development relating to enterprise culture, education and entrepreneurship, especially among women and immigrants; but there is no appreciation of how identity or sense of place might affect emotions, feelings and meaning with positive consequences for innovation. Another key policy document also fails to mention this crucial aspect: the national skills strategy or *Tomorrow's Skills: Towards a National Skills Strategy,* launched in March 2007 and prepared by the Expert Group on Future Skill Needs.[78] This proposes a vision of what it calls 'a competitive, innovation-driven, knowledge-based, participative and inclusive economy with a highly skilled workforce by 2020.'

Joe Lee, in his inimitable style, nicely expresses the challenge of moving Irish educational thinking away from cosy assumptions about its role in serving the needs of multinational companies and towards fostering a spirit of national self-reliance:

> We need a shift in our whole mental axis, but not one that sacrifices our residual scraps of identity for nothing better than servility to subsidized squatters, instead of fostering the self-reliance that requires an education of intellect, imagination and character. When the foundations are fragile, the frantic effort devoted to keeping up the paint work is doomed to futility, however lucrative it may be for the decorators of the day.[79]

Observers have drawn attention to human factor deficiencies they maintain prevent the creation of a sustainable Irish enterprise culture. In 1993, sociologists Paul Keating and Derry Desmond put this down to the inadequacies of the cultural values of Ireland's entrepreneurial establishment.[80] Michael Casey, former assistant director general of the Central Bank, says that people should not be surprised at Ireland's failure, outside of a few exceptional individuals, to generate high-calibre entrepreneurs.[81] He sees the key issue as the mindset: risk aversion is hard-wired into Irish people. It is no surprise, he says, that a country so wounded physically, morally and spiritually during long years of oppression will naturally find it difficult to produce people of confident risk-taking ability. After independence, the new State and the Church acted as forces of conservatism and there is no doubt many enterprising people emigrated, especially to the US. Then, just as social and cultural norms became more welcoming to the emergence of an entrepreneurial class, the prevailing model of enterprise became one of 'cunning and stroke play'. The heroes were those who pulled strokes, that is, made money for little effort or risk, usually on the basis of cronyism and inside information; profit was not the return on risk but the pay-off for being 'in the know'. Casey says that, despite tribunals of enquiry, the lure of stroke play is still strong, appealing to something in the Irish character. From the standpoint of development, this is disastrous since no communal value is added by such behaviour. To take risks is to be courageous; the entrepreneur must be willing to take responsibility for his or her decisions. Yet, according to Casey's harsh verdict, it is in the area of responsibility that the Irish appear weakest. The private and public sectors seem populated by managers and executives who find it difficult to take responsibility for their actions.

The presence in the workplace of so-called generation Y workers, those born after 1980, who may have different motivations and expectations than their parents, has major implications for the leadership and management of learning and innovation within Irish enterprise. These young people are often concerned with opportunities for development, both inside and outside the workplace. Job security is not a significant concern for them since they expect to work with multiple organisations throughout their careers.[82] They increasingly seek more meaningful and interesting work which means companies need to move from a command and control world where rules and procedures are important to one where relationships, conversations and team-working matter.[83] Generation Y workers need constant praise and feedback and are used to getting answers to their questions immediately. Social networking platforms can play a very important role, for instance in combating high turnover, rewarding work well done, answering questions in a speedy manner and allowing more senior employees to act as mentors.[84] The goal must be to create what Lynda Gratton, professor of Management Practice at London Business School, calls 'hotspots'.[85] These are places where young people are energised and excited and infused with a co-operative mindset. They value others and want to work on meaningful projects that transcend disciplinary boundaries.

Public Sector

To achieve productivity improvements by means of learning organisations in the public sector, a value-led framework must also be the starting point. A public learning organisation, unlike the traditional or bureaucratic one, is capable of reinventing itself when necessary, continually improving its ability to be more effective in meeting goals important to its members. The key concept is continuous improvement, even improving how improvements are made, which means once-off triumphs do not necessarily cut it. Leadership has a different hew – not depending on some extraordinary leader to effect change, it relies largely on a bottom-up rather than a top-down approach. The role of the change leader is to encourage people to question assumptions, develop ideas, strive to reach their potential, work well together and remove barriers that hinder innovation.

The central idea is that there is sufficient talent and energy at the grassroots to make significant improvements in the organisation, but long experience with barriers means people become frustrated and discouraged, which leads them to believe that change is impossible. The secret of good leadership in public sector organisations is to harness the fact that most people working there really do care about making things better and improving the lives of others. The bureaucratic model works on a basic formula that defines how to run everything in the organisation, seeing its role to transform inputs into outputs. The strategy is to follow a formula, not innovate or please the customer. The structure is hierarchical with a clearly defined vertical chain of command. This is different in a learning organisation characterised by a horizontal or matrix structure and in a state of permanent change, with people constantly thinking about how and why things are done a certain way. In this environment, networking is crucial. These two models can be contrasted on several other fronts.[86] Under the bureaucratic model, skills are narrowly specialised, whereas people are versatile and cross-trained in the learning organisation model.

There is role clarity and work is conducted in a dispassionate manner in the bureaucratic model while, in the learning organisation model, there are flexible job boundaries and individuals feel passionate about their work. In the bureaucratic model, systems are formalised, co-ordination is by the rule book and standard operating procedures are very important. In the learning organisation model, systems are informal and coordination is by mutual consent. In a public learning organisation, people fulfil a shared mission through creative work within a community, whereas in the old-style bureaucracy they administer programmes and policies authorised from the outside.

The quality and range of Ireland's public services lag behind those of many of its less prosperous neighbours in Europe. Yet a well-managed innovative and efficient public sector is essential to drive Ireland's productivity growth rates. Paul Tansey makes a distinction between administration, which is passive, and management, which is active.[87] Public services, he argues, are over-administered but under-managed. Management is a professional skill, acquired only with time, effort and experience, and usually backed by professional qualifications. In order to achieve the type of growth rates in productivity necessary in the future, he believes the most important item in public sector reform is the management of public services.

After independence, Ireland inherited the old British imperial civil service model structured around secrecy with little regard for political and public inquiry, and with structures so complex it was impossible to isolate responsibility.[88] Such rigidities have largely been untouched by public sector reforms carried out to-date. Innovators often go unrewarded and are sidelined with many parts still working within grade-based hierarchies and structures that originated in the nineteenth century; there is little interchange of personnel between different parts of the public service and between the public and private sectors.[89]

Whatever might be said about the wisdom of Irish economic policy or the fairness of Irish society in the past, public servants seem to have been largely motivated by the goal of serving the public interest. Todd Andrews, activist on the Republican side during the Civil War and later chairman of CIÉ, illustrated well his own attitude to service in his autobiography *Man of No Property*.[90] Like many of his generation, Andrews was determined to shape the new nation after release from internment in 1924. An ethic of public service also shines through the book *Interests*, the autobiographical sketches by T.K. Whitaker.[91] The visionary exploits of those who ran semi-state bodies like Bord na Móna or the ESB in the decades after independence were inextricably linked with boundless commitment to ideals of national self-determination, pride and patriotic zeal. Through much of its history, the State relied on a bureaucracy trained in civic duty as its primary motivation. Public servants saw themselves, and were viewed by both politicians and the public, as having a different ethos to those working in the private sector. Money was not the primary motivation. Different internal dynamics of the public and private sectors were obvious in how each was made accountable and standards maintained.

Contrast this with the recent decision by the Government to sanction significant pay increases for chief executives of commercial State bodies such as the ESB, CIÉ, RTÉ and An Post as a consequence of a report from external consultants. The criteria used were that the majority of companies in the commercial State sector are too 'far away from matching, or indeed approaching comparable private sector total cash packages at CEO level.'[92] The implication is that suitably qualified candidates cannot be lured from the private sector unless they are paid comparable salaries. Under the new pay policy, the board of the ESB, for instance, will be able to pay its CEO between €395,760 and €494,700 per annum. Health insurer VHI sought Government permission to pay its new CEO €650,000 per annum, more than twice the approved salary. This was the second top level in the public sector to receive significant increases under these reviews. Late in 2007, the Government accepted a report of a review group that also recommended significant pay rises for themselves, other politicians, many senior civil servants as well as chief executives of non-commercial State bodies. Yet this all happened at about the same time as another review that recommended that most rank-and-file civil and public servants receive no special increases in pay. A problem with such a benchmarking process is that it links public sector salaries to comparable positions in the private sector where the gap between the top echelons and ordinary workers has widened considerably in recent years.[93]

Kieran Allen contrasts the way performance in public services is increasingly assessed.[94] In health services, for instance, a high degree of quantification is now commonplace, with measurements and prices imposed on everything from surgical operations to nursing care. Allen insists that health professionals are primarily motivated by something more than money so, when offered the opportunity to work within a culture that sustains their civic and humanitarian instincts, they respond with better health care. He sees a sense of purpose being replaced by a cult of performance in the way the recently set up Health Services Executive (HSE) operates. Advocates of the new approach, he says, refuse to accept a distinction in organisational philosophy between private corporations and the public sector. Under the 'business model' increasingly being applied, however, both are seen to have 'suppliers' and 'customers'. The two organisation types are managed through business plans, using incentives to motivate top managers. Instead of professional trust that cultivates an ethos of civic responsibility, audits and benchmarks are used to monitor compliance to business-style targets. He argues that, as a result of such 'marketisation', the quality of Irish health services is now worse and more costly than ever.

In recent decades, managerialism seems to have proliferated in the Irish public sector. This began with reforms, originally known as 'new public management' or NPM, designed to organise the public service in a more 'business-like' manner.[95] Beginning in 1994 with the Strategic Management Initiative (SMI), other plans and blueprints to improve delivery of public services from the Department of the Taoiseach included the Quality Customer Service Initiative, the Performance Management and Development System (PMDS), the Management Information Framework (MIF), and so forth. Top civil servants now seem skillful at setting targets and devising ways of measuring achievements. The question is: has this approach really improved the quality and value of public services?

Granted, a more collegial form of governance in services like health and education was not without problems. For instance, it was difficult to remove professionals who were clearly not performing. But as UK researcher Ralph Stacey asserts, the new approach does not lead to authentic quality.[96] The basic trouble happens when organisations are seen as things rather than as ongoing patterns of relationships between people. To Stacey, the best way to address this issue is from the perspective of complex adaptive processes that take account of the essentially local nature of human interaction. Organisations are really processes for negotiating conflicts in ordinary, everyday situations. Rather than importing mechanistic notions of quality from the world of business, industry and manufacturing, a key question is: what do value and quality actually mean in the local situation in which, for example, health services or education are delivered?

Ultimately, a small country like Ireland has to make an intangible ethic of excellence, service or quality the core of its productivity and innovation policies.[97] This is why clean streets, well-run public facilities and quality public goods and services are as important as business in driving national competitiveness. This ethic of quality is especially important in public services. While quality is not easy to define, as the classic book *Zen and the Art of Motorcycle Maintenance* maintains, everybody still knows what it is! Here is the exquisite logic the book uses to explain why defining quality is practically impossible:

> Quality is a characteristic of thought and statement that is recognized by a nonthinking person. Because definitions are a product of rigid, formal thinking, quality cannot be defined.[98]

A 'person of quality' is close in spirit to the ancient Greek concept of *arete* which signifies 'excellence' or 'virtue'. *Arete*, however, was not a sense of duty towards others; it was a duty towards one's self with respect for the wholeness of life, in other words 'integrity'. A good description of what the subjective inner quality called personal excellence should mean in health, for instance, is described by Seán Brophy, based on his experiences as a patient over nineteen Irish hospital admissions during a fifty-five year lifetime.[99] He observed different types of people, those doing jobs, those pursuing a career and people with a calling or vocation. He wrote that work provides meaning in people's lives, helping to define them as people. For those with jobs or careers, their work is largely instrumental to other goods in their lives. Individuals with a calling, on the other hand, see work as a passionate commitment to work for its own sake and as an end in itself. They view it as contributing to the greater good, to something larger than themselves, fulfilling in its own right and independent of money and advancement.

In the Irish health services, people with a calling find meaning in relationships at a personal level at work. They define themselves fundamentally as human beings relating to other human beings, in addition to carrying out the technical features of their work. Just doing a job or pursuing a career is limiting to such individuals; having a calling through a philosophy of personal excellence allows a person to continually push out the limits of his or her own experience of work and to convey ever more meaning to their own lives. So how can a doctor, nurse or similar health professional attain such personal excellence? Brophy sees this as akin to asking how a person can live a 'corporate value' of quality. Firstly, they need to provide themselves with an incentive – their own happiness. Secondly, they need to discern those strengths within themselves that facilitate them being excellent in their own personal way. Meaningfulness comes from using these signature strengths and virtues in the service of something greater than oneself. Professionals need to be aware of their own particular gifts or strengths, those that fill them with vitality. When they craft their jobs to employ these capabilities in the service of others it makes them feel fulfilled. The person's identity therefore comes not from his or her role as a doctor or nurse but as somebody practising a particular gift, a calling, where excellence and quality are the constant goals.

Quality or integrity implies commitment and this is the embodiment of successful public services innovation in a learning society. Giving individuals meaning in their lives, continuity with the past and a sense of place in the present results in a more trusting, caring and higher quality environment. Standards then become internal, deriving impetus from personal values, wholeness and integrity. They are not driven by the need to satisfy others through quality 'standards' or 'benchmarks'. A core component of a rooted Irish-global identity is attention to tradition, community, empathy and intergenerational solidarity. Nurturing a culture of rootedness offers individuals an opportunity to reflect on their place in the world. This helps them better understand and manage risk or uncertainty about the future. Since value is determined by the attitude to risk, a work environment that fosters a rooted Irish-global identity also helps to increase value for money. Productivity, innovative public services and a high quality of life are best generated by a combination of idealism and practical patriotism, operating within an environment with high levels of social capital or trust. Public services development must be driven by a striving for sustainable innovations within learning organisations where inspiration, imagination and an ethic of discovery are at the core.

Sustainability and Learning Organisations

Sustainable Innovation

A growing body of research suggests that economic competitiveness, social equity and environmental performance are compatible, if not mutually reinforcing. Michael Porter presents evidence indicating that the environmental performance of countries correlates positively with their competitiveness.[100] Social and environmental problems often signal low productivity in the use of resources, and display themselves prominently when competitiveness is low. Discarded packaging, for instance, wastes resources and adds costs. Customers bear additional costs when using products that pollute or waste energy. Conversely, low pollution and efficient energy usage are signs of a highly productive use of resources. Policies that stimulate improvements in environmental quality may actually foster improvements in technology and competitiveness. For example, Germany and Japan implemented strict anti-pollution laws in the past and kept making them stricter. The result is that firms from these countries today have a huge edge in pollution-control equipment.[101] Similarly, lax clean-air laws in the US meant that within twenty years that country went from leading the world in wind-energy manufacturing to lagging badly. Companies in countries like Germany, Denmark and Spain grabbed the technological lead and now hold approximately 80 per cent of a market growing at a rate of over 25 per cent a year.

The new paradigm of international competitive advantage therefore rests not on a static model involving a trade-off between the environment and the economy, but on a dynamic one based on innovation. Innovation allows companies to use a range of inputs more productively, from raw materials to energy to labour, thus offsetting the costs of improving environmental impact. Ultimately, it is enhanced resource productivity that makes companies more competitive, not less. Business lobbyists, fighting proposed regulations, often focus on the actual costs of eliminating or treating pollution. It might be more fruitful to shift their attention to include the opportunity costs such as wasted resources and reduced value to the customer.[102] This is where Ireland needs substantial improvement. By employing a system-wide or holistic perspective centred on a sustainability ethos, Ireland could build an inimitable competitive advantage.

The potential for enhancing Ireland's international competitiveness through nurturing sustainable innovation is enormous. A recent report from the Irish Council for Science, Technology and Innovation (ICSTI) bolsters the case for placing science, technology and innovation firmly on the sustainable development agenda in order to enhance Irish competitiveness.[103] The report lays particular emphasis on the need to move from a tight disciplinary approach in current science and technology structures to greater integration and strengthening of the linkages both within science and technology and holistically with Government policy development. It is in Ireland's interest to be among the innovators and early adopters, not the laggards.[104] Innovation, after all, is what successful organisations do, whether they are in the public, private or community sectors. They constantly reinvent themselves in the face of changing circumstances.

Apart from the opportunities offered by regulations on issues like climate change, pollution and health concerns, sustainability can itself be a potentially powerful driver of innovation due to its potential for creating discontinuous conditions, an ideal context for stimulating innovation. As the book *Managing Innovation* points out, most of the time innovation takes place within a set of rules of the game which are clearly understood, involving players trying to innovate by doing what they have been doing all along but better; yet the 'rules of the game' are accepted and do not change.[105] However, these 'steady-state' conditions are sometimes punctuated by discontinuities, which occur when some basic conditions such as technology, markets or regulatory environment shift dramatically, thereby changing the 'rules of the game', threatening existing incumbents and opening up opportunities for new entrants. Sustainability is an excellent example of such potentially disruptive innovation. Discontinuities or disruptions open up opportunities as well as challenge existing arrangements, since they have major system-level implications. Such innovations arise within complex social, political and cultural contexts, with a high risk of failure if these elements are ignored.

The development of wind energy again provides a nice example. While the USA had been the traditional leader in this area, and still spends huge amounts on R&D, development in Denmark followed a simpler small-scale approach matched to meeting the energy needs of small and local communities.[106] This enabled the Danish industry to develop significant competence through interacting with a growing user base and building technological sophistication from the bottom up. After the 1970s oil crisis, the Danish State encouraged the provision of local renewable energy sources and development of associated technologies. This led to enormous benefits in international trade for a wide range of products and services based on these technologies.

The development of urban transport in Sweden provides a further example. As Brendan Keenan points out, Dublin should aim, like Stockholm, to be an integrated sustainable city.[107] All of Stockholm's city centre buses run on biogas. Part of this biogas, methane, is pumped from the city's sewage treatment plants straight to the pumps in the nearby bus depot. This innovation required a whole-systems mindset notoriously absent in Ireland. Ireland should emulate the Swedish strategy, which perceives the environment as a great business opportunity and a driver of the Swedish stock market. Seeing the climate challenge as a central part of industrial and technology strategy, rather than merely a problem for the government, as Keenan puts it, 'to footer about with', might make the country not only richer but greener as well.

Some of the most successful Irish companies already recognise the potential of sustainable innovation. Treasury Holdings, for instance, restructured its operations to take advantage of emerging environmental challenges that are creating a demand for high-quality, eco-friendly developments that support sustainable living.[108] In China, for instance, the Treasury spearheaded a revolutionary €1.2 billion 'eco city', destined to be a low energy, sustainable and environmentally friendly city.[109] The company also acquired the German waste management group Herlof, which specialises in mechanical and biological recycling technologies to recover valuable products from waste, in a deal worth more than €20 million.[110] Irish company NTR, which is expected to report profits of more than €1 billion in 2008, is involved in toll roads, waste management and electricity generation. The group, which owns waste management business Greenstar, has recently begun shifting its focus from developing and operating infrastructure in Ireland to becoming a leading international developer of sustainable solutions in renewable energy and recycling waste management.[111] It recently sold its interest in the Westlink toll bridge to the Irish Government. It invested €120 million in 2006 in a new biofuels division that it believes will deliver €300 million in annual revenues within three years.[112] In 2006 it launched the company Bioverda to develop new businesses in biofuels and bioenergy generation in Ireland, Germany and the Americas.

Rural Enterprise

Since the agri-food sector is Ireland's largest indigenous manufacturing sector, developments here are especially worthy of note. EU structural reforms are decoupling subsidies from production, promoting sustainability in land use and the diversification of the rural economy. At the same time, there are public concerns about balanced regional development, loss of diversity, ecosystem damage, animal welfare, food safety and traceability. Sustainability is also increasingly recognised as the key challenge for Irish researchers, farmers and the entire food chain.[113] For researchers, it is to provide the best science-based knowledge for cost-effective sustainable and welfare friendly animal production; for farmers it is to deliver quality produce at competitive prices in an environmentally friendly way; and for the food chain it is to have a unified approach to ensuring food safety and quality standards. Innovative policies are needed to achieve profitability in agriculture and food processing, while sustaining viable rural communities.[114]

In particular, consideration needs to be given to the introduction of initiatives to encourage farmers to manage the rural landscape and optimise the public goods value of agriculture and its contribution to the rural economy. A holistic approach to development and prosperity will be necessary if a knowledge-based multifunctional agriculture sector and a 'living countryside' are to be achieved in rural Ireland.[115] Some initiatives in this direction are now being undertaken. For instance, Donegal Creameries, in an attempt to develop a branded organic dairy and food portfolio, recently announced the transformation of its 2,500-acre An Grianán estate in Donegal to what may someday become the biggest organic farm in Europe.[116]

With the estimated number of Irish full-time farmers projected to drop to 10,000 in coming years, a culture of diversification, entrepreneurship and innovation within the farm gate seems the best strategy to ensure viability.[117] Gerry Boyle, director of Teagasc (Agriculture and Food Development Authority), recently announced his intention to place the agri-food sector at the centre of the knowledge economy.[118] To achieve this, according to Larry Murrin, chief executive of Dawn Farm Foods, the R&D model used for developing the food sector over the past two decades will not work in the future. As Liam Donnelly, director of Moorepark Food Research Centre, Ireland's oldest, largest and probably most successful non-university applied research institute, puts it, 'There is a world of difference in innovation content between a research project which has knowledge as its prime output and one which is primarily targeted at innovation.'[119] Moorepark, which employs some 90 researchers, is a public non-profit institute that receives its funding mainly from the Department of Agriculture, Food and Rural Development for food-related research projects in competition with the university sector.[120] In 1993 it set up Moorepark Technologies Limited (MTL), an innovative joint venture with the major Irish dairy processors. This was the first and probably is still the most significant partnership in Ireland between private enterprise and a public research body. Donnelly points out that, historically, information was regarded as the central research output quantified by publications. In an innovation-driven culture, however, the emphasis is on ensuring usefulness. He believes the reason academic institutions have difficulty with the pursuit of innovation is because the value system is dominated by an ethos of academic freedom. Universities, as argued earlier in the chapter, tend to be inefficient in translating primary knowledge into useful products, processes and services.

Since education at both school and higher levels plays a special role in nurturing a culture of innovation, the next chapter is devoted to examining human resource development and learning for the creation of sustainable competitive advantage in the context of education.

Notes

1. Title page quote by Belgian Government Minister M. Briavionne in Kane, R. (1844), *The Industrial Resources of Ireland*, Dublin: Hodges and Smith, p. 394.
2. For explorations on relationships between knowledge and action in different settings, see, for example, Cannon, S. (2005), 'Reconciling Local Initiative with National Policy in Teacher Professional Development', unpublished Doctor of Management thesis, University of Hertfordshire, UK.; Dunne, J. (1999), 'Professional Judgment and the Predicaments of Practice', *European Journal of Marketing*, 33(7/8), pp. 707–19 and Lillis, S. (2001), 'An Inquiry into the Effectiveness of my Practice as a Learning Practitioner-Researcher in Rural Development', unpublished Ph.D. thesis, University College Dublin.
3. Sweeney, G. (ed.) (2001), *Innovation, Economic Progress and the Quality of Life*, Cheltenham, UK: Edward Elgar, p. 8.
4. 'Hiring the Best Talent Money Can Buy', *Irish Times*, 21 December 2007.
5. Graeber, D. (2001), *Toward an Anthropological Theory of Value*, Palgrave: New York.
6. Hart, K. (1999), *The Memory Bank: Money in an Unequal World*, Profile Books: London.
7. Capra, F. (2002), *The Hidden Connections: A Science for Sustainable Living*, London: HarperCollinsPublishers. Capra points out that nothing is meaningful in itself: *Webster's Dictionary* defines meaning as 'an idea conveyed to the mind that requires or allows of interpretation', and interpretation as 'conceiving in the light of individual belief, judgement or circumstance'. People interpret something by putting it into a particular context of concepts, values, beliefs or circumstances. In other words, to understand the meaning of anything, individuals need to relate it to other things in its environment, in its past or in its future.

8. Bawden, R.J. (1992), 'Systems Approaches to Agricultural Development: The Hawkesbury Experience', *Agricultural Systems*, 40(1), pp. 153–76.
9. Quinn, F. (1990), *Crowning the Customer: How to become Customer-Driven*, Dublin: The O'Brien Press.
10. This conceptualisation benefited from ideas outlined in Hopwood, A.G. (1988), 'Production and Finance: The Need for a Common Language', Proceedings of the 1st Industrial Summit on New Manufacturing Imperatives, 12–15 January, London, UK.
11. Standard finance textbooks demonstrate these techniques. For instance, Brealey, R.A., Myers, S.C. and Allen, F. (2006), *Corporate Finance,* 8th edition, New York: McGraw-Hill/Irwin.
12. For approaches to value creation decision making on IT projects, refer to Curley, M. (2004), *Managing Information for Business Value*, Oregon, USA: Intel Press; Tiernan, C. and Peppard, J. (2004), 'Information Technology: Of Value or a Vulture?' *European Management Journal*, 22 (6), December, pp. 609–23. For a practical illustration in preparing energy investment proposals, refer to Sustainable Energy Ireland (2004), 'Investing in Energy: A Practical Guide to Preparing and Presenting Energy Investment Proposals', Dublin.
13. Ryan, B. (2007), *Corporate Finance*, London: Thomson.
14. Moore, M.H. (1995), *Creating Public Value: Strategic Management in Government*, Cambridge, MA: Harvard University Press.
15. Moore, *Creating Public Value,* p. 293.
16. 'Business "Strung up in Red Tape Bias"', *Irish Independent*, 19 July 2007.
17. 'Quinn Empire Profits Surge €107m to €433m', *Sunday Business Post*, 16 November 2007.
18. For reviews of cost-benefit analysis within the Irish context, see CSF Evaluation Unit, Department of Finance (1999), *Proposed Working Rules for Cost-Benefit Analysis*, Dublin: CSF Evaluation Unit; Honohan, P. (1998), *Key Issues of Cost-Benefit Methodology for Irish*

Industrial Policy, ESRI, General Research Series, No. 172, November; Mulreaney, M. (1999), 'Cost-Benefit Analysis' in M. Mulreaney (ed.), *Economic and Financial Evaluation: Measurement, Meaning and Management*, Dublin: IPA, pp. 177–204.

19. Allen, F. and Bradley, F. (2007), 'Transporting Individuals – Transforming Communities', *Studies*, 96(383), Summer, pp. 145–53.
20. For a review of PPPs in Ireland refer to Farrell Grant Sparks and Goodbody Economics Consultants, in association with Chesterton Consulting (1998), *Public Private Partnerships*, Dublin: FGS; Bradley, F. and Allen, F. (2001), 'Value for Money in Public Private Partnerships (PPPs): Myth & Reality', *Administration/ Journal of the Institute of Public Administration*, 49(1), Spring, pp. 46–58.
21. Allen, F. and Bradley, F. (2002), 'The Potential of Public-Voluntary Partnerships for the Delivery of Quality Social Services, *Studies*, 91(364), Winter, pp. 371–80.
22. See, for instance, Frank, R.H. (1988), *Passions within Reason: The Strategic Role of the Emotions,* New York: W.W. Norton; Ridley, M. (1996), *The Origins of Virtue*, London: Penguin Books.
23. Elias, R. (1998), 'Game Models' in S. Mennell and J. Goudsblom (eds.), *Norbert Elias: On Civilization, Power and Knowledge*, Chicago: The University of Chicago Press, pp. 113–38.
24. Bradley, J. (2007), 'Small State, Big World: Reflections on Irish Economic Development', *Dublin Review of Books*, 3, Autumn, available at: <http://www.drb.ie/sept_smallstate.html>.
25. Smith, A. (1910, 1776), *The Wealth of Nations*, New York: Everyman's Library.
26. Darwin, C. (1966, 1859), *The Origin of the Species*, Cambridge, MA: Cambridge University Press.
27. Smith, A. (1966, 1759), *The Theory of Moral Sentiments*, New York: Kelley.
28. Darwin, C. (1873), *The Expression of the Emotions in Man and Animals*, New York: D. Appleton.
29. For a look at the fascinating life and economic theories of Schumpeter, refer to McCraw, T.K. (2007), *Prophet of Innovation:*

Joseph Schumpeter and Creative Destruction, Cambridge, MA: Belknap Press/Harvard University Press. Renowned economist and former President of Harvard University Larry Summers says that if Keynes was the most important economist of the twentieth century, Schumpeter may well be of the twenty-first ('Creative Destruction's Reconstruction: Joseph Schumpeter Revisited'), *New York Times*, 7 December 2007.

30. The following book, Nalebuff, B.J. and Brandenbuger, A.M. (1997), *Co-opetition*, London: HarperCollinsBusiness, offers a strategic way of thinking that combines competition and co-operation, based on the concept of *added value.*
31. Lambooy, J. (2005), 'Innovation and Knowledge: Theory and Regional Policy', *European Planning Studies*, 13(8), December, pp. 1137–52.
32. Sabau, G. (2003), 'The Knowledge-Based Economy – Sustainable Development Nexus', paper presented at the conference, 'The Knowledge-Based Economy and Regional Economic Development', St. John's Newfoundland, Canada, 3–5 October.
33. Available at: <http://www.intentblog.com>.
34. Magee, B. (1973), *Popper*, London: Fontana Press, p. 70.
35. Magee, *Popper,* p. 69.
36. Lester, R.K. and Piore, M.J. (2004), *Innovation – The Missing Dimension*, Boston, MA: Harvard University Press.
37. Suri, J.F. and Howard, S.G. (2006), 'Going Deeper, Seeing Further: Enhancing Ethnographic Interpretations to Reveal More Meaningful Opportunities for Design', *Journal of Advertising Research*, September, pp. 246–50.
38. The first comprehensive attempt was: Ireland (in association with OECD) (1965), *Science and Irish Economic Development: Report of the Research and Technology Survey Team appointed by the Minister for Industry and Commerce in 1963*, Dublin: The Stationery Office.
39. Enterprise Strategy Group (2004), *Ahead of the Curve: Ireland's Place in the Global Economy*, Dublin: Forfás.
40. Government of Ireland (2006), *Strategy for Science, Technology and Innovation, 2006–2013*, Dublin: The Stationery Office.

41. Government of Ireland (2007), *National Development Plan 2007–2013: Transfoming Ireland*, Dublin: The Stationery Office.
42. There is also evidence that recently an increasing share of public research funding in Ireland is going to physical infrastructure rather than to building knowledge capacity. For instance, it is reported that the Programme for Research in Third-Level Institutions (PRTLI), Cycle 5, will allocate only 20 per cent of total funds to building knowledge capacity, compared to about 50 per cent in the previous round (Cycle 4) (see 'Capital Intensive Funding of Third Level Research', *Business & Finance*, 15 February 2008, p. 7).
43. Forfás (2008), *The Higher Education R&D Survey 2006 (HERD)*, March, Dublin: Forfás.
44. Forfás (2008), *The Higher Education R&D Survey 2006 (HERD)*, March, Dublin: Forfás.
45. Government of Ireland (2006), *Strategy for Science, Technology and Innovation, 2006–2013.*
46. Jordan, D. and O'Leary, E. (2007), 'Is Irish Innovation Policy Working? Evidence from Irish High-Technology Businesses', paper presented to a meeting of the Statistical and Social Inquiry Society of Ireland (SSISI), Dublin, 25 October; Jordan, D. and O'Leary, E. (2005), 'The Roles of Interaction and Proximity for Innovation by Irish High-Technology Businesses: Policy Implications', *Quarterly Economic Commentary*, Summer, pp. 86–100. For a summary of these findings, refer to 'Innovation is not Academic' (2008), *Innovation* (*Irish Times* Business Magazine), January, p. 10.
47. 'Third-level Research has "Limited Effect" on Business Innovation', *Irish Times*, 13 January 2008.
48. 'Opinion – Frank Gannon' (2008), *Innovation* (*Irish Times* Business Magazine), February, p. 10.
49. 'Onus Now on Business to Exploit Funding for Scientists', *Irish Times*, 18 December 2007.
50. Ryan, É. (2007), 'Commercialising our R&D', *Business & Finance*, 25 January, p. 56.
51. Trench, B. (2007), 'Irish Media Representations of Science' in J. Horgan, B. O'Connor and H. Sheehan (eds.), *Mapping Irish Media:*

Critical Explorations, Dublin: University College Dublin Press, pp. 128–41.

52. Trench, B. (2003), 'Science, Culture and Public Affairs', *The Republic*, 3, July, pp. 53–63 (see p. 58).
53. Kandybin, A. and Kihn, M. (2004), 'Raising your Return on Innovation Investment', *Strategy & Business*, 35, Summer, Booz Allen Hamilton, New York, available at: <http://www.strategy-business.com>; Jaruzelski, B., Dehoff, K. and Bordia, R. (2005), 'The Booz Allen Hamilton Global Innovation 1000 – Money Isn't Everything', *Strategy & Business*, 41, Winter, Booz Allen Hamilton, New York, available at: <http://www.boozallen.com/media/file/151786.pdf>.
54. IBM Institute for Business Value (2006), 'The Power of Many', IBM Global Business Services, available at <http://www-935.ibm.com/services/us/gbs/bus/pdf/g510-6335-00-abc.pdf>; Economist Intelligence Unit (2007), 'Sharing the Idea: The Emergence of Global Innovation Networks', EIU for IDA Ireland, Dublin.
55. 'New Thinking on How to Innovate', *Irish Times*, 12 November 2007.
56. 'Blood, Sweat and Innovation', *Business & Finance*, 15 February 2008, pp. 40–1.
57. Ó Riain, S. (2006), 'Nurturing Many Knowledges to Grow Ireland's Knowledge Society', paper delivered at Irish Universities Association (IUA), Humanities and Social Sciences Conference, Dublin, 23–24 October.
58. Forfás (2005), *Making Technological Knowledge Work: A Study of the Absorptive Capacity of Irish SMEs*, report conducted by Technopolis, February, Dublin: Forfás.
59. 'Michael Polanyi and Tacit Knowledge', available at: <http://www.infed.org/thinkers/polanyi.html>.
60. Refer to Polanyi, M. (1974), *Personal Knowledge: Towards a Post-Critical Philosophy*, Chicago: University of Chicago Press and Polanyi, M. and Prosch, H. (1975), *Meaning*, Chicago: University of Chicago Press.

61. Information Society Commission (2002), *Building the Knowledge Society: Report to Government*, Dublin: Department of the Taoiseach, pp. 19–20.
62. Seely Brown, J. and Duguid, P. (2000), *The Social Life of Information*, Boston: Harvard Business School Press.
63. Eisner, E.W. (2002), *The Arts and the Creation of Mind*, New Haven: Yale University Press, p. 213.
64. Eisner, *The Arts and the Creation of Mind*, p. 214.
65. Boyte, H.C. (2000), 'The Struggle against Positivism', *Academe*, 86 (4), July–August.
66. Lester, R.K. (2005), 'Universities, Innovation and the Competitiveness of Local Economies', *Summary Report from the LIS Project-Phase 1*, MIT Industrial Performance Centre, Working Paper 05-010. For the Irish situation, UCC researcher Declan Jordan agrees, arguing that teaching and the traditional role of the university are suffering because of the focus on research. The best way to get knowledge out of the university, he says, is 'by hiring an undergraduate' (see Gilmartin, S. (2008), 'Educate! Innovate! Agitate!' *Business & Finance*, 1 February, p. 48).
67. Lester, R.K. and Piore, M.J. (2004), *Innovation – The Missing Dimension*, MA: Harvard University Press.
68. There are hopeful signs this may be changing. The concept of the 'science shop' brings together researchers and communities by encouraging groups with a problem to approach their local university The university then arranges for students and researchers to investigate the problem. Supported by EU funding, a European network of science shops has grown in recent years. A science shop has been in operation at Queen's University Belfast since the 1980s and others started recently at DCU, UCC and NUIG.
69. Johnston, R.H.W. (2003), *A Century of Endeavour*, Dublin: Tyndall Publications/The Lilliput Press.

70. M'Gonigle, M. and Starke, J. (2006), *Planet U: Sustaining the World, Reinventing the University,* Gabriola Island, British Columbia, Canada: New Society Publishers.
71. Ó Riain, S. (2006), 'Competing State Projects in the Contemporary Irish Political Economy', in M. Adshead, P. Kirby and M. Miller (eds.), *Contesting the State*, Manchester: Manchester University Press, pp. 165–85.
72. Advisory Council for Science, Technology and Innovation (2007), *Promoting Enterprise-Higher Education Relationships*, Dublin: Forfás.
73. O'Connor, N. (2007), 'Industry-Academia Collaboration: A Competence Centre Approach for Ireland?', *Studies in Public Policy*, No. 22, The Policy Institute, Trinity College Dublin.
74. Government of Ireland (1992), *Report of the Industrial Policy Review Group – A Time for Change: Industrial Policy for the 1990s [The Culliton Report]*, Dublin.
75. Enterprise Ireland (2007), *Transforming Irish Industry: Enterprise Ireland Strategy 2008–2010*, Dublin.
76. 'How an Enterprising Attitude Pays Off', *Sunday Business Post*, 23 December 2007.
77. Forfás (2007), *Towards Developing an Entrepreneurship Policy for Ireland*, Dublin: Forfás.
78. 5th Report of Expert Group on Future Skills Needs (2007), *Tomorrow's Skills: Towards a National Skills Strategy*, Dublin: Forfás.
79. Lee, J.J. (1985), 'Centralisation and Community' in J.J. Lee (ed.), *Ireland: Towards a Sense of Place,* Cork: Cork University Press, p. 95.
80. Keating, P. and Desmond, D. (1993), *Culture and Capitalism in Contemporary Ireland*, Aldershot, UK: Avebury.
81. 'Fear and Cultural Quirks to Blame for Ireland's Lack of Enterprise', *Irish Times*, 23 May 2006. Micheál Martin, Minister for Enterprise, Trade and Employment, offered a trenchant reply, stating Casey is 'fundamentally mistaken' and many high quality, high growth potential businesses are emerging in Ireland ('The Flourishing Irish Entrepreneurs', *Irish Times*, 26 May 2006). He offers as evidence a *Global Entrepreneurship Monitor 2005*, which says Ireland ranks as the fifth most entrepreneurial society in the

world. A recent *New York Times* article suggests Ireland is alive with enthusiasm for entrepreneurs, who 'seemingly rank just below rock stars in popularity' (see 'Entrepreneurship Takes Off in Ireland', *New York Times*, 17 January 2008).

82. Deloitte Management Briefing (2007), 'Growth Through Leadership: Creating Leadership Capacity to Support Business Growth', November, Dublin: Deloitte.
83. Generation Y workers need constant praise and feedback and are used to getting answers to their questions immediately. Social networking platforms can play a very important role, for instance, in combating high turnover, rewarding work well done, answering questions in a speedy manner and allowing more senior employees to act as mentors.
84. Fuscaldo, D. (2008), 'Innovation: Corporations Embrace Social Networking', Fox Business, 8 February (available at: <http://www.foxbusiness.com/story/markets/innovation/innovation-corporations-embrace-social-networking/>). Richard Delevan points out that the recent rage by the business lobby group ISME (Irish Small and Medium Enterprises Association) against workplace use of networking sites is misguided. For every news release from a business lobby, he says, 'stuffed with platitudes on the need for Ireland to become a so-called "knowledge economy" there is another declaring as anathema any evidence of movement towards that state of bliss.' ('False (Knowledge) Economies', *Business & Finance*, 1 February 2008, p. 63).
85. Gratton, L. (2007), 'Hotspots – Why Some Companies Buzz with Energy and Some Don't', *TimesOnline*, MBA Podcasts, Week 5, available at: <http://extras.timesonline.co.uk/mba/mba-final-week-table.html>.
86. Sugarman, B. (2000), 'A Learning-Based Approach to Leading Change', The PricewaterhouseCoopers Endowment for the Business of Government, December.
87. 'Public Sector Reform would Aid Productivity', *Irish Times*, 23 November 2007.

88. 'Who is Taking Responsibility for the Crises in the Country?' *Sunday Business Post*, 25 November 2007.
89. 'Public Service can Help Shape Future', *Irish Times*, 23 November 2007.
90. Andrews, C.S. (1982), *Man of No Property*, Cork: Mercier Press.
91. Whitaker, T.K. (1983), *Interests*, Dublin: IPA.
92. 'Salary Rises Approved for Heads of Commercial State Firms', *Irish Times*, 9 January 2008.
93. Fintan O'Toole sees the significance of benchmarking is that by replicating the income disparities of the private sector, inequality has now become official State policy. He says the underlying assumption is that inequality is an inevitable side-effect of a dynamic economy. In reality, he argues, inequality damages economies by leading to poor labour relations, low staff morale and decreased productivity. It also has negative political consequences ('Inequality Now Official Policy', *Irish Times*, 15 January 2008.
94. Allen, K. (2007), *The Corporate Takeover of Ireland*, Dublin: Irish Academic Press.
95. 'Pay Hikes and Cock-Ups', *Sunday Business Post*, 4 November 2007.
96. Stacey, R. (2006), 'Ways of Thinking about Public Sector Governance' in R. Stacey and D. Griffin (eds.), *Complexity and the Experience of Managing in Public Sector Organizations*, London: Routledge, pp. 15–42.
97. A comment made by former Managing Director of the Kerry Group Denis Brosnan is relevant. He said, 'Irishness I define as the capacity of the Irish to accept and/or deliver standards which appal many of us.... It is the antithesis of quality', *Irish Independent*, 29 November 1986, quoted in Lee, J.J. (1989), *Ireland 1912–1985: Politics and Society*, Cambridge: Cambridge University Press, p. 679.
98. Pirsig, R.M. (1974), *Zen and the Art of Motorcycle Maintenance*, London: Vintage, p. 210.

99. Brophy, S. (2006), '"Personal Excellence" as a Value for Health Professionals: A Patient's Perspective', *International Journal of Health Care*, 19(5), pp. 372–83.
100. Esty, D.C. and Porter, M.E. (2001), 'Ranking National Environmental Regulation and Performance: A Leading Indicator of Future Competitiveness?' in *The Global Competitiveness Report, 2001–2002*, New York: Oxford University Press.
101. 'For Economic Growth, *Tougher* Environmental Laws?' *Christian Science Monitor*, 24 February 2005.
102. Porter, M.E. and Van der Linde, C. (1995), 'Green and Competitive', *Harvard Business Review*, September/October, pp. 120–34.
103. Irish Council for Science, Technology and Innovation (2004), *ICSTI Statement – Sustainable Development in Ireland: The Role of Science and Technology*, Dublin: Forfás.
104. In March 2008, the Irish Government announced it intended investing €200 million over five years in energy-related R&D in order to develop environmental solutions and products and to become one of the leading green economies in the world. It cited a study showing that, by meeting its 2020 national energy efficiency target, economic benefits would outweigh costs to Ireland by close to €300 million per annum.
105. Tidd, J., Bessant, J. and Pavitt, K. (2005), *Managing Innovation: Integrating Technological, Market and Organizational Change*, 3rd edition, Hoboken, NJ: John Wiley & Sons.
106. In the US the realisation has already set in of the huge opportunities in the renewable energy field. With the decline in many old manufacturing industries, 'green collar' jobs are seen by many as the future (see '"Green Collar" Jobs Seen As Prosperous', *New York Times*, 2 February 2008).
107. 'Follow Swede Success and We Would be Flush with New Wealth', *Irish Independent*, 16 November 2007.
108. 'Treasury Announces Restructuring Plan', *RTÉ Business*, 13 November 2007, available at: <http://www.rte.ie/business/2007/1111.treasury.html>.

109. 'Treasury to Build China's 'Eco-City', *Irish Independent*, 5 July 2006.
110. 'Treasury Moves into Waste Business', *RTÉ Business*, 8 October 2003, available at: <http://www.rte.onbusiness.ie>.
111. 'NTR Shifts its Focus to Energy and Recycling', *Irish Times*, 4 April 2006.
112. 'NTR to Invest €120m in Biofuels', *Irish Independent*, 8 March 2008.
113. 'Research Funds "Vital" for Agriculture', *Irish Examiner*, 27 August 2007.
114. Some of the most powerful advocates of farming communities such as Kentucky farmer, writer and philosopher Wendell Berry and organisations like the International Society for Ecology and Culture (ISEC), see <http://www.isec.org.uk>, have written powerful arguments on the need to protect and rebuild agricultural diversity, especially for rebuilding local food economies. For examples refer to Berry, W. (1995), *Another Turn of the Crank*, Washington, DC: Counterpoint; Norberg-Hodge, H., Merrifield, T. and Gorelick, S. (2002), *Bringing the Food Economy Home: Local Alternatives to Global Agribusiness,* London: Zed Books.
115. Downey, L. and Purvis, G. (2005), 'Building a Knowledge-Based Multifunctional Agriculture and Rural Environment' in C. Mollan (ed.), *Science and Ireland – Value for Society*, *Volume 2,* Dublin: RDS, pp. 121–39.
116. 'Creamery Sets up Organic Enterprise', *Irish Examiner*, 5 December 2007.
117. 'Part-time Farmers Encouraged to Utilise Skills Learned in Commercial Workplace', *Irish Examiner*, 23 February 2008.
118. 'Teagasc Makes Plans for Bio-Economy', *Irish Examiner*, 3 December 2007.
119. Donnelly, W.J. (2000), 'Public Research: Managing the Innovation Process', *International Journal of Dairy Technology*, 53, November, pp. 149–55 (see p. 152).
120. Cogan, J. (2007), 'Moorepark Food Research Centre: The Challenge for Open Innovation – Case Study', National Institute of Technology Management (NITM), UCD.

CHAPTER 5

Education in the Learning Society

> The same rule of self-destructive financial calculation governs every walk of life. We destroy the beauty of the countryside because the unappropriated splendours of nature have no economic value. We are capable of shutting off the sun and the stars because they do not pay a dividend.
>
> John Maynard Keynes, 1933[1]

INTRODUCTION

The late economist Patrick Lynch maintained that the distinction between utilitarian and cultural education was not valid.[2] Lynch argued that education should teach people to think resourcefully as well as memorise, and to understand not just changing techniques, but the application of principles to changing conditions. He paraphrased the French philosopher and political thinker Jacques Maritain, who held that the trouble with purely utilitarian education was that it was not utilitarian enough![3] Education has a much wider role than accelerating economic growth. A key goal is to promote social and cultural development, thereby helping an individual fit into the community and environment in order, as he put it, to 'arrive at a national identity and to obtain a better basis for a wider understanding'.[4]

Ireland needs a different approach to education if it is to build the foundation for a sustainable and successful learning society. This chapter focuses on how the school and higher education sector can develop powerful learning environments. Central to this is that students be helped define a life purpose, understand the value of tangible and intangible resources, and appreciate how science and technology might be applied to solve societal problems. Perhaps most importantly, they must be given the opportunity to undergo a transformative experience guided by a sense of identity founded on place.

Of course, the development of a learning society is not limited to third-level educational institutions. Ireland requires a new kind of educationally rich experience at all levels, driven by self-discovery and exploration, if it is to adapt successfully to the evolving global competitive environment. In the innovation age, learning to learn, learning to transform information into new knowledge and learning to transfer new knowledge into applications are more important than memorising facts.[5] Primacy must be given to meaning, emotions, feelings, analysis, reasoning ability, critical thinking and problem solving skills.[6] Working in multidisciplinary teams, thinking holistically, and engaging in interactivity, relationships and networks while developing the ability to cope with risky change are among the most valuable skills in a learning society. The education process should be based on helping individuals develop the capacity to find, access and apply information and knowledge, especially to projects in local communities. Young people, in particular, should be helped to develop core values to guide them as responsible citizens in an increasingly complex and multicultural society. The unifying purpose of higher education should be nothing less than to help students develop to their full potential. The current approach generally falls short of this, neither stimulating creativity and communication skills, nor fostering a culture of lifelong learning.

Education should help individuals to reflect on, determine and implement a considered personal response to an increasingly risky and challenging international environment. They should be helped answer such questions as: 'how do I know I am doing the right thing?' or 'how do I improve my work practice to achieve a desired result?' Ireland's education system, still based largely on the old industrial model, is out of step with the kinds of innovative learning required to serve the needs of modern business and society. A radical overhaul is urgently required.

Higher Education

Culture of Discovery

Kerry poet Brendan Kennelly, in the Preface to his collection of poetry entitled *The Little Book of Judas*, writes:

> I wonder if many people feel as I do – that in the society we have created it is very difficult to give your full, sustained attention to anything or anyone for long, that we are compelled to half-do a lot of things, to half-live our lives, half-dream our dreams, half-love our loves? We have made ourselves into half-people. Half-heartedness is a slow, banal killer. It is also, paradoxically, a creepy pathway towards 'success', especially if half-heartedness is of the polished variety….I believe our tragedy is the viability of our half-heartedness, our insured, mortgaged, welfare voyage of non-discovery, the committed, corrosive involvement with forces, created by ourselves, that ensure our lives will be half-lived. There's a sad refusal here. A rejection of the unique, fragile gift.[7]

The most fundamental task of universities is to develop critical minds and to expose their students to processes of both self-discovery and discovery of the world about them. A spirit of exploration should be at the core of this experience if a knowledge-based society with a high quality of life is to be achieved. Without exposure to processes of exploration and self-discovery, students are unlikely to emerge as creative, engaged and responsible citizens. If a proper culture of inquiry and exploration was initiated in the early years, it could also enhance the creative output during the postgraduate period. Yet undergraduate research experience is not just for those interested in an academic career; students should not have to wait until they are postgraduates to enter the exciting world of discovery. Exposure to inquiry could prepare students for life and work in a range of sectors and occupations. As the Irish Government Information Society Commission points out, employers in both the public and private sectors will seek future graduates who are independent, inquisitive and sufficiently flexible to apply knowledge gained in one area of specialisation to others.[8]

Students are entitled to experience the excitement of creative endeavour but many get no realistic opportunity to do so. Most leave universities never having been exposed to the riches of research.[9] Academics often view their own research and undergraduate teaching as existing in different worlds, with lessons and insights derived from research-based inquiry not shared with students. Even though vast resources are pored into research in Irish universities, their presidents still maintain they face a funding crisis. This is partly due to the fact that most researchers hired under SFI-funded programmes do little or no teaching, certainly not at undergraduate level.[10] The problem is not confined to Ireland; evidence in Britain shows, for instance, that while professors and lecturers read current journals for their research, their lecture notes are largely taken from textbooks.[11] While academics' own research offers deep personal satisfaction and recognition, undergraduate teaching is often seen as a chore. Many fail to imbue these young people with a passion, or even an appetite, for exploration.[12]

This issue has plagued US elite institutions such as Harvard and Stanford for years. The Boyer Commission advocated a new model of undergraduate education urging that students become active participants, not passive receivers, so the skills of inquiry, analysis, synthesis and evaluation generated in the research process become hallmarks of a good education. Calling most research universities 'archipelagos of intellectual pursuit rather than connected and integrated communities'[13], the Commission's view is hard hitting:

> Universities are guilty of an advertising practice they would condemn in the commercial world. Recruitment materials display proudly the world-famous professors, the splendid facilities and the ground-breaking research that goes on within them, but thousands of students graduate without ever seeing the world-famous professors or tasting genuine research. Some of their instructors are likely to be badly trained or even untrained teaching assistants who are groping their way toward a teaching technique; some others may be tenured drones who deliver set lectures from yellowed notes, making no effort to engage the bored minds of the students in front of them.[14]

Allan Bloom charges academics with abandoning their principles and their purpose.[15] Often these kind of attacks come from outside the academy as in journalist Charles Sykes' book *ProfScam*.[16] He maintains that university teaching has become a lucrative racket where the most important responsibility, undergraduate teaching, has been abandoned in favour of trendy research, the pursuit of personal or political agendas, outside consulting contracts and the drive for tenure. Yet even an enthusiastic establishment figure like New York University President John Sexton maintains that an unhealthy separation exists between the ideal and reality of the US research university. He says it would be difficult to classify most as communities of scholars and learners dedicated to a common enterprise.

While admittedly the situation in Ireland is not directly comparable with the US, policy-makers appear intent on pursuing the same model.[17] The danger is that Irish academics will come to view themselves as little more than independent contractors without any sense of loyalty to their institutions or students. Instead, their primary allegiance may be to their own disciplinary area. This phenomenon could accelerate even further as technological advances offer faculty membership in virtual communities that span the globe.

In 1990, Ernest Boyer, head of the Carnegie Foundation, and after whom the above Commission was named, wrote a seminal treatise questioning the dominance of research as the pre-eminent measure of academic scholarship.[18] His rationale was that the mission of universities should expand to reflect a changing world; traditional empiricist research was too narrow to encompass the new emerging social order. Boyer saw education as a seamless web that extends beyond the lecture room door and campus gate to embrace the larger community. Calling for campuses to be more energetically engaged in the pressing issues of communities, he suggests a broader idea of scholarship:

> We should recognize that scholarship means the discovery of knowledge through research but also we should recognize that scholarship means integrating knowledge, and let us also recognize the scholarship of applying knowledge, finding ways to relate information to contemporary problems, and above all let us recognize the scholarship of presenting knowledge though advising, counseling and teaching.[19]

There are signs of change internationally, even if many may not yet have appeared in Ireland. Boyer's work has persuaded many US universities to substitute 'discovery' for 'research' in their mission. Therefore, even though Boyer's work has liberated many US academics from the confines of positivism, Irish universities still uncritically embrace an outdated model even as US academia is trying to move away from it. There is also an active debate within academia regarding the discovery processes possible at undergraduate level to stimulate knowledge creation, interdisciplinarity and inquiry-based learning. Many innovative approaches are being tried. For instance, 'world-courses' at the University of Maryland are team-taught and integrate natural sciences with humanities or social sciences perspectives. Undergraduates at the University of Chicago participate in a wide variety of research projects in multiple disciplines. The University of Delaware has adopted problem-based learning in all its basic science classes to promote active learning and connect concepts to applications. Students are not given all the information they need to solve open-ended, real-world problems but are responsible for finding and using appropriate sources. They work in teams with access to an instructor. Trained graduate or even undergraduate students help lead some groups.

Three years after its original publication, the Boyer Commission surveyed US research universities to gauge progress on implementation of its recommendations.[20] The response showed that the topic of research had become more embedded in the experience of undergraduate education. While conversion to a new model is by no means complete, faculties and administrators are undoubtedly moving towards developing inquiry-based techniques. Yet substantial use of this form of learning remains limited in the US. While opportunities to participate in research activities are becoming an established component of many undergraduate programmes, efforts have been largely directed at the best students. Moreover, the definition of research is still narrow and laboratory-centred, excluding a host of other potentially creative and innovative activities. Not surprisingly, undergraduate research appears to be more developed in the laboratory sciences and engineering than in the social sciences and the humanities.

In Europe things are also slowly changing. All teaching at Aalborg University in Denmark, for instance, is interdisciplinary, problem-centred and project oriented. Interaction between theory and practice through cooperation with the external environment is emphasised. A project starts with a real-life problem. Students work in project groups under supervision, analyse and formulate a goal and solve the problem. During the first year, students are organised into groups of eighty students, six to ten teachers and a secretary. The students are then split up into sub-groups of five to seven students which constitute the basic working unit, the project group. A group has its own room and each student a fixed working place. Students undertake three or four projects in the first year and this continues in a similar manner in subsequent years, with gradual specialisation permitted over time.

Interdisciplinarity

Theologian Enda McDonagh holds the view that the pursuit of truth, beauty and the good is what gives meaning, value and purpose to university education.[21] He says all university disciplines combine a sense of beauty with a sense of truth if staff and students are alert enough to appreciate it. Patrick Lynch argued that various academic disciplines should be bound closer together in higher education so that society consists of people who can communicate intelligibly with one another.[22] Echoing the concerns of C.P. Snow and others he says that the educational system and intellectual life are characterised by a split between two cultures, the arts or humanities on the one hand, and the sciences on the other.[23] He believes the positive impact of either could be increased by associating with the other and stresses the danger of seeing science as something apart. He sees the divorce of technology from a system of values as one of the main explanations for the predicament facing mankind, and academic adaptation essential if universities are to humanise society. Lynch saw that genuine interdisciplinary studies have to be problem oriented to be really effective.[24] Consistent with the vision of Thomas Jefferson and Benjamin Franklin that a university has an obligation to the society that supports it, he argues that institutions should be confronted with problems requiring collaboration between disciplines and should be charged with applying this knowledge to the service of the community and society. To him, interdisciplinarity will remain a vacuous cliché or unattainable aspiration at Irish universities unless the importance of problem solving that calls on the skills of different disciplines is accepted by the academic establishment. He sees that what is needed is a Centre of Innovation, quite different in principle to a Centre of Excellence, which usually grows around the work of one scholar and embodies the approach used today by SFI. Lynch's centre would be staffed by people of different disciplines, working there on a temporary basis, using a range of skills that could vary as the nature of the problems they worked on changed.

Both art and science involve instinct, intuition and imagination. Interdisciplinary studies are crucial to innovation but, compared to many other countries, as Brian Trench puts it, 'Ireland has an especially bad case of the cultural splits.'[25] He says the gap in Ireland between the sciences and culture is large and may even be growing larger to the detriment of both. In many languages, the arts and humanities have names containing 'science' such as *sciences humaines* in French and *Literaturwissenschaft* in German. In Finnish, 'science' is translated as *tiede* (from the verb *tietää*, to know) an art as *taide* (from the verb *taitaa*, to make something known). Finns see the connection between these fields so that any politician there who pronounces the word *tiede* almost instinctively adds the word *taide*.[26]

It is no surprise that the current promotional campaign of IDA Ireland entitled 'The Irish Mind', with a Celtic-inspired logo and tagline 'Knowledge is in our Nature', is selling potential investors an image of a creative, imaginative, flexible and agile Irish mindset.[27] As its former Chief Executive Seán Dorgan points out, the Irish psyche has an innate creativity, manifested in literature and music, a curiosity that is interested in others and seeks to build relationships, and a greater tolerance for ambiguity and ability to handle it than most other people.[28] He notes these characteristics are especially valuable in the modern, fast-moving world in which quick, instinctive solutions are needed to solve problems when only imperfect information is available.

These IDA Ireland claims hearken back to the inherent creativity of the Irish literary and artistic tradition. Yet, because of the academic structuring of knowledge into the separate disciplines, integrated programmes that draw on the arts, humanities, science and technology are especially difficult to develop in Irish universities. This is a major obstacle to nurturing an innovative culture within institutions, many of which have evolved, not to satisfy real local needs, but in circumstances more suited to other societies and cultures. Breaking down the barriers between specialisations can foster academic diversity and thereby individual creativity. As E. Estyn Evans once put it, 'it is at the fences, along the borders, that discoveries are likely to be made.'[29] It is not surprising that an artificial border like the one between Northern Ireland and the Republic could prove a spur to creative endeavour. Peter Quinn says his own youth in Fermanagh and south Cavan taught him a lot about cross-border trade.[30] He puts it, 'we knew which side to buy and which side to sell and how to get things from one side to the other.' As the border ran through the Quinn fields and the fields of their neighbours, he said, 'we got to know every gate, every ditch, every lane, and where to leave things when we got to the other side.'[31]

The modern dichotomy between knowledge areas would have been incomprehensible to Irish scholars of long ago. There were no divisions between art and science, mathematics and music, when Irish monks founded Clonmacnoise and Iona or wandered the Continent during the Dark Ages. From the earliest times, Richard Kearney writes, 'the Irish mind remained free, in significant measure, of the linear, centralising logic of the Greco-Roman culture which dominated most of Western Europe.'[32] He argues that to appreciate fully the integrity of the Irish mind, the conventional practice of rigidly separating the artist and the thinker, imagination and reason, must be questioned. He shows how James Joyce, especially in *Finnegans Wake*, subverted the established modes of linear thinking in order to recreate a mode of expression that would foster rather than annul heterogeneous meanings. Seamus Heaney, like Joyce, is another who juxtaposes the foreign and the familiar, being both at exile and at home, practising the art of, as Kearney puts it, 'making contradictions dance'.[33]

The aesthetic faculty is underdeveloped in Ireland, as can be seen from problems such as litter, dumping, environmental desecration and so on. The litter, decrepit buildings, and development eyesores seen in Irish towns and countryside do not just affect the senses. They reflect a mind frame and an attitude to place, value and resources that is simply intolerable in a quality learning society.[34] Improving this will not emerge from the individualist culture promoted in the arts, business, or the natural and social science programmes delivered in the Irish higher education system. In Gerry Sweeney's view, there is a need to cast aside the academic individualist mindset and structure of teaching. This approach to higher education is a major factor in the loss of the traditional *meitheal* culture of team-working and mutual help, historically a strong force in Irish social cohesion. He says indigenous enterprises will only reach their true innovative potential if native culture is strengthened by linking a sense of place with creativity.

Improving this state of affairs will not easily come about, given the lack of integrated thinking within the Irish third-level system. Sweeney points out that the low level of indigenous industry illustrates the need for an education system to shift from the teaching of theory to application, and to provide the skills to which experience would add the tacit know-how necessary for innovative and entrepreneurial development.[35] The challenge is to nurture an innovative culture in Ireland that fosters academic diversity and promotes individual creativity. The perspectives of the humanities, of disciplines such as anthropology, geography, linguistics, psychology and sociology, are therefore crucial if we are to arrive at any comprehensive sense of 'who we are and who we might be.'[36] If a culture of innovation and creativity is to be developed, integrated programmes that draw on the arts, humanities, science and technology must play a crucial role. Universities themselves now seem to realise there are major deficiencies and a rethink is overdue. The president of the University of Limerick, for instance, admitted recently that not much in undergraduate education had changed in decades. He urged more breadth and less depth in programmes. He was frank about the deficiencies in nurturing creativity and effective communication skills, suggesting that today 'employers seem closer to Newman than the universities!'[37]

Overhaul

It is difficult for any outside observer to identify a consistent theme flowing through Irish third-level education. Programmes of study, even those within the same institution, appear to share no common mission or unifying narrative that can inspire or give meaning to the educational experience.[38] Even though access to information is now widespread on the Internet, traditional lecturing, sometimes to classes of hundreds of students, is still the norm. The assumption, as educators Abbott and Ryan put it, is that 'no learning is taking place unless students are being taught.'[39] The Boyer Commission maintained that what is learned can often not be carried beyond the classroom, so even students with highly developed knowledge of a subject find it difficult to put that to use except in the artificial world of university examinations. Students often lack a coherent body of knowledge, fail to see connections, and possess no clear sense of how one course is related to another. As the Commission said, many graduate 'without knowing how to think logically, write clearly or communicate coherently'.[40]

Granted, a lot of faculty experience, discussion and hard work are put into determining course content and combining individual modules to form a programme. However, as Neil Postman explains, the *means* by which young people learn is merely an engineering or technical problem.[41] The more fundamental problem is a metaphysical one, the *why* or *reason* for education. If students are confident at creatively dealing with change and open to new possibilities, they are better prepared for a network society. People who create change expect to succeed while those less willing to be innovative do not believe their vision can affect the world.[42] The more practice and experience students have of contacting and exploring their inner emotional world, the more confidently they can creatively deal with change and be open to new possibilities. Learning should be based on cultivating the natural curiosity and impulse to learn of individuals rather than rewarding them for performing for the sake of others. This means learning in order to attain one's own goals, guided by one's own values, not the approval of an outsider such as a lecturer or teacher. The Boyer Commission argued that all students should clearly understand from the time they arrive on campus the reason they are at university: it is to become a *discoverer*.[43] Inquiry, exploration and investigation should be at the heart of their educational experience. Former Cornell University President Frank Rhodes puts it as follows:

> The notion that you 'receive' [education] passively is just a total falsehood. Education is something you create for yourself. And you no more receive it than you can receive a career, you have to create it for yourself. And the student who prospers will be one who is endlessly inquisitive, endlessly curious, endlessly persistent in pursuing faculty members, in mining information from every source, from reaching out to the richness of experience that campus life provides.[44]

Rhodes feels that, while the undergraduate experience should be one of the most important foci within academia, in reality it constitutes a great failure of the research-driven university. According to him, two factors are primarily responsible for this state of affairs. The first is that undergraduate education has become more 'pre-professionalised', in other words it merely prepares students for careers in the likes of accounting or engineering, thereby narrowing, quantifying and squeezing curricula into a scientific mould. The second is that faculties have given up on any agreement as to what the purpose of an undergraduate education is, or what it should provide. This lack of attention is understandable given the burdens placed on academics to excel in publishing as they scramble for grants and struggle to keep up with the explosive growth in knowledge within their own disciplines.

Education should mean more than simply preparing students for a job or cultivating intellect. Educators should be concerned with students' personal values and welfare, as well as their interpersonal and intercultural skills. Fostering self-esteem, healthy relationships and socially responsible behaviour is a priority. Educators should imbue ethical behaviour or, to repeat Horace Plunkett's somewhat old-fashioned word, *character* within the education experience. Students should learn to think holistically, work in multidisciplinary groups, cope with change and develop systems and products that are sustainable and caring of nature and humanity.[45] Too much emphasis on technical skills rather than the formation of quality relationships is flawed, with this kind of education being (to use American philosopher Mortimer Adler's phrase) 'preparation for earning a living, instead of preparation for living well'.[46]

Irish universities should strive to form stronger connections between faculty research and undergraduate teaching and learning. Yet, without changes in the wider institutional and structural context, curricular reform or programme design alone are probably insufficient to ensure the provision of the proposed approach to higher education. However, rebalancing the weights allotted to research versus teaching in academic promotion decisions would undoubtedly make a difference.

Perhaps the best way to nurture creativity and innovation would be for each Irish third-level institution to pursue a clearly defined interdisciplinary purpose, in effect a roadmap to guide all its research and learning activities. The key challenge for educators is to structure programmes that would connect to this shared institutional mission through a seamless web or network of exploration. Across the university, whether in the arts, humanities, social or physical sciences, this is a challenge if higher education is to respond appropriately to the education needs of a learning society.

Many scholars question the relevance of the traditional model of university education described in Newman's classic *The Idea of a University*.[47] At the same time, there is general agreement that in the knowledge age the case for the value of the university has never been stronger. However, the university should not be a place where knowledge discovery and research are confined to elite postgraduate and faculty research programmes. At its core it must offer an inquiring environment to all its community members, especially its undergraduates. A knowledge society is ultimately one that is inclusive and participative, concerned with values, culture and quality of life. Brendan Tuohy argues that a liberal education is of particular importance; value is created more by intangible assets such as ideas, ways of working, emotions and community than through either information or knowledge acquisition per se.[48] The undergraduate experience should be characterised by a sense of purpose and excitement, and develop in students a strong mission or vocation to motivate them. It is only when young people believe their vision can change the world that they are willing to lead change and be innovative.

Two recent reports, the *Skilbeck Report*[49] and the *OECD Review*,[50] highlight the global challenges facing the Irish universities and institutes of technology. While the emphasis in each is different, both recommend structural and institutional reform such as stronger links with industry and the wider community, development of an entrepreneurial ethos, an enlarged student intake, more access for the disadvantaged, a focus on quality and development of new funding sources. The *OECD Review* sees Irish third-level institutions as being crucial to continued prosperity and to a smooth and rapid transition to a knowledge society. It warns that Irish universities could be marginalised in an increasingly competitive international environment unless there are sweeping internal changes such as new-style management, cost efficiency, transparency and accountability. It recommends that, in return for change, institutions should be supported by a huge leap in funding. In response, the Irish Universities Association (IUA), representing the heads of all seven Irish universities, recently published a framework committing to 'produce a new breed of entrepreneurial third-level graduate entering and improving the workplace and the wider society'.[51] The IUA promises to develop what it is calling the 'new graduate', designed to secure an international competitive advantage. In response, the Government has increased significantly the resources devoted not only to university research but is backing the IUA commitment with a €510 million strategic innovation fund committed over the period 2007–2013 to reward colleges that push through structural reforms that make them more responsive to economic and social needs. We argue that the required innovative culture cannot be generated without a fundamental revamp of Irish university education.

Some may feel that the overhaul advocated in this book, affecting both the mission and the operation of university education, is too expensive to implement, since this will generally require small interactive environments. In fact, the opposite is likely to be true if innovative approaches are used to determine which courses might be delivered face-to-face and which online. Indeed, some might be taken by the students at another institution altogether since many of the most crowded undergraduate courses, such as introductory modules, are the same ones taught at most higher education institutions. This could result in better inter-institutional collaboration, facilitating student mobility and thereby reducing overall costs.

The Futures Academy at Dublin Institute of Technology (DIT) develops and applies futures methods and techniques to explore and imagine Ireland's future. In its report *Imagineering Ireland*, published in 2005, it looked at various scenarios for Ireland in the year 2030.[52] It concluded that the type of mindset required was one that could tackle complexity, uncertainty and change. This implies minds oriented to process rather than to structure, ecologically rather than hierarchically driven, value-added rather than competitive, holistic rather than functional and collaborative, and innovative rather than adversarial and derivative. For such a future, a radical new approach to third-level education in Ireland is essential. Students graduate today into a world of global risk, environmental degradation, values conflict and cultural confusion. Great opportunity and wealth exist alongside deprivation and poverty. Natural resource depletion and the dangers of global warming offset the benefits of medical and biotechnology advances. Forming a culture of inquiry, research and innovation within a framework that stresses intercultural understanding, sustainability, equitable sharing of resources and enhanced civic responsibility presents an enormous challenge for educators. The transformation proposed could prove a significant competitive advantage internationally. It would also offer protection to Irish universities so that they could continue to receive public support within a highly uncertain future environment. This will ensure these institutions make the kind of contribution to society that is consistent with the special intellectual role they have been offered by the Irish State.

Business and Technology Education

Sustainability and Systems Thinking

Dynamic, leading-edge organisations now design products, services, processes and systems to create prosperity founded on the healthy co-evolution of human and natural systems, so-called *profits, people* and *planet.*[53] The successful evolutionary company incorporates a new type of whole systems perspective to improve this triple bottom line. It tries to do more and better with less, or redesign products and services on industrial ecology models that mimic biological behaviour to eliminate waste. Innovations that minimise the use of materials, support biodiversity and increase resource productivity are at the core of this values-led culture. Since humans are intimately connected with the fabric of life, a unified systematic understanding that integrates cultural, social, cognitive and biological dimensions of life is essential.

The changing priorities and perspectives are depicted in Figure 4. Sustainability represents a fundamentally different way of envisioning human progress, shifting human values and societal rules from economic efficiency towards social equity and from exclusion to equality of opportunity. This implies a change from individual rights to collective responsibilities, from independence to interdependence,

Figure 4: Changing Priorities and Perspectives

Efficiency	→	Equity
Exclusion	→	Opportunity
Rights	→	Responsibilities
Independence	→	Interdependence
Luxuries	→	Necessities
Short-Term	→	Long-Term
Growth	→	Vitality
Income	→	Well-Being
Quantity	→	Quality
LINEAR	→	SYSTEMIC

from luxuries to necessities, from short-term to long-term thinking, and from growth that benefits a few to development or vitality that benefits all. It also, not coincidentally, shifts the focus from income to well-being and from quantity to quality. Overall, this implies a movement from a linear to a systemic way of thinking.

Science is moving from a focus on mechanics to one of dynamics, evolutionary development and the emergence of complex adaptive systems.[54] Everything in this world is connected with everything else. Recent scientific discoveries indicate all life is organised along the same basic patterns and principles, namely the *network*. The academic focus likewise needs to change from a focus on tangible products or things exchanged to *processes* and *relationships*.

An organisation's informal networks and 'communities of practice' are often the sources of novelty, creativity and flexibility. As Fritjof Capra argues, the vitality of an organisation, its flexibility, creative potential, innovativeness and learning ability, reside in these informal 'communities of practice'.[55] Leaders learn how to support and strengthen such informal networks. Traditional managers believe they control the organisation through their knowledge of how its different components and departments interact; they choose to ignore the living network of their employees. But Capra explains that there is a crucial difference between a living system and a machine; a machine can be controlled while a living system can only be disturbed. In other words, organisations cannot be controlled through direct interventions or instructions but they can be influenced by impulses such as guiding principles and indicative directions. He says, 'There is no need to push, pull, or bully it to make it change. Force and energy are not the issue; the issue is meaning. Meaningful disturbance will get the organisation's attention and will trigger structural changes.'[56]

As mentioned, the correct framework for examining and fostering innovation is not the traditional equilibrium analysis favoured by economists but a qualitative learning organisation or learning region approach. This is founded on the concept of generative learning, a systemic way of thinking that is more about creating than controlling. It is based on cultivating people's natural curiosity and impulse to learn rather than rewarding them for performing for the sake of others.[57] It requires discerning the systems that control events and grasping the systematic source of problems. It is this type of learning that is badly needed in Ireland in order to stimulate true creativity, rather than adaptive learning, which is about coping with present events.

Multidimensional policies that use whole systems thinking, taking into account the interconnectivity of all life forms, will be most successful in a network society. One-dimensional thinking has plagued Irish development since the foundation of the State. Pride in place, cultural traditions, language, music and sport along with a new emphasis on sustainability and biodiversity should form the foundation for Ireland's learning society. Broader social and environmental relationships, the keys to achieving a sustainable future, must be at the centre of Ireland's development policy. Policymakers are beginning to realise that a shift in emphasis from research, science, information and knowledge to the broader concept of learning is necessary.

A learning society is fundamentally concerned with fostering personal growth, capability and creativity. This suggests, as a consequence, that current approaches to educating Irish business and technology professionals are flawed.[58] These are generally based on a managerial or mechanistic paradigm, overlaid by a utilitarian market philosophy. Participants often fail to see connections and patterns. In an ecological or whole-systems view of the world, the emphasis is on relationships. Thinking in a learning society is systematic rather than linear, integrative rather than fragmentary, concerned with process, emphasising dynamics rather than cause-effect and pattern rather than detail. It is fundamentally concerned with recognising wholeness. A change of educational culture towards the realisation of human potential and the interdependence of social, economic and ecological well-being is often transformative and constructive. It engages the student in true learning rather than a transmissive methodology that concerns itself mostly with the transfer of information, which is merely instructive and imposed. It includes education of the mind, the heart and the hand, balances intuition with the analytic, focuses on character and community, and cultivates wisdom rather than the mere accumulation of facts.[59]

Increasingly, educators in business schools in particular are questioning both the kind of teaching and the nature of scholarship within their institutions. Scholarship in recent decades has pursued society's economic objectives much more than its social ones so that the public interest, as distinct from the private interests of capital and labour, appears to hold a tenuous place in management scholarship.[60] Yet individual growth in organisations furthers the public interest, independent of its value for firm performance. The challenge is to bring the role of society into organisational scholarship and construct a philosophy in management education that integrates social and economic objectives.

Effective management is above all a *practice*. Management educator Henry Mintzberg urges that three elements should feature centrally in business education, namely craft (or experience), art (or imagination) and science (or analysis).[61] Since innovation is about applying knowledge to create value, in order to stimulate institutional links between research or knowledge generation, teaching and practice, universities need to give value creation a prominent role in their institutional mission. This would also likely lead over time to more integrated structures since it would clearly identify how the arts, sciences and humanities contribute to the creation of value through interrelationships between financial, human, social, cultural, technological and natural resources.

Nurturing a sustainable culture through diversity and interdisciplinary studies should be a guiding principle. Helping students understand how all sources of capital, whether financial, human, social, cultural, technological, natural or financial resources, create value through innovation is the best foundation on which education can be built. This way of thinking is illustrated in Figure 5.

To develop such an innovation culture, science, technology and business programmes should be radically re-designed so that practical value creation, rather than knowledge transfer, is placed at the centre. Transformative learning occurs when students are placed in

Figure 5: Learning for Innovation

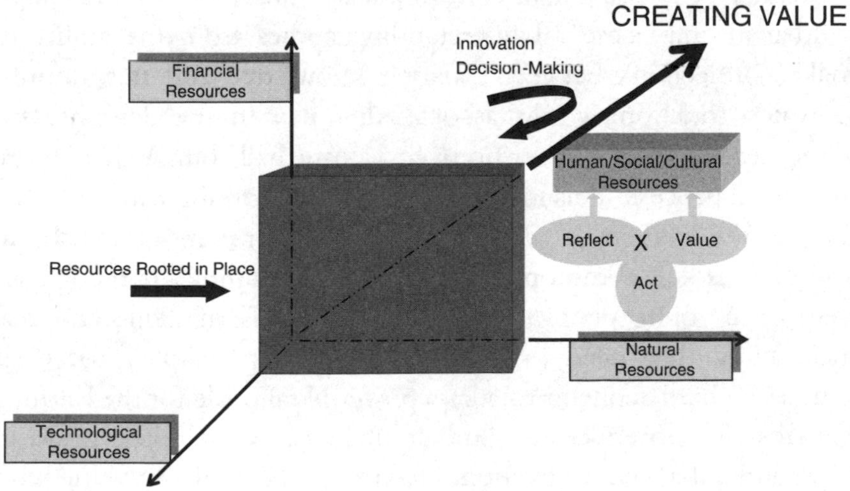

practical situations, such as conducting projects of interest to local enterprises and communities, and are required to make decisions. Students then gain a better understanding of the often conflicting relationships between individual, community and market values. Rather than being required to remember facts, students learn to create and share value largely defined by themselves, based on the outcome of discussion, problem solving, project work and reflection. The students then discover for themselves, perform their own research, solve real-life problems and make decisions. Their own values and interests, along with those of their colleagues, lecturers, the greater university itself and the wider society, form the basic dynamic of situations in which different stakeholders learn the essence of what it means to compete, co-operate and trade. Students in such situated learning discover the appropriate circumstances in which to apply what they are taught. They learn where, when and why a concept fits or does not fit a particular situation. This, not passively 'taking' courses, constitutes the heart of such a learning enterprise. However, at present, learning in order to attain personal goals, guided by one's own values rather than the approval of a lecturer, is hardly visible in Irish university education.

Experience is an effective teacher and the best way to learn something is by doing it, as educationalists John Dewey and Eduard Lindeman emphasise.[62] Understanding comes from the ability to make connections between existing knowledge and new inputs. Learning traditionally was associated, not with the de-contextualised setting of the classroom or lecture hall, but with a more integrated process. This involved the scholar working with the master, or the craftsman working with the apprentice.[63] Such an approach is still common in medicine, for example. It recognises that, once young people acquire certain levels of skills and real motivation, they need to be given more responsibility for their actions. Richard Sennett provides a powerful rationale for the learning benefits of apprenticeship and craftsmanship, including pride in work and enhanced motivation. He argues that, while working with materials, human beings may be inspired to receive meaning through their actions, which also helps them understand more about themselves.[64]

Radical changes would be necessary to assess student performance in this kind of environment. Innovative assessment methods, based on subjective or qualitative criteria rather than traditional testing by means of examinations, should be the norm. For instance, in the case of a collaborative project involving the local community, this might be assessed not only by using quantitative criteria such as its economic return but also by its social and environmental contribution to the long-term sustainability of the community.

Sustainability and Service

In a learning age, it is outdated to make a distinction between goods and services or to see manufacturing as different from and somehow superior to services. Essentially, goods can be characterised as tangible services, or the application of specialised competencies. People do not buy either products or services; they buy offerings in order to obtain valuable services. In this sense, customers no longer buy things; instead, they buy fulfilment or meaning. Value is co-produced through a complex relationship among parties. Emphasis should not be on the tangible product or good itself but on this co-creation of value and the relationship between the parties involved. Characteristics like utility, meaning and performance determine value. As a result, intangible qualities like creativity, ideas, flexibility, emotions, feelings, aesthetics, tradition, identity and community must be at the heart of a culture of services innovation. The purpose of a firm is to serve customers, not to produce things to sell. Making money (or profits) merely indicates how well it is fulfilling its core mission: to create, share, exchange and sustain value.

Previously, the idea was that intangibles existed to create value out of tangibles. Today, this thinking is reversed: the function of tangibles is to create value out of intangibles! Depending on the uniqueness and inimitability of intangibles, this is why the difference between the accounting or book value of a firm and its market value can be substantial. The market value of a firm is no longer largely determined by its physical assets but by its intangible resources. For instance, the market values of high technology US companies like Microsoft or Intel are several multiples of their book values; the opposite is true for US automobile companies like Ford or General Motors.[65] This conveys some idea of how much the market values resources embedded in an organisation. Such resources take the form of human knowledge, networks of relationships, and the trust implicit in a company's name, brand, products and services. The crucial aspect is that intangible resources, whether resident in a nation or an organisation, possess value because their characteristics are central to creativity and innovation and are rare, not imitable or easily substituted by competitors.[66]

Yet, while the Irish economy is increasingly dependent on intangibles, and services employ far more people than manufacturing, public policies on research and innovation still focus unduly on tangible products. Universities in particular seem poorly equipped to deliver a suitable education in the field of services. Services tend to receive a low priority in Irish academia since they centre on the subjective rather than the objective or scientific. Services are also interdisciplinary by nature and, as pointed out previously, Irish educational institutions are especially weak at developing research and teaching across disciplines. Language departments, for instance, often operate separately from business departments, and find it difficult to co-operate to develop traditional programmes, not to mind ones centred on services. Prefixes like 'financial', 'health' or 'public' associate services with a particular discipline, yet such segmentation often results in academic communities having no shared sense of what service is all about.[67]

The complex nature of the services sector demands learning environments that foster the development of personal skills, competencies and conceptual thinking within a student-centred reflective environment. However, the higher education sector emphasises codified or objective knowledge, delivered using a traditional lecture format, rather than tacit knowledge, communicated in a dynamic human-centred environment. For services, learning must focus on intangibility, relationships, meaning and purpose, and application of science and technology, enacted in multilingual, culturally diverse environments. The development of collaborative and problem-solving skills, aesthetics, taste, character and an ethic of quality are crucial. Individuals need self-knowledge as well as appreciating connections, patterns and relationships among various phenomena.

To achieve a proper learning environment, institutions should attempt to draw on the spirit and sensitivity of *both* the scientific and the artistic mind. Yet the fields of science and the arts often comprise people with widely different cultural backgrounds. The scientist is generally a team player who is part of a powerful institution while the artist works alone, often with a high degree of personal risk to his or her profession. As one physicist put it, 'an artist uses the first person singular, a scientist the first person plural…beauty does not belong solely to art, nor truth solely to science.'[68] For a good education in services, students should be exposed to both the objective or rational and the subjective or emotional to get the richness of both perspectives.

For example, the threat of global warming is changing the academic landscape in the US where professors and students from a range of different disciplines now actively collaborate in studying the environmental ramifications of production and consumption decisions.[69] Institutes like the Kenan-Flagler Center for Sustainable Enterprise at the University of North Carolina address global cultures, business ethics and corporate social responsibility, along with environmental issues. Individuals passionate about the environment have funded many of these initiatives. For instance, during the past ten years, philanthropists Frederick and Barbara Erb have donated some $20 million to fund the Erb Institute for Global Sustainable Enterprise at the University of Michigan. Companies are also involved: ExxonMobil, General Electric, Schlumberger and Toyota are financing the Stanford University Global Climate and Energy Project, the Shell Oil Foundation supports Rice University's Shell Center for Sustainability and giant retailer Wal-Mart is committed to funding the Applied Sustainability Center at the University of Arkansas.

In Ireland, there is little evidence to date of support for these sorts of sustainability-led initiatives. Irish-American donors have long contributed to the strengthening of ties between the Irish at home and in the US. Many wish to do more but, as former President of Coca-Cola Donald Keogh recently warned, Ireland is becoming more mentally distant for Irish-Americans.[70] He wondered whether the seventy million people of Irish ancestry worldwide are regarded as an important asset for the country's future. He urged Ireland to become more attentive to the Scots-Irish, a group that might look, along with the descendants of Roman Catholic emigrants, to Ireland, North and South, as their ancestral home.[71] The best way to foster such a potentially invigorating cultural, economic and political relationship is to redefine the basis of Irish identity. This involves opening up a dialogue with the Diaspora to centre on rootedness, sense of place and sustainability.

Reforming Business Education

For the past decade and more there has been an international debate among academics and executives about the most appropriate model for business education. Essentially there are two contrasting schools of thought. The most common one used on MBA programmes draws heavily on scientific research and analytical problem-solving techniques. A recent article in the *Harvard Business Review*, however, regards this as inadequate and based on the flawed assumption that business is an academic discipline like chemistry or geology, when in reality it is a profession like medicine or law.[72] The authors contend that the 'dirty little secret' at most of today's top US business schools is that they chiefly serve the faculty's research interests and career goals but pay little regard to the needs of other stakeholders. The intellectual premise on which the scientific school model rests is that the role of universities is to help society advance by supporting scientists who push back the boundaries of knowledge. Such schools see their objective as conducting scientific research, whereas most issues facing practitioners are questions of judgement that cannot be shoe-horned into formulae or equations. Practical implications are therefore left to others.

Nevertheless, business academics generally like this approach, since it utilises the considerable skills and statistical competence they possess, and requires no great insight into complex social and human factors. They themselves also need to spend little time in the field discovering problems facing practising managers. Yet, when the outcome of this teaching is applied to the real world of business where judgements are made with messy and incomplete data, methodological wizardry can actually blind rather than illuminate. The aura of quantification, however, masks the fact that the variables not included, ignored because they cannot be measured (such as human factors relating to wisdom, experience or ethics and many strategic and competitive issues), are exactly what makes the difference between good and bad business decisions.

This approach, described by one CEO as leading to a 'vast wasteland' of effort, means many students graduate from these schools ill-equipped to wrangle with complex, unquantifiable issues, the real stuff of management. The main problem is *not* that business schools have embraced scientific rigor but that other forms of knowledge, especially tacit forms, are ignored. It is also ironic that this approach ignores areas of science that hold the greatest promise for business, such as cognitive science where some fascinating work is being done on issues like how trust impacts economic decisions. What is needed, say critics, is another approach that provides a better balance between scientific rigor and practical relevance, with emphasis on vocational, skill-based or clinical approaches.

Yet this alternative approach also has detractors such as Tom Cooley, dean of the Stern School of Business, New York University.[73] Cooley attacked a recent proposal of the Association to Advance Collegiate Schools of Business (AACSB) to move towards what he labelled a 'backward-looking practice-based approach'. He says a research mindset brings a powerful focus to business education, is forward looking and thereby moves 'education away from teaching students a collection of *facts* to teaching them how to *think* … from a stultifying 'best practice' mentality toward developing *analytical* ability [emphasis in original].' Cooley says the goal of business schools is to teach not only the current accumulation of knowledge but to be actively engaged in creating new knowledge that will drive business in the future. He sees new codified (note, not tacit) knowledge as the key to success in business and only by developing tools and analytical techniques is such success possible.

There is merit on both sides of the divide but neither approach addresses the fundamental and paradigm-shifting mentality required in the education of Irish global managers. The mentality we advocate is close to that advocated by business professor Robert Chia.[74] He argues that the cultivation of the 'entrepreneurial imagination' is the most important contribution business schools can make to the enterprise sector. The entrepreneur, a word that comes from the terms *entre* ('to penetrate in between') and *prendere* ('to seize hold of'), signifies individuals who penetrate the spaces between established boundaries, seizing opportunities overlooked by others and making their mark by deliberately flouting conventional wisdom. Chia says the focus on a discipline-based curriculum mirroring the research interests and aspirations of academics reinforces a thought style and mental attitude that pays too much attention to narrow priorities and analytical rigour. This is done at the expense of a loss of imagination and resourcefulness in dealing with practical concerns. Yet, in the innovation age, imagination leads to a truly distinctive and inimitable competitive advantage. Academics should instead cultivate an intimate sense of the power and beauty of ideas, and the relationships between them. He advocates a recourse to literature and the arts to provide the means of stimulating the powers of association in fertile minds. The scientific mentality emphasises the simplification of complex experiences in manageable principles or axioms, whereas literature and the arts stress the opposite thereby sensitising individuals to the subtle nuances of contemporary life. Such heightened 'aesthetic consciousness' cultivates a critical sensitivity to hidden assumptions and subtle relationships in social situations, crucial if the entrepreneurial imagination is to flourish.

The dominant thought style in business schools manifests itself through the research process and rigidity in the curriculum. Chia advocates that business schools should 'weaken' this thought process to encourage and stimulate the entrepreneurial imagination and direct attention to the webs of relationships that define social situations. This would lead to an understanding of management theories and knowledge as *imaginative* products of sense-making or meaning, human inventions rather than how things 'really' are. It would also allow human situations to be open to critical questioning, reinterpretation and reconceptualisation. Students should be encouraged to 'forget' what they think they know, giving themselves over to chaos, ambiguity and confusion, which can offer them deeper insights and understanding. To Chia, such a paradigm-shifting educational strategy is more likely to produce entrepreneurial managers who are capable of 'thinking the unthinkable' and inventing new patterns of thought out of the chaotic unpredictability, volatility and dynamism of the current global environment.

The American educationist, philosopher and mathematician Alfred North Whitehead maintained that a university 'is imaginative or it is nothing'.[75] Therefore, in properly functioning business school classrooms, students and faculty should be engaged in the imaginative acquisition of knowledge. Whitehead maintained that a university can only be justified if it preserves the connection between imagination and 'zest for life'.[76] He held that universities, which fail to impart information imaginatively, have no reason to exist; university education should be directed towards the opening of vision so new ways of thinking and understanding are possible. As he told a gathering of business academics, the real tragedy is that those who are imaginative have little experience and those who are experienced have little imagination! The main mission of the business school is to ensure that imagination and experience coalesce.

This is why Irish university classrooms need to become more akin to the learning organisations or 'communities of practice' originally championed by Senge[77] and Wenger[78], respectively. Wenger uses the phrase the 'negotiation of meaning' to characterise the process by which people experience the world and engage with it in a meaningful manner. He argues that the primary unit worthy of study is neither the individual nor social institutions but informal communities of practice which people create as a shared enterprise to nurture meaning and identity. Education should not just be formative or informative but rather *transformative*, in order to help students explore what he calls 'new ways of being that lie beyond our current state'.[79]

Peer to peer learning is especially important. Rather than an individual experience, learning should become a team effort. Dermot Desmond, a prime driver in the late 1980s of the International Financial Services Centre (IFSC) in Dublin and founder of a leading supplier of corporate e-learning content, agrees.[80] Learning, knowledge and community, he argues, are tightly bound together. He maintains that learning is a collaborative and reflective activity that takes place best in informal networks where ideas are generated, shared and exchanged. People learn by watching experts, sharing reflections with others, problem solving and applying knowledge in new contexts. Students should acquire knowledge in order to achieve group objectives or balance conflicting goals, just as they would in most places outside the rarefied atmosphere of a college. The traditional role of lecturer should become closer to that of facilitator and coach with the emphasis on creating a motivating culture of mutual respect, co-operation and idealism, while de-emphasising the presentation of facts and the acquisition of information.

Educating the Irish-Global Manager

Enterprise Ireland (EI) argues that leadership, allied to innovation, is fundamental to driving the growth of indigenous Irish enterprises. Therefore, it actively promotes management capabilities and innovation for Irish business by providing tailored, results-oriented management development programmes. These include the 'Leadership 4 Growth' programme, conducted in association with Stanford Graduate Business School and the Irish Software Association. It also promotes an 'International Selling Programme' in association with the DIT. The agency's latest strategy identifies leadership as one of the core enablers and key competitive differentiators for the achievement of scaled international growth.[81] This stresses that leadership and management are critical to the successful adoption of innovative business models, practices and processes, as well as the commercialisation of innovative new products and services.

The issue of business education is also being addressed by the Management Development Council (MDC), established in 2007 to advise the Government on the adequacy and relevance of management development provision in Ireland. In a recent address to members of the MDC, Minister for Enterprise Trade and Employment Micheál Martin said:

> We need to ensure that there are no barriers to our companies gaining the additional management skills that they need to give them a competitive edge in trading both at home and abroad. The ability of an enterprise to launch innovative products and services and to expand successfully into international markets depends heavily on the capability of the company's management team.[82]

MDC Chairman Frank Roche, of the UCD Smurfit Business School, says the MDC has a vision of Ireland as a country internationally recognised for its excellent business managers, with all SME managers having access to high quality management development that meets their needs. He says the MDC believes this vision is achievable. Yet this seems unlikely to occur without radical changes in how Irish business schools conceptualise their role in the innovation process. Irish business education differs in no material way, in theory or practice, from anywhere else in the world. There is nothing specifically Irish about the ethos at business schools at Trinity College/Irish Management Institute (IMI), Dublin City Uiversity, National University of Ireland, Galway or University College Dublin.[83] The historical, cultural or societal context from which Irish enterprise operates is regarded as irrelevant in the education these schools offer. Such schools need to fundamentally revamp their offerings to prepare managers to face a future completely different to the past. Management development programmes should be built around learning environments that nurture an appreciation of Irish identity and place through the study of the interplay between the local and the global. The global manager must be helped to develop a strong sense of identity, with deep respect for Irish heritage and traditions, blended with a global cosmopolitan outlook.

Some educators recognise things have to change. Writing jointly in the *Irish Times*, Gerard McHugh, head of the School of Business, Trinity College and Tom McCarthy, chief executive of the IMI, argue that executive education requires a global perspective driven by local innovation obtained by marrying management practice, learning and culture.[84] They appear to accept the international evidence that innovation sticks locally once the right conditions are in place, and programmes that focus on action learning yield the highest results. The challenge facing Irish business, they contend, is for both indigenous companies and multinational subsidiaries to remain globally competitive through achieving productivity growth. What has not been taken on board, at least till now, is that the best way to do this is through enhancing intangible assets informed by local knowledge, research, identity, culture and tradition.

Environments that support integrity or wholeness, by mediating relationships not only between the local and the global but also the material and the immaterial, are especially important to nurture in Irish higher education. Support for this perspective was given recently by two eminent UK academics. Colin Mayer, dean of the Said Business School at Oxford, points out that, while the dark side of globalisation tends to destroy relations of trust, the countries that can combine the benefits of globalisation with local relations of trust are the ones that will prosper most from it.[85] Dame Sandra Dawson, professor of Management at the Judge Business School at Cambridge, holds that leaders of the future need an education that exposes them to the relationships between the material and emotional worlds.[86] Programmes should be designed so students are sensitive to difference and appreciate others' needs and motivations. This would help build trusting relationships across collaborative networks, which are crucial if a culture of creativity and innovation is to be established.

Sample Irish-Global Innovation Programme

We now illustrate how a resource-based innovation programme, founded on the New-Revival framework, might operate in practice. As depicted in Figure 6, *Workshops in Reflective Practice* are at the centre of the learning environment, designed to enhance learning by crossing many disciplines and assisting students to see connections between different courses of study. Creating value, both for the participants as individuals and the organisations for which they work, is at the heart of the programme. All elements of the programme, which centres on understanding how each form of capital or resource contributes to value creation, come together to form a cohesive core. Since everything is connected to everything else (e.g. the dynamic interplay between business organisations, the economic system and the natural environment), a systems

Figure 6: Resource-Based Innovation Learning

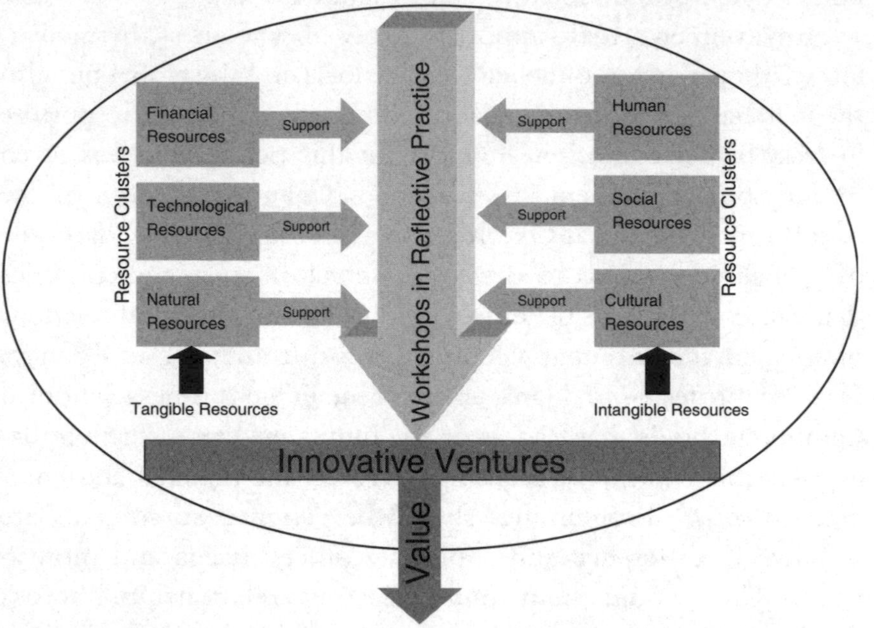

approach is critical and workshops are ideal for such a role. This is where a community of practice discusses, debates and reflects on learning and meaning. Specialisations in business, science, engineering or technology would be possible through an interdisciplinary and collaborative learning environment fostered by this approach. It would help marry within the one programme students working on technology-based innovations, for example, with projects on energy conservation and social ventures. Such an approach would create a practical and *unique* ethos.

The workshops provide a powerful learning infrastructure consisting of progress reports, interdisciplinary projects, case studies, simulations and presentations by guest speakers. In order to ensure graduates are capable of stimulating ventures, either inside or outside organisations, students should also be regularly exposed to presentations and seminars by leading entrepreneurs, industrialists, artists, community leaders, spiritual thinkers and others working in a host of creative arenas. Debates between class members on a range of societal issues would help students see connections among different disciplines. This means they would likely become more reflective, stimulated perhaps by engaging in volunteer work with local communities, becoming involved in political action or the initiation of social ventures. In this way, students would develop ventures that balance economic/financial viability, social equity and environmental sustainability.

A further elaboration on the layout of such a rooted Irish-global innovation programme specifically designed for managers in private, public and community organisations is depicted in Figure 7. As before, Workshops in Reflective Practice are the core around which the programme is built. Alongside these Workshops, managers would be exposed to two categories of courses that support the value creation process, namely studies in a) *Managing Innovation Investment* and b) *Fostering Rooted Irish-Global Identity*. The first would help them understand how to identify new opportunities, manage risk, launch and manage ventures and build them into viable projects and companies. The second is intended to expose them to issues of identity

Figure 7: Rooted Irish-Global Innovation Programme

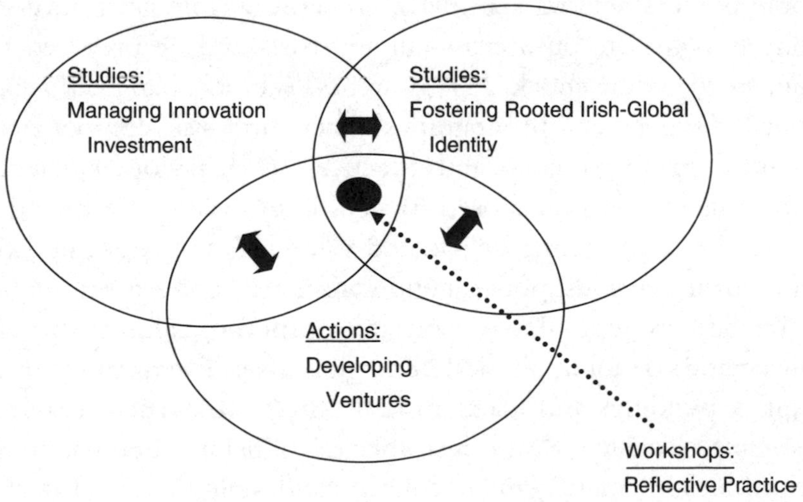

and meaning, nurture a sense of wholeness and help them appreciate biophysical and socially sustainable practices and stewardship. Learners would develop distinctive competencies that heighten their sensitivity to cultural and geographic differences, bedding this down with an intimate sense of their own identity and rootedness. The participants would also work in groups on *Developing Ventures* and present their proposals to an assembled gathering of academics, senior management and potential investors at the end of the programme. They would demonstrate how they created value, while pinpointing aspects like the viability and sustainability of their venture.

Not long ago geopolitics in international business was regarded as passé, especially in the financial services industry where quantitative models were dominant.[87] What people in various countries wanted or why interests might differ for cultural reasons in different parts of the world seemed not to matter. Today, that way of thinking appears outdated, especially as the impact of the global credit crisis hits home. Global managers nowadays require a wide range of knowledge and skills to handle situations encountered in different countries. Education should provide an opportunity to learn and practice negotiating techniques in a cross-cultural context by refining skills, habits of mind and competencies. Students should possess cultural sensitivity, empathy, adaptability, have the ability to negotiate on a cross-cultural basis and be prepared for exposure to culture shock. This awareness is best enhanced through applied management programmes that emphasise competencies grounded in the theory and practice of behavioural science. Individuals should be exposed to significant events in a country's history, the fundamental beliefs and values of its people, and the institutional, religious, political and commercial context.

In the emerging global economy, corporate value is increasingly embodied, not in physical or tangible assets like manufacturing facilities, buildings and telecommunications infrastructure, but in intangible assets like R&D, customer relationships, brands, imagination, insight, management courage and agility.[88] The Internet has amplified this trend, making it global and ensuring intangibles are more mobile and tradable. In the e-world, competing involves a completely new way of thinking, particularly in the conceptualisation of service delivery. For many companies, since intangibles are their great untapped source of competitive advantage, a different mindset is required on how to create sustainable value. The key challenge that a manager faces is to build a framework that links the company's resources with the new economy, assessing and capitalising on the critical intangibles that matter most.

As the significance of the material diminishes and capacities of the mind become more and more a crucial competitive factor, human attitudes and meaning, which are heavily influenced by community, society and tradition, become key resources. The philosopher and economist Friedrich Hayek explained that tradition is not something arbitrary, mindless or accidental but the product of millions of human trials and errors.[89] Hayek held that humans become intelligent because they learn from tradition, which lies between instinct and reason. This is why it is important that Irish business education embeds the latest academic theories within a practical environment where students learn to reflect on their own identity and the local context. Exposure to their country's history, culture, language and so on should be essential components of their education. This would help individuals, whether full-time undergraduates or part-time executives, navigate between the local and the global and be of inestimable assistance in developing new international markets for Irish enterprise.

School Education

Radical Reform

It is not just at third level that Irish education needs radical redesign, enhanced quality and a focus on identity. A learning society promotes tolerance, inclusion, well-being, social skills and knowledge that ideally begins in childhood. Such lifelong skills are key determinants of competitiveness and productivity in the globalised economy. Education scholars Arthur Chickering and Linda Reisser assert that in the global society of the twenty-first century, where change is the only certainty, identity formation should be the central task of education.[90] Yet Pádraig Hogan argues that, since the time of Plato, Western education has been serving the interests of some ideology.[91] He says that in many countries education policy is now an active accomplice in furthering acquisitiveness and the accumulation of material advantage. Education thinking emphasises control and curriculum, with the learner's identity viewed as the 'property' of the educational institution. He maintains that a greater emphasis should be placed on the learner's identity, with teaching and learning a shared experience. In Howard Gardner's theory of multiple intelligences, analytical intelligence is only one of seven measures (the others are linguistic, logical/mathematical, spatial, musical, bodily/kinesthetic, intrapersonal and interpersonal).[92] Daniel Goleman in his book *Emotional Intelligence* redefines intelligence, arguing that attributes such as self-awareness, self-discipline, motivation, empathy, character and compassion mark out people who excel at relationships and at work.[93] Others have emphasised various reasons, many centred on sustainability, for why spiritual intelligence is crucially important in today's workplace.[94]

The above work shows that feelings, sentiments and unconscious thoughts crucially impact human behaviour. These help young people achieve meaning in their lives and make sense of the world. Yet only in recent years (and quite tentatively) have feelings and emotions have been recognised in the Irish school curriculum. A subject titled SPHE (Social, Personal and Health Education) is now mandatory at junior cycle level. The basis of SPHE is quite revolutionary in Irish education: young people have interconnected needs that encompass the physical, emotional, social and spiritual aspects of their lives, and they need to develop the requisite skills to handle them.[95]

In order to create the kinds of rich learning communities required to prepare for the challenges and opportunities of a learning era, the industrial age Irish school system, driven by a functional philosophy exemplified by the CAO points system, needs a complete shake up. More of the reform exemplified by SPHE is needed. For instance, little support is presently given to arts education at national policy level. A total of only two hours per week at primary level and no mandatory provision for the arts at secondary level is regarded by many concerned educators as completely inadequate for fostering creative childhood experiences, long-term interest in the arts and facilitating new ways of thinking about a familiar world.[96]

According to UCD economist Moore McDowell, the Leaving Certificate does not work properly and is merely a test of memory, not a proper reflection of a student's ability.[97] Jumping through mental hoops, he says, replaces the ability to demonstrate analytical skills, rote learning replaces inquiry and 'covering the course' replaces reading into a subject. Personal competencies such as the ability to be a collaborative, self-starting, quick-thinking and risk-taking individual should be developed. Such skills and attitudes are more naturally developed in the rich problem-solving environment of apprentice-type learning than in a formal classroom, which emphasises timetables, curricula, tasks, schedules, measurable results and disconnected activities.

There is a decided imbalance in the investment committed to education in many countries, and Ireland is no exception: far more resources per student are devoted to higher education than to primary or secondary schools. Resources should be redistributed from first, second, third and fourth levels towards the elementary school level to have the most impact in creating a learning society.[98] New forms of instruction should accompany this. From their earliest years, it should be obvious to learners that, as they progress, they will be held more responsible for the development of skills they already have, while being supported in higher order skills (such as how to reason, solve problems and develop strategies for thinking ahead) only until they can perform these themselves.

A key element of such learning communities is a greater commitment to the places from which young people come, and for which a sense of identity and responsibility can be fostered. Another is forming learning relationships between young people and adults in communities to replace the isolation from real life that makes current schools so ineffective. The traditional role of education, at present instructional and teacher moderated, should be replaced by empowered minds wishing to discover and individuals learning to learn themselves, both independently and collaboratively. Aided by sophisticated multi-media digital networks, the social world of learning would then be much more about problem solving, talk, practical involvement and experimentation.

However, in Ireland today, as Patricia McDonagh, president of the National Association of Principals and Deputy Principals (NAPP) points out, education and schools are being treated more like market commodities.[99] The language of business is used to evaluate the work of Irish schools, for instance terms like 'whole school evaluation' and 'subject inspection'; both students and parents are regarded as consumers. The language should instead be one used in regard to communities, for instance: care, nurture, creativity, imagination and exploration. The key to effective schools is the strength of the relationships among teachers, school leaders and students. To prepare students for the future, she says, 'It is not so much what we teach as much as how we teach and it is not what they learn as how they learn to evaluate, process and appreciate information that matters.'[100]

There is certainly an acceptance that transformation is needed in Ireland. After wide consultation with various stakeholders, in 2003 the National Council for Curriculum and Assessment (NCCA) proposed a radically different vision of second-level education.[101] Under the student-centred plan, a revolution in school culture would occur, with the relationship between teachers and students changing to one of equality and mutual co-operation.

Students would be taught to think and communicate rather than to amass knowledge, there would be more time for independent and group learning, and students would even be allowed to choose their own dress code. The UK Qualifications and Curriculum Authority (QCA) is on a similar radical tack regarding the ways students learn. It recently proposed to abandon the traditional school timetable altogether and replace it with an approach whereby subjects would be taught together, with entire weeks or days turned over to single subjects. This would ensure students were not turned off learning in the crucial first years at secondary school, as many are at present both in the UK and in Ireland. As in third level, interdisciplinarity is sought: teachers would be encouraged to engage in joint subject teaching across a range of subjects with lessons divided into different lengths, some lasting no more than a few minutes. Timetables could be adapted for different groups of children. Those, for example, entering secondary school might do swimming in games and PE until they can swim. Those who can swim already could experiment with a range of subjects. The director of the authority likened the new approach to the preparation of a mixed salad:

> The way you put them [ingredients] together to create the salad is the crucial bit in making it appetising. There is nothing to say that a school has to offer 40 minutes of tomatoes, followed by 40 minutes of lettuce, followed by double onions.[102]

Culture and Identity

Much could be learned from a major Irish competitor for global investment – Singapore. Using the slogan 'Thinking Schools, Learning Nation' Singapore has embarked on an ambitious plan to develop the nation's ability to learn, recognising this will have an enormous bearing on its future well-being.[103] By making learning a national culture, it is trying to create a total or systemic learning environment that will include students, teachers, parents, workers, companies, community organisations and government. It sees the task of education to provide the young with core knowledge, skills and habits of learning that will enable them to learn continuously throughout their lives, equipping them for a future nobody can predict. With good broadband access, something Ireland still finds hard to deliver, much knowledge content is readily available over the Internet. Therefore, Singapore's Ministry of Education is studying how to cut back on the amount of content that students are required to learn, encouraging teachers and students to spend more time on projects that can develop thinking and learning skills for the future. This is also designed to develop a stronger desire in students to contribute to something larger than themselves.

Singapore recognises that learning goes beyond simply maximising an individual's potential and that a nation's culture and its social environment shape what learning means, and determine its impact. Like the Japanese did for decades, the Singaporeans are now trying to get every organisation to recognise that each individual, regardless of status, has a contribution to make towards improving the organisation. By putting learning and the development of human resources at the centre of its philosophy, the country is hoping this will lead to an incredibly innovative and highly productive learning society. Yet, while espousing innovation, the country also cherishes time-honoured values that are integral to Singapore's society and which made the country what it is. Balancing change with rootedness means innovation can co-exist with history and tradition and thereby help create a highly productive economy going into the future.

There is a lesson here for Irish education, as there is from another country, Finland, which consistently ranks at the top in international education.[104] It is instructive to compare the role in education of the national epic of Finland, the *Kalevala*, with Ireland's closest equivalent, the *Táin Bó Cúailnge*. The *Táin*, a centre-piece of the eighth century Ulster cycle of heroic tales, could also act perhaps as a unifier of traditions in Ireland, but is virtually ignored in education north and south of the border. Contrast this with Finland where the *Kalevala* is studied extensively in schools at all levels, serving as an ethnic memory for the Finns and providing a coherent national identity. By presenting a compelling view of the Finnish past, it has provided a guide to the modern development of Finnish culture. It is at the root of Finnish consciousness, shaped the language, inspired independence and served as the source of the flowering of Finnish art and literature. It also fosters the Finns' strong pride in place and respect for nature. Finns today name their children, their towns, streets and companies after legendary figures in the *Kalevala*.[105] As one *Kalevala* scholar put it,

> Finnish history is not something dead and over. It is always alive, always growing, always unfinished – and every Finn today has his or her own contribution to make to the great fabric of tradition and hope which binds all Finns, dead and living and yet to be born, in a common faith and a common destiny.[106]

In Ireland, there is no comparable attempt at developing an ethnic memory within the education system that develops the imagination while offering a guide to young people in the contemporary world. Official concern is most exercised on issues like the declining uptake of science by students at first and second levels.[107] Former Tánaiste Mary Harney recently proposed what she calls a 'civic science', defined as a science 'engaged with and invited into the national dialogue', as a key mission for Ireland in the twenty-first century. We need citizens, she said, 'whose imagination grips them with an interest in science.'[108] Urging that science have a central place in Irish culture, she says this would lead to a different concept of identity or citizenship, strengthen Irish culture and inspire the creativity of new generations. She feels the country should inspire and support a scientific culture in the same way it embraces artistic exploration in literature, music and art. In our view, such a perspective is too narrow and lacks historical context to generate a true learning society.[109] Innovation requires the sciences and humanities to be linked, but primary emphasis should be on emotional development and the cultivation of meaning and rootedness. In other words, self-knowledge, exploration and identity, integrated with scientific and technological knowledge, hold the key to transformational learning so Ireland can become a truly successful innovation society.

The focus in this chapter has been on the capabilities of individuals, although some emphasis was placed on the social and cultural environment within which powerful learning occurs. In the next chapter, the specific potential of cultural and social capital to enhance innovation and competitiveness is examined using the examples of language and community, respectively.

NOTES

1. Keynes, J.M. (1933), 'National Self-Sufficiency', *The Yale Review*, 22(4) June, pp. 755–69.
2. Lynch, P. (1979), 'Whither Science Policy?' Seventh Kane Lecture, Science Policy Research Centre, UCD, p. 3.
3. For a review of Maritain's views on education, see Tierney, M. (1944), 'M. Maritain on Education', *Studies*, 33(129), March, pp. 21–9.
4. Lynch, 'Whither Science Policy?' p. 13.
5. Salmi, J. (2001), 'Tertiary Education in the 21st Century: Challenges and Opportunities', *Higher Education Management*, 13(2), pp. 105–31.
6. Alan Mortiboys points out that to be fully effective in higher education, teachers need to teach with emotional intelligence. Students need to be engaged and feel valued and trusted. This emotional dimension of learning and teaching is often overlooked. The emphasis is on the cognitive level with knowledge of the subject the only thing that seems to matter. See Mortiboys, A. (2005), *Teaching with Emotional Intelligence*, Oxford, UK: Routledge Falmer.
7. Kennelly, B. (2002), *The Little Book of Judas*, Tarset, Northumberland, UK: Bloodaxe Books.
8. Information Society Commission (2005), *Learning to Innovate: Re-perceiving the Global Information Society*, Dublin: Department of the Taoiseach.
9. Some educationists argue that search engines like Google are dulling students' sense of curiosity, stifling debate and producing a generation of students who get by on a diet of unreliable information. Students often drift to the first site returned through Google. As one put it, 'Google is filling, but it does not necessarily offer nutritional content.' The challenge is to develop dynamic and critical thinkers so emphasis should be on interpretative rather than technological skills ('Google: White Bread for Young Minds?' *Irish Independent*, 30 January 2008).
10. 'University Heads Warn of Crisis through Lack of Funding', *Irish Times*, 18 March 2008.
11. Sweeney, G. (2002), 'The Skilbeck Report and the Need for Change', *Céide*, April/May, pp. 18–9.

12. Boyer Commission (1998), *Reinventing Undergraduate Education: A Blueprint for America's Research Universities*, Stony Brook: State University of New York, New York.
13. Boyer Commission, *Reinventing Undergraduate Education*, p. 9.
14. Boyer Commission, *Reinventing Undergraduate Education*, pp. 5–6.
15. Bloom, A. (1987), *The Closing of the American Mind: How Higher Education has Failed Democracy and Impoverished the Souls of Today's Students*, London: Penguin Books.
16. Sykes, C. J. (1990), *ProfScam: Professors and the Demise of Higher Education*, New York: St. Martin's Griffin.
17. Government of Ireland (2006), *Strategy for Science, Technology and Innovation, 2006–2013*, Dublin: The Stationery Office.
18. Boyer, E. (1990), *Scholarship Reconsidered: Priorities of the Professoriate*, New Jersey: The Carnegie Foundation for the Advancement of Teaching.
19. Glassick, C.E. (1999), 'Ernest L. Boyer: Colleges and Universities as Citizens' in R.G. Bringle, R. Games and E.A. Malloy (eds.), *Colleges and Universities as Citizens*, Boston, Allyn & Bacon, pp. 17–30 (see p. 21).
20. Boyer Commission (2001), *Reinventing Undergraduate Education: Three Years after the Boyer Report*, Stony Brook: State University of New York.
21. McDonagh, E. (2005), 'University Reform in Ireland', unpublished manuscript, St. Patrick's College, Maynooth.
22. Lynch, P. (1972), 'Interdisciplinarity in the Universities', *Irish Journal of Education*, 6(1), pp. 3–8.
23. Snow, C.P. (1998), *The Two Cultures*, Cambridge: Cambridge University Press; Kelleher, D. (1985), 'The Alienation of Science: An Irish Cultural, Industrial and Political Problem', *The Crane Bag*, 9(1), pp. 63–9.
24. Lynch, P. (1979), 'Whither Science Policy?', Seventh Kane Lecture, Science Policy Research Centre, UCD.
25. Trench, B. (2003), 'Science, Culture and Public Affairs', *The Republic*, 3, July, pp. 53–63.
26. 'Tiede-Taide, Two Cultures' (2004), *RTD Info* (Magazine for European Research), March, p. 3.

27. IDA Ireland (2006), *Ireland, Knowledge is in Our Nature*, Dublin: IDA.
28. Dorgan, S. (2006), 'How Ireland Became the Celtic Tiger', *Backgrounder*, The Heritage Foundation, Washington, DC, No. 1945, 23 June.
29. Evans, E.E. (1992), *The Personality of Ireland*, Dublin: Lilliput Press, pp. viii–ix.
30. 'Business "Strung up in Red Tape Bias"', *Irish Independent*, 19 July 2007.
31. 'Business "Strung up in Red Tape Bias"'.
32. Kearney, R. (1985), 'Introduction: An Irish Intellectual Tradition?' in R. Kearney (ed.), *The Irish Mind: Exploring Intellectual Traditions*, Dublin: Wolfhound Press, pp. 7–14.
33. Kearney, 'Introduction: An Irish Intellectual Tradition?' pp. 7–14.
34. 'Our Streets are a Holy Show', *Irish Times*, 17 August 2002, presents a depressing low down of dirt-filled Dublin streets, litter wardens afraid to work on weekend nights in case of being attacked doing their job, tourists who regularly complain about filthy Irish towns and businesses that refuse to pay bin charges, creating a serious rat problem. One person wondered whether there is some kind of unwitting balancing act in the Irish psyche whereby the predilection for the *craic* and a laid-back lifestyle militates against rules and orderliness.
35. Sweeney, G. (2002), 'The Skilbeck Report and the Need for Change', *Céide*, April/May, pp. 18–19 (see p. 20).
36. Cronin, M. (2004), 'The Unbidden Ireland: Materialism, Knowledge and Interculturality', *The Irish Review*, 31, Spring/Summer, pp. 3–10.
37. 'Mind the Quality and Feel the Width: Third-Level Rethink Overdue', *Irish Times*, 16 October 2007.
38. Of course, there are several exceptional institutions and unique programmes of study in Irish higher education. One exciting example, for instance, is the Furniture College, located at Letterfrack, a remote part of Co. Galway. The site once housed a reform school run by the Irish Christian Brothers. Since 1987, the Galway-Mayo Institute of Technology (GMIT) runs courses in Letterfrack in

partnership with Connemara West (a community and rural development organisation based in North-West Connemara). The aim is to enable its graduates to contribute to, and influence, the fields of design processes and manufacture of furniture in ways that are innovative, creative and responsive to the needs and development of a quality Irish furniture industry. The college attracts applicants from all over Ireland and Europe. A second example, applying a philosophy much in tune with our rooted Irish-global identity, is the Irish World Academy of Music and Dance, University of Limerick.

39. Abbott, J. and Ryan, T. (2000), *The Unfinished Revolution: Learning, Human Behaviour, Community and Political Paradox*, Stafford, UK: Network Educational Press, p. 218.
40. Boyer Commission, *Reinventing Undergraduate Education*, p. 6.
41. Postman, N. (1996), *The End of Education: Refining the Value of School*, New York: Vintage Books.
42. Walley, P. (1993), *Learning the Future – A Brief Guide to the Knowledge Society*, Galway: Meitheal Mhaigheo, City of Galway VEC.
43. Boyer Commission (1998), *Reinventing Undergraduate Education.*
44. Kreisler, H. (1999), 'Adaptation and Change in the American University', conversation with Frank H. T. Rhodes, in *Conversations with History Series*, Institute of International Studies, UC Berkeley, 31 March, p. 4, available at: <http://globetrotter.berkeley.edu/people/Rhodes/rhodes-con0.html>.
45. Cooley, M. (1993), 'Skill and Competence for the 21st Century', IITD 24th National Conference, Galway, April.
46. Adler, M. (1957), 'The Deterioration of American Education', from a lecture, 'Liberal Education in an Industrial Democracy', presented to the Industrial Indemnity Insurance Company, San Francisco, 1957, available at: <http://www.chariscorp-wordgems.com>.
47. Turner, F.M. (ed.) (1996), *The Idea of a University – John Henry Newman*, New Haven, CT: Yale University Press.
48. Tuohy, B. (2002), 'A Liberal Education for a Technology World', paper presented at the Conference on Values in Education and

Public Policy, University of Limerick, Centre for Culture, Technology & Values, April.

49. Skilbeck, M. (2002), *The University Challenged: A Review of International Trends and Issues with Particular Reference to Ireland*, Dublin: HEA/ CHIU.
50. Organisation for Economic Cooperation & Development (2004), *Examiner's Report – Review of National Policies for Education: Review of Higher Education in Ireland*, Paris: OECD.
51. Irish Universities Association (2005), 'Reform of Third-Level and Creation of Fourth-Level Ireland: Securing Competitive Advantage in the 21st Century', Dublin: IUA.
52. The Futures Academy (2005), *Imagineering Ireland: Future Scenarios for 2030*, October, Dublin: Dublin Institute of Technology (DIT).
53. Nattrass, B. and Altomare, M. (1999), *The Natural Step for Business: Wealth, Ecology and the Evolutionary Corporation*, Gabriola Island, British Columbia, Canada: New Society Publishers.
54. Vargo, S.L. and Lusch, R.F. (2004), 'Evolving to a New Dominant Logic for Marketing', *Journal of Marketing*, 68 (January), pp. 1–17.
55. Capra, F. (2002), *The Hidden Connections: A Science for Sustainable Living*, London: HarperCollinsPublishers.
56. Capra, *The Hidden Connections*, p. 98.
57. Senge, P. (1990), 'The Leader's New Work: Building Learning Organizations', *Sloan Management Review*, 32(1), pp. 7–23.
58. Stirling, S. (2001), *Sustainable Education: Re-Visioning Learning and Change*, London: Green Books.
59. Hart, T. (2001), *From Information to Transformation: Education for the Evolution of Consciousness*, New York: Peter Lang.
60. Walsh, J.P., Weber, K. and Margolis, J.D. (2003), 'Social Issues and Management: Our Lost Cause Found', *Journal of Management*, 29(6), pp. 859–81.
61. Mintzberg, H. (2004), *Managers: Not MBAs,* London: FT/Prentice Hall.

62. Dewey, J. (1938), *Experience and Education*, New York: Touchstone/ Simon & Schuster; Lindeman, E.C. (1926), *The Meaning of Adult Education*, New York: New Republic.
63. Over-emphasis in Ireland on 'academic' or 'graduate' qualifications means apprentice-style craft training programmes are relatively ignored. Note the response of the chief executive of the HEA to the likelihood that many young construction workers face long-term unemployment: 'Ireland needs more graduates, lots of them.' ('80,000 Jobs at Risk', *Irish Independent*, 8 January 2008).
64. Sennett, R. (2008), *The Craftsman*, London, UK: Penguin/Allen Lane.
65. Interestingly, in the case of former Irish State airline Aer Lingus, which recently went public, it is estimated its net assets exceed its market valuation by at least €200 million ('Assets Outstrip Aer Lingus Market Valuation by €200m', *Irish Independent*, 3 January 2008).
66. For a comprehensive analysis of the valuation of intangible resources in an Irish telecommunications company, refer to Millett, A.J. (2007), *Developing an Intellectual Capital Report for a Technical Product Development Organisation*, MA Thesis, NUI Maynooth, unpublished.
67. 'A Failing Grade for the Innovation Academy', *Financial Times*, 24 September 2004.
68. 'Interview with Jean-Marc Lévy-Leblond: Science and the World, Art and the Ego' (2004), *RTD Info* (Magazine for European Research), March, pp. 5–7.
69. 'A Threat So Big, Academics Try Collaboration', *New York Times*, 25 December 2007.
70. 'Irish-Americans Growing "Distant" from Ireland', *Irish Times*, 8 November 2007.
71. The Scots-Irish or Scottish-Presbyterians came to Ireland in the seventeenth century. Many descendants crossed the Atlantic where they formed the vanguard of the great army of pioneers who pushed the frontier westward. Famous names in American history came from this stock: frontiersmen Davy Crockett and

Kit Carson, Civil War generals Stonewall Jackson and Ulysses S. Grant, businessmen like the Gettys and the Mellons and US Presidents like Andrew Jackson and Woodrow Wilson. For a fascinating if unabashedly biased account, see Fitzpatrick, R. (1989), *God's Frontiersmen: The Scots-Irish Epic*, London: Weidenfeld and Nicolson.

72. Bennis, W.G. and O'Toole, J. (2005), 'How Business Schools Lost their Way', *Harvard Business Review*, May, pp. 96–104. A recent piece in the *Financial Times* ('Why Business Ignores the Business Schools', 7 January 2007) points out that, unlike professions such as law, medicine or engineering, chief executives in business pay little attention to what business schools do or say. One academic admitted that most of what is published is not even cited by other academics. The inability to research and write about their work in a way that business people can understand and use has frustrated many academics for years, but things don't seem to be changing much. Irish business schools seem to be moving further in the direction of making an ability to publish in prestigious peer-reviewed journals, where accessibility is of no relevance, a key criterion in promotion decisions.
73. Cooley, T.F. (2007), 'The Business of Business Education', *Stern Business*, Fall/Winter, pp. 23–5.
74. Chia, R. (1996), 'Teaching Paradigm Shifting in Management Education: University Business Schools and the Entrepreneurial Imagination', *Journal of Management Studies*, 33(4), July, pp. 409–28.
75. Whitehead, A.N. (1932), *The Aims of Education*, London: Williams & Norgate.
76. Whitehead, *The Aims of Education*, p. 139.
77. Senge, P.M. (1990), *The Fifth Discipline: The Art and Practice of the Learning Organization,* London: Random House.
78. Wenger, E. (1998), *Communities of Practice: Learning, Meaning and Identity*, Cambridge, UK: Cambridge University Press.
79. Wenger, *Communities of Practice: Learning, Meaning and Identity*, p. 263.

80. Desmond, D. (2004), 'The Future of Learning', talk given at National College of Ireland (NCI), 29 April.
81. Enterprise Ireland (2007), *Transforming Irish Industry: Enterprise Ireland Strategy 2008–2010*, Dublin.
82. Available at: <http://www.managementdevelopmentcouncil.ie>.
83. There are centres at both DCU and NUIG, *Fiontar* and *Acadamh na hOllscolaíochta Gaeilge*, respectively, that run enterprise programmes through the Irish language. The artificial division that Declan Kiberd complains about (Kiberd, D. (1979), 'Writers in Quarantine: The Case for Irish Studies', *The Crane Bag*, 3, pp. 9–21) that persists between writing in Irish and English could be applied to these; they operate outside mainstream business schools at these universities.
84. 'Educating Executives Vital to Growth', *Irish Times*, 9 December 2005.
85. Mayer, C. (2007), 'Globalisation, Financial Markets and Trust', *TimesOnline*, MBA Podcasts, Week 1, available at: <http://extras.timesonline.co.uk/mba/mba-final-week-table.html>.
86. Dawson, S. (2007), 'Management and Leadership in the Global Economy', *TimesOnline*, MBA Podcasts, Week 2, available from: <http://extras.timesonline.co.uk/mba/mba-final-week-table.html>.
87. 'Global Forces take Command', *Sunday Business Post*, 2 December 2007.
88. Read, C. *et al.* (2001), *eCFO: Sustaining Value in the New Corporation*, Chichester, England: John Wiley & Sons.
89. Zinsmeister, K. (1997), 'Tradition Works', *The American Enterprise Online*, March/April, available at: <http://www.taemag.com/issues/articleid.16200/article_detail.asp>.
90. Chickering, A.W. and Reisser, L. (1993), *Education and Identity*, 2nd edition, San Francisco: Jossey-Bass.
91. Hogan, P. (1995), *The Custody and Courtship of Experience: Western Education in Philosophical Perspective*, Blackrock, Co. Dublin: The Columba Press.
92. Gardner, H. (1993), *Frames of Mind: The Theory of Multiple Intelligences*, New York: Basic Books.

93. Goleman, D. (1996), *Emotional Intelligence: Why it Can Matter More than IQ*, London: Bloomsbury.
94. See, for example, Benefiel, M. (2005), *Soul at Work: Spiritual Leaderhip in Organizations*, New York: Seabury Books; McGeachy, C. (2001), *Spiritual Intelligence in the Workplace*, Dublin: Veritas.
95. 'Social and Emotional Skills must be on Curriculum', *Irish Independent*, 14 November 2007.
96. 'Creative thinking', *Irish Times*, 10 March 2008.
97. 'Failures of the Leaving Cert', *Sunday Business Post*, 19 August 2007.
98. Abbott, J. and Ryan, T. (1998), 'Upside Down and Inside Out: A Challenge to Redesign Education Systems to Fit the Needs of a Learning Society', *The American Administrator*, January.
99. 'Schools "Treated more like Factories"' *Irish Examiner*, 8 March 2007.
100. 'Schools "Treated more like Factories"'.
101. 'Plan for Shake-up at Second Level Unveiled', *Irish Times*, 24 September 2007.
102. 'All Change as Schools Rip up the Timetable', *TimesOnline*, 5 February, available at: <http://www.timesonline.co.uk/tol/news/uk/education/article1329328.ece>.
103. 'Shaping our Future: Thinking Schools, Learning Nation' (2007), Speech by Prime Minister Goh Chok Tong at the opening of the 7th International Conference on Thinking, Singapore, 2 June.
104. When it comes to quality of education, it is not more money that seems to matter. The OECD's Programme for International Student Assessment (PISA) compared school systems across the world. Korea spends less per student than Ireland and performs better, while the US spends considerably more and performs worse. Nor is it study time: Finnish students begin school later and study fewer hours than in other rich countries, yet the quality is in the top rank ('In My Opinion: Quality of Education cannot Exceed Quality of Teachers', *Irish Independent*, 9 January 2008).
105. The names the Irish give streets, housing estates and children is an indication of cultural identity. The top five baby names in 2006

were: for boys – Sean, Jack, Conor, Adam and James; for girls – Sarah, Emma, Katie, Aoife and Sophie ('Sean and Sarah most Popular Baby Names Last Year', *Irish Independent*, 2 August 2007).

106. Friberg, E. (translator) (1988), *The Kalevala – Epic of the Finnish People*, Helsinki: Otava Publishing Company, p. 19. For the *Táin*, refer to Kinsella, T. (translator) (1969), *The Táin*, Dublin: Dolmen Press.
107. Royal Irish Academy (2005), *School Science Infrastrastructure: Can Ireland Deliver?*, RIA Workshop, Dublin, May 2005.
108. Harney, M. (2003), 'Towards a Civic Science: A Mission for the 21st Century', address to the RIA, Dublin, 20 January.
109. This perspective is common at all levels in Government thinking. For instance, Mary Hanafin, the former Minister for Education and Science, writes, '*We know* [our emphasis] that science education is at the heart of developing Ireland as a knowledge economy'. See 'Education is Still Fostering Future Success', *Sunday Business Post*, 23 March 2008.

CHAPTER 6

Realising the Potential of Cultural and Social Resources

Ní neart go hiontaoibh is níl iontaoibh go cur le chéile.

There is no strength without trust and there is no trust without working together.

Nie ma siły bez zaufania i zaufania bez wzajemnego poparcia.

No hay fuerza sin confianza y no hay confianza si no se trabaja unidos.

Donla Uí Bhraonáin, 2007[1]

INTRODUCTION

The core concept in the framework outlined in Chapter 3 is that development of human, cultural and social capital features prominently in competitiveness and learning organisations. The previous chapter discussed the first of these, human capital, by describing how innovative mindsets can be fostered within the education system. This chapter examines these two other capital sources.

Cultural capital, a set of common values expressed through art, language, music, song, poetry or other forms of cultural expression, is the fundamental building block of social capital. Social capital in turn is generated by feelings of belonging, relationships, trust and civic responsibility, a kind of glue holding society together. It is not always clear how social and cultural capital contribute to creativity (or, for that matter, how the impact of one differs from another). Yet a couple of things are clear. First, creativity and innovation have more to do with social group dynamics and the cultural context rather than individual capability or effort. Second, social and cultural practices, identity, motivation, negotiated meaning, conversation and communities of practice are critical elements in this process.

The development of cultural capital is a firm basis for developing the innovative potential of humans, leading to a high quality of life.[2] The links demonstrated earlier between identity, tacit knowledge, emotions, intuition, meaning, creativity and innovation are why language in Ireland is used as an example of cultural capital. Even with globalisation, national identity will remain a relevant force for the foreseeable future and Irish is still a critical expression of identity for many people on the island of Ireland. With dramatic recent changes in ethnic composition, will the relationship between language, culture and identity in Ireland undergo radical redefinition in the years to come? This book agrees with the argument that the best hope for Irish is if a sense of pride in things unique to Ireland itself is engendered which includes not just the language but also, say, special areas of conservation and archaeological treasures.[3]

There is a dynamic interaction between communities, a civic culture, creativity and innovation. A strong cultural identity emerges when individuals address questions such as: Where do I come from? Who are my people? What were their values? Establishing such an identity means individuals are more aware of their own capabilities, competencies, feelings, emotions and values. A sense of roots in a particular cultural and historical context means people are also likely to appreciate the traditions of other cultures. Developing self-confidence and self-reliance through an enhanced identity is consistent with becoming more trusting of others. By having a better sense of themselves, of being part of a community, people are also likely to be more open and tolerant of difference. Yet, as Peter Sutherland points out, while a country needs to set the rules of the game by which norms evolve, values themselves should not be fixed.[4] A national identity has to be a dynamic process that is able to change and adapt so the society can accommodate newcomers. The evidence is that societies with strong social capital, called earlier a 'trusting milieu', tend to be happier places to live, with positive implications for both people's employment prospects and their learning abilities.[5] This chapter therefore also looks at the development of communities to examine the role of social capital as an catalyst for innovation.

CULTURAL CAPITAL: LANGUAGE IN IRELAND

Irish and Innovation

One of the greatest disappointments of modern Ireland has to be the failure to create a bilingual society, especially when much energy and resources were (and still are) devoted to the revival of Irish. Yet the argument for the value of Irish made by writer Sean Ó Faoláin in an editorial in *The Bell* magazine more than sixty years ago is still relevant:

> Unless we can communicate, even if it be only in stumbling, half-understood whispers, with those drops that are part of the whole stream that fed us, we are, to put it no higher than the coldly intellectual plane, the less wise as to our own natures, so variously and often so incongruously formed by the flux of history....Those who have not had this – if one may call it – 'romantic' experience of association with the immemorial past cannot imagine how illuminating it is to discover that, by virtue of it, even the most plebeian memories, the most vulgar tales, the most humble customs, suddenly become in the literal sense venerable, indeed sanctified, by becoming an intimate part of one's own inheritance, one's own story, one's own nature.[6]

Declan Kiberd contrasts the speed and rigour with which people mastered English in the nineteenth century with their utter failure to re-master Irish in the twentieth, despite massive support from the State.[7] While many historical reasons have been cited for the loss of Irish (the Famine, the example of Daniel O'Connell, the indifference of the Church and the effect of English in the national schools), these do not include the most potent factor of all: Irish declined when large numbers decided themselves not to use it. During the Revival, Douglas Hyde and D.P. Moran, by emphasising Irish culture and the language, questioned contemporary assumptions in sociology and economics. The central insight of Douglas Hyde and the Gaelic League was that the Irish would never develop to their potential until the people learned a sense of self-confidence and self-respect.[8] Restoring Irish was central to that vision. Yet, while the Gaelic League was a key element in sparking creativity, it failed to explain precisely how the Irish language, as the central component of cultural identity, actually affected the development process. John Walsh suggests there is perhaps a similar conceptual weakness today in the analysis of innovation. The theory of a national system of innovation, a model of development urged by Lars Mjøset in a 1993 NESC study, is a key element in the government development strategy.[9] Walsh maintains, however, that this fails to identify what role 'national culture' plays in innovation, even though Mjøset identifies national factors such as workforce, infrastructure and existing resources as critical components of such a system.

The book *Why Irish?* by sociologists Hilary Tovey, Damian Hannan and Hal Abramson, holds that Irish is needed to reconstruct a sense of cultural and historical distinctiveness which recognises what is central and unique to the Irish variant of human experience.[10] The authors maintain that alternatives to Irish, even in the language's current attenuated and threatened condition, cannot offer the same richness and potentially liberating links to the past. The language remains the most effective basis for claiming the Irish as distinctive people, linking the past to the future and commonality to diversity in a creative and dynamic way. When continuity is established through the living language, the past is dynamically connected with the present. The more Irish is treated as just another element of heritage, the more this encourages distancing and fossilisation, preventing a dynamic connection between past, present and future. If Irish was relegated to a merely symbolic position in the identity system of the majority, as it increasingly appears to be, it will deprive people of valuable resources. Yet, in drawing attention to the rich resources available from Irish, the authors of *Why Irish?* do not suggest that access to the English speaking world is not also valuable. Genuine bilingualism would increase the capacity for Irish people to move between different realities and points of view, with enriching and liberating effects on their capacity to deal with a range of social and economic problems.

The Irish language has enormous potential as a resource for nurturing sensitivity to difference, meaning and aesthetic qualities in young people. There is strong evidence that a network of complex forces links innovation, self-confidence and a host of psychological and sociological phenomena based on identity. In order for professionals and enterprises to achieve a competitive edge, deep self-confidence must be present, the product of internal motivation driven by meaning and sense of purpose. No one conjures up self-confidence on demand. The main determinants of self-confidence are personal identity and national identity. Finland achieved this entrepreneurial spirit and a desire to develop self-reliance through the special circumstances it faced: its relationship with the Soviet Union, a desire to emulate their wealthy neighbours the Swedes, and a difficult language. The pioneers of the American West had a similar spirit, based on the need for self-sufficiency and, even more, the desire to 'win'. This self-confident spirit came partially from a profound sense of national identity.

Irish is potentially a valuable resource for business since it is likely to accentuate positive qualities and make people more self-confident. Damien Hannon, former research professor of Sociology at the ESRI, makes just such an argument.[11] Hannon maintains that language is an incontestable symbol linked to self-confidence and identity. In Ireland, he says, people have a 'leaky' identity, partly because the English spoken there no longer differs greatly, except in accent, from English spoken elsewhere. He maintains that it is only through a self-confident identity that a person gains the necessary self-confidence and skills needed for success in enterprise.

In his classic text, Joe Lee argues that the loss of the Irish language carried a host of psychological consequences.[12] He claims this loss affected the national personality, fostering an inferiority complex that retarded Irish economic performance during most of the twentieth century. Attempts at language revival were surely, he maintains, not to blame for the country's unimpressive performance in the pre-Celtic Tiger phase:

> It would be agreeably reassuring to feel that the economic failure of the state, taking one decade with another, could be attributed to the diversion of the time and energy of outstanding 'practical men' into a hopeless revival crusade. That is one excuse that even a people prolific in excuses have yet to dream up. Nor did the revival fail because 'practical men' were too busy creating a name for their country in other areas. The 'practical men' might even have been justified in their distain for the revival – if only they had succeeded as 'practical men'. Despite occasional impressive individual performances, they did not. They simply had not got the class. The failure of the revival was more obtrusive than other failures, but it was cut from the same cloth.[13]

Lee shows that the assumption that industrialisation and economic success are incompatible with minority languages derives little support from the European record. He illustrates this by examining the marketing performance of Irish firms in English-speaking countries. Ireland's performance has been (and undoubtedly still is) generally unimpressive compared to its counterparts in other small countries like Denmark, that, in Lee's words, 'had not the wit to abandon its language'.[14] For instance, Denmark's superior economic performance in the British butter market of the late nineteenth century linked neatly with its own national revival. Denmark's growing sense of identity and loyalty to its native language did not inhibit its performance. Knowledge of English, of course, was indispensable for selling in this market. Nevertheless, competitors from a more 'backward' culture eclipsed the allegedly linguistically progressive Irish! The failure to grasp market opportunities was surely not because the Irish 'clung to an obscure, petty, peasant patois'.[15]

The reason countries like Denmark, Finland, Norway and Japan are among the most successful marketers in the world is that, perhaps by having a good understanding of themselves, they more easily understand others. Ireland's virtually exclusive use of the world language, English, ironically seems to exert a parochial influence, impeding both language learning and learning in general. For revival in Ireland, both the cultural and economic are intertwined. Declan Kiberd argues that 'if the native culture of a people is devalued and destroyed for the sake of material progress, what follows may not be material progress of the kind hoped for, but cultural confusion and a diminished sense of enterprise.'[16] Sweden, Denmark and Finland have shown it is possible to retain one's own language yet also acquire excellent English as a second (or even third or fourth) language.[17] These countries have managed to build a strong competitive advantage based on research, innovation and hard work, which in reality far exceeds the accomplishments of the Irish State. Israel is another example: it built an economy and revised its culture more or less at the same time, yet Ireland, having failed to protect her cultural identity, still struggles to develop an indigenous high technology industry.

Ireland devotes enormous resources to helping primary and secondary students speak Irish. The value for money of such expenditure seems low if the performance yardstick is the language-speaking ability of youngsters leaving school. Suppose instead that the language's role in fostering meaning, self-discovery and imagination was emphasised instead. If it were, then the prospects for the language might be far brighter. It might become a vital component of a movement for economic regeneration, just as it was originally envisaged by Hyde and the founders of the Gaelic

League. The language offers a valuable resource for achieving a learning society functioning to its full potential. This point is made emphatically by Michael Cronin. He argues that, because of the Irish language's enormous cognitive and aesthetic potential, it is tantamount to political, economic and cultural suicide for the country to now relinquish such extensive and distinctive resources. He holds that to jettison two millennia of resources when the country has in its possession precisely those factors central to value creation in a learning society would be 'the ultimate sacrifice of political realism to the prejudice of impractical monolingualism.'[18] He puts it:

> For even the most aggressively philistine pragmatist, such abandonment would represent a serious narrowing of the basis for any future knowledge society that might be constructed on the island.[19]

Cronin points out that the Irish language has a special role to play in a renewed sense of identity, in nurturing the aesthetic in enterprise and in re-appropriating the places in which people live.[20] Through the close fit between linguistic knowledge and economic influence, the past should be seen as a strength, not a handicap. Using this logic, he makes two key arguments for Irish in contemporary society. The first, *explicative* arguments, are those directly related to the storehouse of aesthetic and cognitive knowledge in the Irish language. Disseminating such resources adds value to society. He says the scholar-intellectual, à la Douglas Hyde and Eoin MacNeill, should be cultivated. These people engage in the public sphere and explain those riches through example after example. The second, *operative* arguments, relate to using the resources of the Irish language in practice to help society discover new ways of looking at its sense of self through, for example, conducting business or creating works of art. He sees operative arguments necessary to counter a:

> …debilitating tendency to present Irish in terms of death, twilight, dusk, a quant lingering on the Wrong Side of the Great

> Divide and to evolve a language and an outlook that are consciously concerned with birth, genesis, beginnings. Again, there is little or no point in telling people that Irish is self-evidently a Good Thing. To operate in this fashion is to depend for results on the dice roll of prejudice or Pauline conversion.[21]

Cronin maintains that contemporary concern with interlingual difference could undermine the strong case that exists for safeguarding and promoting the language. He argues that to rely on Irish as an autonomous and self-sufficient marker of identity is flawed. A more convincing argument can be made on an intercultural basis, focused more upon interdependence than independence, and appreciating how the language shaped as well as was shaped by other cultures. Therefore, the crucial aspect of Irish today is emphatically not the formal structures of the language itself (i.e. the actual words); rather, it is possession of the language embedded in its historical and cultural context that offers Irish people an alternative view of their present reality. This hinges on the language's role in creating meaning, with clear and positive implications for creativity and innovation potential. This language-as-resource role fits in with Zimmermann's phrase, previously cited, that 'resources are not, they become.'

Here is the way Irish can establish a unique role for itself. Yet, ironically, it is through the medium of English that the fate of Irish is now likely to be decided; after all, today it is necessary to make the argument largely through English that Irish is a critical and inimitable rooted resource. Cronin argues that Irish has to be positioned at the forefront of social, cultural and economic renewal with Irish-medium education at third level one of the most effective ways of ensuring the country has the potential to become something different. Yet it seems the Irish Government and educational institutions, especially the universities, have lost sight of this important rationale for having an Irish language policy. Seán Ó Tuama makes a similar powerful argument, saying that even an adequately bilingual society should be based on assuring people that, by giving Irish an important place in the community, they are rendering an inestimable educational service to themselves and to their descendants.[22] The Irish language simply has no rival in Ireland as the key to a unique experience. It opens up a life-experience of over 2,000 years of poetry, song and stories. It sharpens for many an awareness of their inherited patterns of thoughts, feelings and behaviour and increases their capacity for self-knowledge and self-assurance, key aspects in any successful Irish learning society.

Meaning is central to the generation of tacit knowledge and, as illustrated earlier in this book, is in turn a major driver of innovation. Language is a practical and explicit manifestation of cultural and social context, and plays an especially vital role in the construction, interpretation and sharing of meaning. Since ambiguity of meaning features strongly as a driver of creativity, this suggests that dynamic multilingual communities, especially at the interfaces of languages, may be more likely to stimulate new ideas and innovation than monolingual ones.[23] Experiments by social psychologists show that, when hearing certain words, people behave in ways influenced by the meaning they infer from them. For example, hearing words related to the elderly makes people walk slower![24] If this kind of impact can be had by exposure to simple English words, imagine how more powerful the widespread usage of Irish in speech and signage might be in a society where English is the norm. The crucial thing, as professionals in marketing and brand identity discovered a long time ago, is that words impact feelings through the meaning they convey to the listener.

A true innovation culture is founded on a spirit of self-reliance; relationships based on community trust, a sense of place, tradition and civic engagement. Key concepts in the creativity (and innovation) literature are intrinsic motivation, persistence, commitment, meaning and sense of purpose.[25] Using this logic, programmes through the medium of Irish have a special potential to be powerful sources of creativity, innovation and renewal, particularly if imbued with a sustainability ethic. They offer an enabling culture centred on a local response to the challenges of globalisation.[26]

English-Only as a Disadvantage

A good reason English is not adequate as the sole language of everyday life in Ireland is that it is not specific to the country. As a small country, Ireland cannot ever make English its private language – one to provide a bulwark against forces frustrating its attempts to determine its individual expression. While English has largely been the vehicle for Irish cultural survival since the mid-nineteenth century, French language scholar Breandán Ó Doibhlin argues that the long-term effect of committing exclusively to it has consequences for the impoverishment of creative energies as well as blurring and even obliterating anything but a sentimental form of historical memory.[27]

It is clearly in its own interest for the business community to support Irish distinctiveness and identity. However, the role of the Irish language as a unique resource for stimulating innovation and international competitiveness is generally ignored in policy discussions. Even in 1963, five years after the publication of the *First Programme for Economic Expansion*, the key turning point in the country's economic policy formation, Eoin McKiernan wrote, 'a crude utilitarianism is rooting in Ireland which rejects, *a priori*, even the consideration of the case for the language.'[28] He saw the demise of Irish as a lack of will, not of intellect, that affected far more than the survival of the language. McKiernan blamed an obsessive inferiority that plagued the modern Irish character with many of those on the first rungs of success unable to appreciate values beyond, as he put it, 'the clink in the till'.[29]

Almost fifty years on, Ireland is still losing its unique language and culture, fast becoming little different than other English-speaking countries. The attitude of many elite today is bitterly captured by Ó Doibhlín:

> In practical terms, I suppose we are trying to decide what to do about what is, for the elites of our society, that embarrassing relic of a disputable past, the Irish language. There it is like some toothless grandmother, huddled by our hearth, mumbling over days of misery or ancient heroism that we, her forward-looking children, have never known and would sooner forget. We can't in all decency throw her out – she is after all our blood – but we can park her in a geriatric ghetto where she can expire in comfort and in solitude, while we get on with the business of living. So we have given her government commissions to revive her, Gaeltacht grants and schemes to build up her resistance, even her own television service to cheer her last lucid hours.[30]

Of course, English is a highly developed and versatile language and now virtually the universal mode of communication. Yet the exclusive cultivation of the English language by business leaves Irish people, as Ó Doibhlin puts it, 'heirs to the parochial belief that English is in fact universally known'.[31] It has turned the Irish into a monoglot culture; one, he holds, that is better afforded by richer and more powerful states. It is also very risky; the Irish should not be putting all their eggs in one basket. A report commissioned by the British Council and written by applied linguist David Graddol points out that, while no language has ever been as widely spoken as English is today, native English speakers comprise an ever-shrinking minority in the world.[32] Fifty years ago English had more native speakers than any language except Mandarin. Today, both Spanish and Hindi-Urdu have as many native speakers and, by the middle of this century, English could fall into fifth place behind Arabic in the number of native speakers.

The fact that Irish people speak English as their native tongue is touted without fear of contradiction as a competitive advantage since English is clearly the dominant language of international business.

However, being a native English speaker today can actually be a competitive disadvantage. While many international executives speak English, most are not native speakers of the language. There is widespread agreement that native speakers are poor at insuring they can be understood in international discussions. According to Barbara Seidlhofer, professor of English and Applied Linguistics at the University of Vienna, there seems to be widespread anecdotal evidence that business meetings in English run more smoothly when there are no native English speakers present. She quotes an Austrian banker saying it is easier to conduct business in English with partners from countries like Greece, Russia or Denmark who are non-native speakers, but, as the executive phrased it, 'when the Irish call, it gets complicated and taxing.'[33]

There is clearly a relationship between language, meaning and thought, although its precise extent is difficult to articulate. It has been argued that the practice of thinking in atomistic and objective terms, the hallmark of the scientific approach, is a function of the fragmenting tendency of the English language.[34] Physicist David Bohm notes that much Western thought is highly fragmented and attributes this to the way English is structured, specifically into subject-verb-object sentences. This style of thinking pervades the way people also see the world, dividing it into discrete entities. According to Robert Chia, the logical structure generated by English forces people to comprehend the world through conceptual lenses that carve up and give meaning only to discrete entities, suppressing the dynamic and relational aspects of reality.[35] Such 'strong' forms of knowledge give priority to the 'solidity' or 'tangibility' of things, social entities and events such as 'individuals', 'organisations', 'society', 'strategy', 'decisions' and 'strategic advantage'.

It is easy to see where a rooted Irish-global identity is an effective mechanism to counter such thought processes, providing an 'aesthetic logic' primarily concerned with frames of ordering, meaning and relationships rather than knowledge content itself. This is why, as pointed out before, nurturing exposure to the Irish language can be quite advantageous to the innovation process. A key aspect of IDA Ireland's success is its insightfulness regarding identifying international trends. It realises that globally and locally traded services possess enormous competitive advantages for Ireland. Information Technology services, for instance, are based not on technology per se but on intangibles such as trust, problem-solving abilities and human relationships. IDA Ireland is grappling with revising the Irish brand as it attempts to attract savvy foreign investors in an increasingly stiff competitive environment. The theme used in its world-wide campaign, 'The Irish Mind', brands Ireland as a place particularly suited for creative and innovative ventures, yet still rooted in Irish distinctiveness. The IDA notes Ireland's long literary heritage in Irish, but remarks that English 'gradually became the predominant language' – as if the changeover itself had no lasting significance.[36] It suggests the development of IT has been a catalyst that harnesses Irish creativity, and has turned economic underachievement into a world-leading performance. Ironically, while IT itself is the business of communication, the emphasis in the field has tended to be on the technology because of its highly complex nature. However, IDA Ireland suggests that what really matters is the innovative communication of information, prompting the book's intriguing speculation:

> Could it be that the centuries-old Irish genius for creative communication, the basis of literature, provided the catalyst that has propelled Ireland into the knowledge society and made it one of today's leading software producers?[37]

The dominance of one perspective or point of view, through exclusive use of a world language like English and practical obliteration of a local one which resonates strongly with an attachment to place, is unlikely to lead to an innovative and globally competitive enterprise sector, whether in software, services, digital media, or the like. Ireland's creative potential will only fully emerge if it fosters fertile interaction between different language and cultural traditions on the island. This is also the ideal way for immigrants to make a major contribution. The potential for new immigrants to negotiate meaning and contribute to innovation is enormous. This can only happen, however, if people's different cultural and linguistic perspectives can be encouraged through a strong commitment to a shared sense of place or a rooted Irish-global identity.

In the learning society, the rooted-resource perspective illustrates that Irish should really be viewed as a valuable gift or investment, not a threat or a cost.[38] Not using a valuable resource is, after all, equivalent to wasted potential and therefore is destroying value. There is no doubt that many outside cultural influences have enriched Ireland through the centuries, and this certainly includes English. But the issue of language in Ireland is different. The tragedy is that resources lie untapped and the country's potential is not being fully realised since people no longer have access to resources to which they are entitled. An emphasis on Irish does not imply that other languages are diminished. Declan Kiberd argues that the introduction of what IBEC calls a 'business perspective' into Irish education may in turn be creating a crisis in the number of Irish students taking foreign languages in the Leaving Certificate.[39] From 1997 to 2006, those taking Spanish, French, Italian and German dropped from 79 per cent to 72 per cent. According to Kiberd, appealing only to short-term tastes rather than long-term interests may end up costing businesses more. The time spent on Irish is often blamed for these trends, but those proficient in Irish are often also those most likely to also master a foreign tongue.

Kiberd reminds readers of the cultural value of studying foreign languages. This prompts him to ask a wider question, 'Do we Irish have a general sense of culture, or just an obsessive fixation on an economy to be primed?' As Marc Coleman points out, Singapore, with great sophistication, understands that the country's language policy must carefully balance that state's economic and cultural objectives.[40] To preserve their cultural identity, the Chinese, Malay and Tamil languages are taught to children at an early age, an age when a language is easily picked up. As the language of commerce, English is taught for its utilitarian value but, at this stage in its development, it has lost much of the richness it had in previous centuries. This, says Coleman, is the price it had paid for its growing flexibility and widespread use as a language of commerce. However, for Ireland, English should not be the only language that defines Irish people. It is a language Irish people are lucky to possess but only if they also have something else, namely a basic ability to speak their own language. This clearly they no longer possess.[41]

Language and Sense of Place

The quality, uniqueness, integrity, diversity and nature of a place are what make it attractive to creative individuals. If invigorating and creative policies were used effectively the Irish language could be a key factor in promoting a renewed sense of place since it offers a special dimension in the country's economic, social and environmental development. The health of the language belongs in policy analyses alongside sustainability, quality of life, well-being and citizenship if Ireland is to become the kind of 'successful society' NESC seeks to promote. Yet a problem in developing a sense of community in Ireland is that the legacy of colonialism has resulted in a weak sense of identity and an underlying inferiority complex. Critics assert that the colonial image of the master has been adopted by a considerable section of the Irish population, including many influential authors and critics.[42] Some cultural pathologies seen by psychologist Geraldine Moane as characteristic of Irish post-colonialism include high levels of alcohol and substance abuse, denial, doublethink and social irresponsibility.[43] It is intriguing to consider what might be the impact on young people, many of whom suffer from alienation, depression and a weak sense of place, should a concerted effort be made to foster a strong sense of identity and community. As argued earlier, loss of the native language has undoubtedly resulted in reduced creativity from the consequent erosion of national and personal identity.[44]

A powerful way of rooting identity in place is certainly with language, but, of the estimated seven thousand languages spoken around the world today, one dies out every two weeks.[45] Since languages embody history and traditions, their death precipitates a loss of irreplaceable knowledge. Languages hold the key to saving species under threat.[46] In Ireland, the intimacy with nature, founded on the continuous link between language and landscape possessed by the 'old ones,' is disappearing along with the Gaeltacht itself. The vocabulary and expressions of local people contain potentially vital information not often found in databases, libraries or sometimes even in written form. Such tacit knowledge resides only in people's heads and in their language. No doubt, the contemporary disregard for 'marginal' languages reflects a generally narrow definition of 'knowledge' itself.

A learning society, defined by the key elements of sustainability, wholeness and well-being, offers a credible opportunity for the future prospects of the Irish language. Sustainability, after all, is fundamentally about values; so are Irish language revival strategies. Preserving a beautiful landscape, an area of unique scientific interest or a place that makes a significant contribution to biodiversity, while at the same time maintaining Irish as a community language, are related activities. Without a systemic perspective founded on an appreciation of the quality and integrity of a place, revival efforts are unlikely to slow the decline of the language. Creating an innovative dynamic culture that understands the nature of 'value' and of value creation in the broadest sense is the best way to harmonise and achieve seemingly conflicting aims.

Brendán Ó Doibhlin, in what he calls an 'enterprise of the spirit', sees language and community as interdependent.[47] This is why it is not sufficient to replace Anglicised place-names with Irish versions without also including the oldest and deepest traits of Gaelic culture, the sense *of* and the attachment *to* place. He regards a cultural resurgence as a moral requirement in contemporary Ireland. Historically, the forces that maintained the Irish people were a sense of uniqueness, a refusal to accept failure, and a sense of continuity with the past and destiny in the future. A founding principle of life in Ireland used to be the primacy of a territorialised identity and the importance of rootedness and kinship with the land.[48] In modern Ireland, the dilemma is in conceptualising Irish identity and determining how the notion of place fits into it. Indeed, the profound changes in Ireland since the 1960s may have induced what Fintan O'Toole categorises as a sense of internal exile.[49] People now feel less and less at home in Ireland. The country has become somehow unreal, with many people experiencing the familiar becoming unknown or unrecognisable. Almost fifty years of global economic dependency, especially on America, has resulted in a society increasingly seen by young people as a pale imitation of the 'real thing' across the Atlantic.

Place-names reflect two elements – land and language – that were central to the spirit of the Revival. Poet Séamus Heaney views the loss of Irish as a spoken language and the anglicisation of place-names leading to a huge loss of collective memory. John Montague regards the meaning of place-names as a unifying community knowledge now being lost. Yet to poet John Hewitt, from the other tradition, living on shared ground was commonality enough. Today, while loss of the original language has resulted in alienation from the land, as Catherine Nash points out, in Northern Ireland the original place-names offer an unlikely source of cultural reconciliation for both traditions.[50] Since place-names give a sense of place and historical context, even different versions of a place-name and the different cultural traditions these might reflect can help lead to cultural dynamism and diversity. This has exciting potential for breaking down divisive legacies of colonialism, and for defining new forms of belonging, not just in the North but throughout the island. It offers a wellspring for innovative ventures, with place the guiding theme in nurturing the creative spirit. With the keen interest of people of all traditions in understanding place-names the Irish language has the potential to carve out a special role as an all-Ireland unifying force. This might invigorate the role of the language in the Republic's schools where it faces enormous challenges when treated solely as just a linguistic marker of heritage and identity.

A key message of Brian Friel's play *Translations* is that, despite the near destruction of the language, the Irish can still discover a constantly evolving post-colonial identity suited to the global economy.[51] This identity is no less 'Irish' for being in the language of the colonisers. The colonised, in other words, can reinvigorate the old in contact with the new, a point made by E. Estyn Evans who defined the essence of Irishness as the process of renewal under the stimulus of culture contact. Wherever we look, he said, 'we find continuity, a renewal of the old in contact with the new.'[52] If Irish culture is to maintain its historic character, according to Evans, it needs constant renewal through exposure to fresh outside cultural forces.

The implications of a rooted Irish-global identity for innovation and development are profound. However, the nearly exclusive use of English as the language of Ireland has led to a restricted and shallow world-view stripped of tradition. The 'gravitational force' in Irish development is centrifugal rather than centripetal.[53] This means the country has the tendency to absorb second-hand ideas, values and concepts developed elsewhere (and often discarded there), without making the adjustments essential in a genuinely innovative culture.

It is exciting to think the Irish language might become a medium to help root resources in place, a source of emotions that help people discover and explore their complex identities. Such a potent mixture of Irish, English and other languages might foster a unique creative ethos in Ireland. It is where the country's opportunity lies in the global age. Designer John Twomey captured this way of thinking in a *New York Times* article that looked at the way Ireland's economic transformation was playing out in the realms of architecture and design. He wrote, 'People used to worry that the global would destroy the local, but, in fact, the global helps the local to untrap itself.'[54]

It is ironic that the Irish language went from being a major force in the creation of Europe in the early Middle Ages to a role analogous to that of native cultures in Europe's colonies. As Maria Tymoczko and Colin Ireland argue, linking the survival of the Irish language to anti-modernist models of identity in the early decades of the State virtually doomed the language.[55] Yet they also hold that the cultural confidence evident in Ireland today would not have been possible at all without the re-examination of language and power initiated by the Revival and pursued, however inadequately, after independence. Irish cultural assertion expressed in other forms today, such as traditional music, the entrepreneurial endeavours of the Irish business community and Ireland's high-profile role in the EU were made possible by the Revival movement. Tymoczko and Ireland maintain that this movement and the linguistic complexity fostered in Ireland today have secured a strong cultural position for Ireland within the English-speaking world, and a distinct place within the EU and the globalised economy.

Perhaps so; yet the case still remains strong that a dynamic Irish language presence is a good foundation for building the concept of Irish identity while strengthening Ireland's competitiveness and innovative potential within the global economy. What is lacking is a coherent and committed language policy and well-designed programmes implementing this in practice. If handled properly, a rich dynamic, vibrant Irish society, North and South, influenced by recent immigrants, is most likely to emerge from creative interaction between the various language traditions on the island. The great hope is in the open-mindedness of immigrants and the interest many take in learning the language, even in the face of cynicism and apathy from the natives.[56] New arrivals in Ireland, obviously proud of their own languages, are often shocked by the awkward and strained relationship many Irish have with the language and the negativity they display about the 'usefulness' of it at all.[57]

Social Capital: Creative Communities

Valuing Community

A working description of community development is 'intricate networks of purposeful conversations about the issues that matter most to people'.[58] In Ireland, this was illustrated by the *meitheal*, or a joint purposeful communal activity, which nowadays is practically extinct. Every community, no matter how disadvantaged, does possess resources, especially tacit ones, but these are often ignored or underutilised by contemporary communities. In turn, it is counterproductive for policy-makers to encourage communities to dwell on their needs to the exclusion of their resources. Yet this appears to be common in Irish public policy initiatives in the community development arena. Contrast this with America where the phrase 'community development' signifies 'community enterprise development', close in spirit to the word 'adventure' which arises from the French word *aventure* signifying 'venture', 'risk' or a 'voyage of exploration'. It can also be contrasted with the attitude of Horace Plunkett who was not only a firm believer in the principle of self-help, but saw co-operation as a way to develop a community's capabilities and capacity for development. As he put it: 'the poorer a community is the more essential it is to throw it as much as possible on its own resources, in order to develop self-reliance.'[59]

The roots of a tree are a good metaphor for a community: just like the branches and leaves are sustained its roots, community members draw from shared history and values for sustenance. In this sense, rootedness is a prerequisite for a civilised society and the heart of a trusting community. It is the reason why it is also a good basis for social or relational capital. Authentic communities are defined by a common history which offers members a shared meaning. Yet many modern communities exist in a vacuum with no real sharing of identity or common sense of history.

Attempts are being made today to replace the loss of traditional community with communities of interest and cyber communities, but the defining link to *place* cannot be dispensed with.[60] People need this link because of their very nature. Just as human beings need to be surrounded by the sights and sounds of animals and plants of the natural world, they need as a human community to be rooted in a particular place. The contemporary concern for community development largely focuses on the secular aspects that relate to physical and mental well-being, but a spiritual dimension to human community is at its core. The recovery of this element is important if authentic community is to prosper.

According to Finola Kennedy, the Irish economy is moving more in the direction of private enterprise and the market, in other words becoming more akin to Boston than Berlin. This is accompanied, she notes, by a shift out of the home by married women taking up jobs that service the economy.[61] This increases demands on the State to provide services previously provided on a voluntary basis at home, or by religious and voluntary groups. At the same time, there is a reduction in the number of people prepared to devote time to voluntary and community activities. Kennedy calls for the concept of the 'social village' to be realised, which would contain some features of the old physical village, a social environment embedded in a safe and secure physical environment in which lives could be lived and people die within a network of intimate relationships. This could lead to a society in which both government and governed share a common purpose and participation at local level.

Much in the vein of Horace Plunkett's thinking, Dee Hock, founder of VISA (the worldwide credit card network), believes the essence of community is the non-monetary exchange of value.[62] He says community is defined by things people do and share because they care for others and for the good of the place in which they live or work. Community is composed of respect, tolerance, trust, generosity and care; these are things that people cannot measure, do not record and for which they ask no recompense. This arises from a deep, intuitive understanding that self-interest is inseparable from community interest, that individual good is inseparable from the good of the whole. Hock argues that all things are simultaneously 'independent, interdependent and intradependent'. Put another way, he sees the singular 'one' as inseparable from the plural 'one'.

To Hock, there could be no civil society worthy of the name without a true community. He sees all life, all nature and all earthly systems as closed cycles of non-monetary exchanges of value (except for the gift of energy which comes from the sun). When an attempt is made to monetise all value, the most effective system for exchanging value is replaced by the least effective. Because the non-monetary, voluntary exchange of value cannot be measured, the efficiency of the whole or the parts cannot be proven to the rational mind, nor can it be engineered or controlled. The non-monetary exchange of value frustrates a craving for the perfect predictability and control that monetary exchange always promises but rarely delivers. When value is monetised, measurement, however misleading, allows people to calculate the relative efficiency of each part of the system. However, it destroys an extremely effective system whose values cannot be calculated in order to calculate the efficiency of an ineffective system. Attempting to engineer mechanistic societies and institutions based on measurement is fundamentally flawed. Giving and receiving cannot be measured in any meaningful sense. They are not transactions but an offering and an acceptance. In nature, when a closed system of receiving and giving is out of balance, death and destruction arise. It is the same for any society. Hock views community as the marketplace where gifts are given and received. When individual and collective consciousness become receptive to new concepts of organisation which this way of thinking suggests, society is more likely to be in harmony with the human spirit and the biosphere.

Community and Sense of Place

Authentic development, and indeed economics itself, is not primarily about commercial enterprise, business, money or markets.

Its focus is far broader than that; it centres on the provision and protection of ‘qualities’. As economist Thomas Michael Power argues, economic welfare is not just the bundle of market commodities consumed within a locale. A clean environment, excellent schools and a host of other non-market ‘qualities’ increase both individual and community welfare and quality of life.[63] Qualitative or non-commercial aspects of people’s lives are sometimes regarded as non-economic, therefore possibly retarding development. With this perspective, trade-offs or balancing economic progress and ‘non-economic’ features (e.g. cultural heritage, a way of life or a unique landscape) may be viewed as inevitable. However, policies that attempt through informed debate to discover approaches to development that promote *both* money and non-money values may offer the best opportunity for a community to improve the general well-being of its citizens.

Concerns about the preservation of natural areas, the quality of air and water, and the linguistic or social character of communities are legitimate economic concerns. Non-market ‘qualities’ such as public amenities affect the health of communities and should also be considered when examining the characteristics of a ‘successful society’. Creative individual activity, illustrated by those developing innovative ways to improve their communities, is a key to a vital, thriving local economy. Communities place themselves in a much better position to improve individual lives by re-establishing the importance of community itself. They emphasise values and appreciate the limited contribution the commercial part of the local economy makes to overall well-being and prosperity. It is difficult to overestimate the potential of a broad range of co-operative, non-commercial, yet intrinsically economic ventures to foster such overall well-being.

The rediscovery of a sense of place is becoming *more* rather than less important, as people search for psychological security and meaning in a restless world. They realise that material progress alone cannot fulfil them in their search for identity.[64]

Richard Sennett illustrates the rapid transformation of the value of place itself.[65] Instead of the institutionally impoverished experience of the assembly line, poverty now lies within the worker who has not made him or herself of value. As the globalised economy erodes people's sense of self-worth in the marketplace, it also erodes the traditional institutions that protected them against markets. The value of place, argues Sennett, is increasing because it feeds the need to belong not to 'society' in the abstract, but to somewhere *in particular*. In satisfying this need, people develop commitment and loyalty to a place. As economic institutions such as corporations diminish the experience of belonging somewhere special at work, people's commitments to geographic places like nations, cities or localities are likely to increase.

Self-Reliant Communities

The fullest expression of de Valera's vision of Ireland anchors his St Patrick's Day address of 1943. It was his traditional greeting to the Irish Diaspora, broadcast around the world, but fully consistent with his vision of an Irish nation, replete with his notions of spirituality and frugality:

> Let us turn aside for a moment to that ideal Ireland that we would have. That Ireland which we dreamed of would be the home of a people who valued material wealth only as the basis for right living, of a people who were satisfied with frugal comfort and devoted their lives to the things of the spirit – a land whose countryside would be bright with cosy homesteads, whose fields and villages would be joyous with the sounds of industry, with the romping of sturdy children, the contests of athletic youths and the laughter of comely maidens, whose firesides would be forums for the wisdom of serene old age. It would, in a word, be the home of a people living the life that God desires that man should live.[66]

This vision of an Irish nation, speaking its own language, politically and economically independent, and embracing a 'frugal self-sufficiency' was not, in spite of modern notions of economic man, a necessarily unattractive one. Joe Lee makes the point that most of those who laughingly deride de Valera's flights of fancy and his 'maidens dancing at the crossroads' have not troubled themselves to read the actual text of the speech.[67] As Lee claims, it was an ideal shared by most Irish people.[68] Irish politicians also echoed it. It expressed sentiments found at the core of the Revival and the War of Independence.

It was also a rich vision, not incompatible with the contemporary concept of sustainable development. Unfortunately, it is ridiculed today, held up as evidence of a veritable 'cloud cuckoo land' inhabited by de Valera and others who dreamed of a bucolic, pastoral, Irish-speaking backwater, rich in 'saints and scholars' if poor in material possessions and economic efficiency, going along in its own measured tread, with not a thought for the rest of the world. To give fair play to such critics, it is clear that although de Valera had a colourful vision he had no idea how to achieve it. Still, faulty execution should not necessarily be an indictment of the vision or the ideal itself.[69]

Lee notes, 'These images of the good society, their cadences verging on the biblical, were suffused with a sense of place, redolent of rooted people with rooted values.'[70] He goes on to re-evaluate de Valera's speech in terms understandable today, purging it of the archaic expression favoured by de Valera. What is the speech about? It is about enjoying reasonable housing conditions; full employment in life-enhancing, rather than life-destroying, occupations; health care; social capital; links between generations; and a rural vision that was non-industrial. Certainly, as visions go, there is much to recommend it. But the economic underpinning of the vision was 'not grounded in economic reality', as Lee points out, 'and represented, in fact, a society but not an economy.'[71]

De Valera's Ireland was a traditional, Irish-speaking society, with small industries and farms, largely self-reliant, possessing a deep spiritual dimension that overrode the materialist inclinations of human beings. Gaelic games echoed throughout the country, and the sense of place, townland, parish, county and nation was deeply rooted and always in evidence. This vision mirrored the reality of Irish life in certain ways, but not in most and certainly not in all. The ideal remained a simple hope, an exercise in wishful thinking, well lodged though it may have been in the minds of both the leadership and people.

Still, parts of his speech anticipate the fruitful relationships that are possible if a rooted identity were central to an Irish learning society. In his speech, de Valera quoted Thomas Davis, who a century earlier had stated that resources of the mind were more important than material resources in national development:

> Our young artisans must be familiar with the arts of design and the natural sciences connected with their trade; and so of our farmers; and both should have that general information, which refines and expands the mind, that knowledge of Irish history and statistics that makes it national and those accomplishments and sports which make leisure profitable and home joyous. Our cities must be stately with sculpture, pictures and buildings, and our fields glorious with peaceful abundance. But this is utopia! Is it? No; but the practicable (that is, the attainable) object of those who know our resources. To seek it is the solemn, unavoidable duty of every Irishman.[72]

Later in the same speech, de Valera anticipated a core principle of the modern ethic of sustainability, namely resource productivity. He said Ireland's material resources were sufficient for a large population once their use was 'considered with due appreciation of their value in a *right philosophy* [our emphasis]'. The aim of Government should be to offer every citizen at least a decent standard of living. Resources of the mind are inexhaustible and materially well-off individuals should feel obligated to cultivate and mark out the country as distinct. The speech directly links the motivation of those who sought national independence and those who attempt to engender an ethic of sustainability today. This, for instance, is what the 2006 NESC Strategy document says:

> We can use our vision to formulate shared goals only if we update and enrich our account of the Irish economy, deepen our account of Irish society and factor the environment more into our understanding – using these three to offer a better relation between Ireland's economic, social and environmental challenges.[73]

Liam De Paor maintains that de Valera's model was not in itself an ignoble ideal. The decent way of life proposed was deeply rooted in a rural past of egalitarianism, personal independence and sufficiency.[74] Some limited progress towards it was in fact briefly achieved by the early leaders of the State. John Feehan argues that with the enactment of the various Land Acts, Ireland appeared to be on its way to becoming a nation of peasant proprietors, thereby already realising de Valera's vision. But he says there is more to creating a nation than transferring title: 'It involves a relationship with land that is only built over generations, characterised by self-sufficiency, craft and community. It requires the context of tradition within which understanding of the land is acquired, developed and passed on.'[75]

John Waters writes that the essence of self-sufficiency is reliance on the resources of a community, which are greater than those available to just one individual.[76] Therefore, to be forced to rely entirely on one's own resources is not evidence of autonomy and independence. This means that a bizarre paradox of modern attacks on the concept of Irish self-sufficiency is that it has made people even more dependent, less able to call on something beyond themselves at a time of crisis. Joe Lee points out that de Valera's model emphasised the essential links between generations, a core principle behind sustainability. Giving was as important as receiving and service as important as wealth. It was a society, Lee says, with 'generations woven together into a seamless social fabric.'[77] It was one in which rights were balanced by responsibilities and where adults of materially productive years acknowledged their obligations both to those who came before as well as to those who would come after them.

Creative Citizenship

The absence of an ethic of citizenship is one of the largest social problems in Ireland. Citizenship implies sharing resources, not maximising one's own interest. The great Irish natural scientist Robert Lloyd Praeger saw citizenship as the key to environmental responsibility and promoted the idea of a civic culture which was underdeveloped in Ireland. In his 1948 broadcast on RTÉ launching An Taisce, Praeger offered a strong moral message about the relationship between citizenship and education:

> What we want in both town and country is some sense of citizenship; and I think that can come only by early instruction in the home and in the school. I would make elementary good citizenship the most important of all subjects in schools, for till people have acquired good citizenship they are not well fitted to acquire good anything else. Good citizenship works … by eliminating destructiveness, promoting tidiness, and reducing selfishness and carelessness.[78]

Citizenship depends on people having an enduring sense of self-worth, and the Irish education system clearly fails to imbue young Irish people with a sense of practical patriotism. Ways in which such practical patriotism can be fostered and promoted are badly needed.[79] Given the nature and content of Irish education, students are not emerging from either schools or universities with any clear recognition of what it means to be Irish, have no sense of ownership of the country or responsibility to use their knowledge, skills and energy on its behalf. A rationale for an Irish identity is based on the grounds that people hold certain basic values and principles which they believe are worth preserving. Seán de Fréine uses a metaphor: Irish life is like a plant that has been cut back to the roots and which cannot grow again because of being continuously trampled upon. Since the roots are basically sound, it could, given the chance, put up fresh shoots to develop and bear fruit. The majority of the Irish people cherish a separate nationality to preserve and develop things of worth. However, nationality implies more than the right to be independent. It also imposes obligations for doing all that is necessary to provide an appropriate environment for the development of integrated personalities in accordance with community ideals. There is no reason, de Fréine says, to believe the Irish are fundamentally different from the rest of the human race. Therefore, when it comes to preserving and developing their ideals and values, they can only do so using cultural and institutional means found indispensable in other countries.

Character education is the process through which a culture of pride and a climate of success are developed within a learning environment.[80] It is not just one more thing being added to the plate: it *is* the plate. In schools, student learning thrives where there is respect and trust among teachers, support staff and students, and where parents and other community members volunteer their time. Citizenship cannot be taught, but can certainly be learned if educators create an environment where tradition, identity and community are seen as national resources to be respected, valued and harnessed. Here again the Revival message is worth repeating. Plunkett understood well that the key contribution of the Gaelic League and the language revival movement was in the development of character and a civic sense. Plunkett argued that the political, religious and education systems in Ireland at the time missed out on this issue of character. The Gaelic League, by appealing to the people's past, had an enormous impact on the Irish intellect and on interdependence between the practical and the ideal. Plunkett saw the League's role in intellectual regeneration in this light:

> The national factor in Ireland has been studiously eliminated from national education, and Ireland is perhaps the only country in Europe where it was part of the settled policy of those who had the guidance of education to ignore the literature, history, arts, and traditions of the people. It was a fatal policy, for it obviously tended to stamp their native country in the eyes of Irishmen with a badge of inferiority and to extinguish the sense of healthy self-respect which comes from the consciousness of high national ancestry and traditions. This policy, rigidly adhered to for many years, almost extinguished native culture among Irishmen, but it did not succeed in making another form of culture acceptable to them. It dulled the intelligence of the people, impaired their interest in their own surroundings, stimulated emigration by teaching them to look on other countries as more agreeable places to live in, and made Ireland almost a social desert. Men and women without culture or knowledge or literature or music have succeeded a former generation who were passionately interested in these things, an interest that extended down even to the wayside cabin.[81]

Historian Tom Garvin, in his recent book *Preventing the Future*, calls the Gaelic League, which during the Revival was primarily an educational movement, a 'bizarre political phenomena'.[82] Yet he also laments that the Irish polity has never considered seriously the teaching of true citizenship in schools. True, many of the policies to revive the Irish language after independence were misguided and doomed to fail, but it is difficult to see how civics or citizenship can properly take root without the type of intellectual foundation offered by the Gaelic League.

Education for creativity can foster the idealism and identity necessary to invigorate civil society. As the *Report of the Taskforce on Active Citizenship* set up by former Taoiseach Bertie Ahern illustrates, prospering in a multicultural world requires individuals to understand and appreciate their own culture as well as the values of others with whom they must co-operate.[83] Students today must be equipped to live as responsible citizens in complex multicultural societies while still upholding the richness and uniqueness of the local culture and the place in which they dwell. Some twenty years ago, Declan Kiberd argued that wide-ranging courses in Irish Studies, whereby the richness of literature in English and Irish would draw from and gain vitality from each other, should be set up in all Irish schools and universities. This has not happened to any great extent in Ireland, but has taken place in many North American colleges.[84] Kiberd called for an end to what he called a 'quarantine' or partitionist mentality that divided North from South, Unionist from Nationalist and Anglo-Irish from Gael. Such sentiments are even more relevant and timely now. Educators must ensure ethical behaviour, or 'character', is central to the education experience. US Supreme Court Justice Antonin Scalia puts it nicely:

> Brains and learning, like muscle and physical skills, are articles of commerce. They are bought and sold. You can hire them by the year or by the hour. The only thing in the world not for sale is character. And if that does not govern and direct your brains and learning, they will do you and the world more harm than good.[85]

Marc Coleman argues that the State has made no effort to build a cohesive Irish citizenry of young people who can respect each other and accept their respective economic statuses as products of effort rather than privilege.[86] He sees citizen building and cultural development as being as important to education as science and mathematics. A way must be found, he says, to inculcate Irish culture and identity in the young as well as some way of moulding new citizens from abroad. Recent immigrants to Ireland are likely allies in forging an Irish identity which gives them access to the riches of the language and traditions. But into what cultural values will these new immigrants be integrated? Ireland is gradually losing all traces of zidentity and uniqueness, so policies are trying to integrate immigrants into a culture that will soon cease to exist. Far from threatening Irish traditions, most immigrants are, Coleman says, blank sheets of paper, willing recipients of the culture to which they emigrate.

Resources embedded in a community offer enormous potential for learning and innovation if their distinctive cultural and social characteristics are recognised. Resources are not just about taking, but also about giving; social responsibility can indeed be a powerful resource. But as the Archbishop of Dublin Diarmuid Martin says, the relationships between individuals and the communities in which they live now lie at the root of social tensions in Ireland.[87] A market-based economy requires enhancing personal capacity and initiative, which is why it works so well. But the market does not necessarily guarantee equity and solidarity, much less the financial resources which social solidarity often requires. Sustained economic growth on its own does not achieve social progress and tension between market freedom and social responsibility is at the heart of political choices which now must be made in Ireland.[88]

There is now much public comment and debate on what prosperity has meant for Ireland. A newspaper column summed up a current attitude as follows, 'It's not who we are any more, or even what we do. It's what we buy. We identify ourselves by our stuff….'[89] The former moderator of the Presbyterian Church in Ireland said he now saw an obsession with money, sexual expression and keeping up with technology as the main features of Irish life.[90] He urged a new mindset on wealth, and a better balance between private riches and the provision of adequate public goods.

Brian Fallon says that present-day Ireland has lost a sense of cultural identity and self-definition.[91] He compares modern Irish society to a pendulum that, swinging so violently, has become jammed and cannot resume its normal rhythm. He puts it:

> Behind its present economic prosperity and almost manic self-confidence, Ireland is now in certain respects a curiously

> confused and riven country, psychologically ill at ease with itself. Very often, the ultimately unavoidable questions of where it is going, and what it aspires to be, are shelved in a hectic swirl of pseudo-modernity. Almost any normal, un-ideological expression of nationality is pounced upon as regressive nationalism, prosperity is confused with mental maturity, and – saddest of all – dismissive ignorance of the past is confused with liberation from it.[92]

Fallon asks if what he describes as Ireland's 'frenzied internationalism' is merely inverted provincialism, the product of an unsure, partly fledged culture lacking the heart to be itself. Anybody, he says, who believes we are living in a new age of tolerance and international understanding knows little of the realities of human nature and history, not to mention economics. We are living in an era of permissiveness that dominates our accepted codes of behaviour largely because massive commercial and other interests underwrite it.

In the past, Irish distinctiveness was not so much due to a different language, music or sport but because the dominant role of the Catholic Church resulted in people having a different self-image than other countries. Sociologist Tom Inglis contends that society has now moved from a culture dominated by the Church to a consumer society dominated by the market and the media.[93] Irish people have become less obsessed with saving their souls and more obsessed with fulfilling their fantasies and desires; moving from a culture of self-denial to a culture of self-indulgence. They have become similar to other Western societies in that the struggle for self-realisation revolves around an obsession with looks and feelings. People see themselves less in terms of nationality and more in terms of individual personal tastes and lifestyles. But, asks Inglis, is this liberation or just a more subtle form of control?

> Have the Irish simply switched from a Catholic to a consumer form of colonisation? Is an ethical regime of self-obsession and

> self-indulgence more liberating and more sustainable than an ethical regime of self-emptying and self-denial?[94]

By possessing a weak historically grounded and rooted sense of self, Irish people lose an essential ingredient for developing a strong cultural identity and thereby creativity. Such an identity provides the proper foundation to handle the benefits of increased prosperity and personal freedom. People then become less vulnerable to charm offensives from advertisers and less likely to pursue fads that in reality are not about freedom but are simply money-making enterprises. The rapid move in Ireland from a culture of self-denial to self-indulgence may be leading to an inability to cope with greater money and freedom. While many struggle to break free from a culture of self-deprecation, self-denial and belittling themselves and others, they are being swallowed up by a culture in which they discover themselves through consumption and self-indulgence. This in turn is leading to a form of self-elimination or loss of a sense of self through addiction, demonstrated by excessive drinking and drugs use. Inglis argues that, in an attempt to express and realise themselves through consumption, Irish people run the risk of eliminating themselves through their addictions.[95] He suggests evidence of this can be regularly seen in the streets of Irish towns and cities where youngsters no longer see a necessity for self-denial and so get 'completely out of it' or 'lose the head'.

Blow-ins often see things clearer than those at home: the German Ambassador caused a minor diplomatic spat when he reputedly described Ireland as a 'coarse place with a sad history where the natives are obsessed with money'.[96] Yet others still see Ireland as somehow special. Thomas Moore, an American psychotherapist and author of several books on the soul, says the Irish are among the few remaining on earth in whom an alternative, soul-filled approach to ordinary living is still alive and possible.[97] He believes the Irish people possess strong roots in an ancient past of enchantment, an alternative to the mechanistic philosophies of vast worldwide corporations. People look to Ireland for its spirituality, hoping to siphon it off to feed their souls that are hungry for something other than consumerism. But Moore sees Ireland itself fast becoming like the rest of the world. He puts it wistfully: 'People hungry for spirit are looking avidly to Ireland and Ireland is looking voraciously at them.'[98] He wonders how long people will protect the natural landscape and traditional stories, and refuse to enter unthinkingly and wholeheartedly into a mechanistic life offering 'lures like a devil bargaining for the Irish soul'.[99] He fears Ireland is already reduced, as he puts it, 'like the rest of modernist society to hyperactive brains in demystified bodies on trashy terrains'.[100]

One of the best predictors of the health of a neighbourhood is the degree to which adults respond to the misdeeds of other people's children.[101] Some level of constraint is good for human beings, while absolute freedom is not good at individual, community or societal level. As people in the West have become wealthier, old ideas about virtue and character, such as the necessity for hard work, self-restraint and sacrifice for the future and for the common good, have fallen out of favour. *Anomie*, the word coined by Émile Durkheim, the French sociologist, signifies normlessness as the condition of a society in which there are no clear rules, norms or standards of value. In such a society people do as they please without any clear standards, or any respected social institutions to enforce standards.[102] *Anomie* breeds feelings of rootlessness and leads to an increase in amoral and antisocial behaviour; this ultimately causes social collapse. When community standards are enforced there is constraint and co-operation. It is when all mind their own business and look the other way that there is freedom in one sense but *anomie* in another.[103]

One way of visualising humans is as multilevel systems (that is, bodies and brains) from which minds somehow emerge, and it is from minds that cultures and societies form.[104] To understand people fully, all three levels, the physical, psychological and socio-cultural, must be studied. Individuals have a sense of meaning when their lives cohere across these three levels. But meaningfulness does not just happen; it emerges automatically from cross-level coherence and it is tradition and practice that are keys to a healthy community:

> To the extent that a community has many rituals that cohere across the three levels, people in the community are likely to feel themselves connected to the community and its traditions. If the community also offers guidance on how to live and what is of value, then people are unlikely to wonder about the question of purpose within life. Meaning and purpose simply emerge from the coherence, and people can get on with the business of living. But conflict, paralysis and anomie are likely when a community fails to provide coherence, or worse, when its practices contradict people's gut feelings or their shared mythology and ideology.[105]

A sound rationale links social responsibility and innovativeness; the social animal innovates when there is room for individual commitment and a sense of belonging to a community.[106] Influencing attitudes and values such as responsibility, tolerance, and ethical decision making requires something different than what the Irish examination-oriented system presently demands. As mentioned, when young people believe their vision can change the world they become motivated, willing to lead change through innovation. Progressive European countries like Denmark and Norway find that the fundamental building block to create an entrepreneurial, innovative and learning culture is to give students a sense of place in the scheme of things, a firm familiar foothold or a strong root from which to grow.[107] This helps them realise that they must utilise the world's natural resources, without interfering with the balance of nature, as well as develop a critical and responsible attitude to social questions. They learn to respect the society and culture of their own as well as those of other countries, thereby tolerating different ways of thinking and fostering a strong ethic of citizenship. There needs to be a similar approach taken to teaching citizenship in Irish schools. Having rooted Irish-global identity and sustainable development as centrepieces of their education is the best way to prepare young people to become innovative thinkers, who appreciate and draw upon their own heritage while being keenly aware of the richness of the heritages of others.

NOTES

1. Uí Bhraonáin, D. (2007), *500 Seanfhocal Proverbs Refranes Przysłów*, Dublin: Cois Life, a collection of well-known proverbs in Irish, with equivalents, or translations if no equivalents exist, into English, Polish and Spanish.
2. For a comprehensive examination of the relationships between social capital and well-being in Ireland, refer to Healy, T. (2005), 'Social Capital and Well-Being in Ireland', paper presented at CORI Conference, Dublin, 5 October.
3. Watson, I. (2008), 'The Irish Language and Identity' in C. Nic Pháidín and S. Ó Cearnaigh (eds.), *A New View of the Irish Language*, Dublin: Cois Life, pp. 66–75.
4. Sutherland, P. (2008), 'A Golden Mean between Multiculturalism and Assimilation', *Studies*, 97(385), Spring, pp. 73–86.
5. National Economic and Social Forum (2003), *The Policy Implications of Social Capital*, Forum Report No. 28, Dublin.
6. Editorial (1942), 'The Gaelic League', *The Bell*, 4(2), pp. 77–86 (see pp. 80–1).
7. 'Make Irish a Gift, not a Threat', *Irish Times*, 7 November 2006.
8. 'How Hyde's Creative Vision was Snuffed Out', *Irish Times*, 2 August 1993.
9. Mjøset, L. (1992), *The Irish Economy in a Comparative Institutional Perspective*, Dublin: NESC.
10. Tovey, H., Hannan, D. and Abramson, H. (1989), *Why Irish? Irish Identity and the Irish Language*, Dublin: Bord na Gaeilge.
11. 'Irish Graduates set to become Fluent Irish Entrepreneurs', *Irish Times*, 8 September 1993.
12. Lee, J.J. (1989), *Ireland 1912–1985: Politics and Society*, Cambridge: Cambridge University Press.
13. Lee, *Ireland 1912–1985*, p. 672.
14. Lee, *Ireland 1912–1985*, p. 663.
15. Lee, *Ireland 1912–1985*, p. 668.
16. Kiberd, D. (1996), *Inventing Ireland: The Literature of the Modern Nation*, London: Random House, p. 652.

17. Coleman, M. (2007), *The Best is Yet to Come*, Dublin: Blackhall Publishing.
18. Cronin, M. (2005), 'Knowing our Place: Irish in a Global Age', *Village Magazine*, 10–16 November, p. 27.
19. Cronin, M. (2005), *Irish in the New Century/An Ghaeilge san Aois Nua*, Dublin: Cois Life.
20. Cronin, M. (2004), 'Welcoming Address', in C. Nic Pháidín and D. Uí Bhraonáin (eds.), *University Education in Irish: Challenges and Perspectives*, Dublin: Fiontar, DCU, pp. 19–22.
21. Cronin, *Irish in the New Century/An Ghaeilge san Aois Nua*, pp. 44–5.
22. Ó Tuama, S. (1972), 'The Gaelic League Idea in the Future' in S. Ó Tuama (ed.), *The Gaelic League Idea*, Cork: Mercier Press, pp. 98–109.
23. Williams, G. (2007), 'From Media to Multimedia: Workflows and Language in the Digital Economy' (Chapter 6) in M.J. Cormack and N. Hourigan (eds.), *Minority Language Media: Concepts, Critiques and Case Studies*, Clevedon, England: Multilingual Matters, pp. 88–106.
24. Bargh, J.A., Chen, M. and Burrows, L. (1996), 'The Automatic Evaluation Effect: Unconditional Automatic Activation with a Pronunciation Task', *Journal of Personality and Social Psychology*, 71(2), pp. 230–44.
25. Abbott, J. and Ryan, T. (2000), *The Unfinished Revolution: Learning, Human Behaviour, Community and Political Paradox*, Stafford, UK: Network Educational Press.
26. For some powerful arguments made for the value of Irish in education, enterprise and innovation, see, for example, Cronin, M. (2005), *Irish in the New Century/An Ghaeilge san Aois Nua,* Dublin: Cois Life; McKenna, L. (1912), 'The Educational Value of Irish', *Studies*, 1(2), pp. 307–26 and Tovey, H., Hannan, D. and Abramson, H. (1989), *Why Irish? Irish Identity and the Irish Language*, Dublin: Bord na Gaeilge.
27. For a review of Ó Doiblin's understanding of tradition as a fundamental force in human life, what he calls 'a living dynamic process', and its importance in modern Ireland, refer to Ó Dúshláine, T. (2007), 'Breandán Ó Doibhlin: Pathfinder' in *Breandán Ó Doibhlin: Saol agus Saothar*, Dublin: Coiscéim, pp. 1–25.

28. McKiernan, E. (1963), 'The Will of the Nation: Ireland's Crisis', pamphlet published by the Patrick Butler Family Foundation, St. Paul Minnesota, USA, p. 12. For an appreciation of the life of Eoin McKiernan, see Rogers, J.S. (2004), 'A Monument More Lasting than Bronze: Eoin McKiernan, 1915–2004', *New Hibernia Review*, 8, Autumn, pp. 9–11; also MacTighearnáin, E. (1987), *Is Treise Dúchas ná Oiliúint* (Translation: *Tradition is Stronger than Learning*), Comharchumann Íde Naofa, Faing, Co. Luimnigh, Méan Fómhair, 1987, which gives an account *as Gaeilge* by Eoin McKiernan on his work setting up the Irish American Cultural Institute, St. Paul, Minnesota, USA.
29. McKiernan, 'The Will of the Nation', p. 12.
30. Ó Doibhlin, B. (2004), 'An Enterprise of the Spirit' in C. Mac Murchaidh (ed.), *'Who Needs Irish?' Reflections on the Importance of the Irish Language Today*, Dublin: Veritas, p. 140–58 (see pp. 144–5).
31. Ó Doibhlin, 'An Enterprise of the Spirit', pp. 140–58.
32. Graddol, D. (2006), *English Next*, London, UK: British Council.
33. 'Whose language: Non-native Speakers give a Twist to the World's Pre-eminent Tongue', *Financial Times*, 9 November 2007.
34. Bohm, D. (1980), *Wholeness and the Implicate Order*, London: Routledge & Kegan Paul.
35. Chia, R. (1996), 'Teaching Paradigm Shifting in Management Education: University Business Schools and the Entrepreneurial Imagination', *Journal of Management Studies*, 33(4), July, pp. 409–28.
36. IDA Ireland (2006), *Ireland, Knowledge is in Our Nature*, Dublin: IDA.
37. IDA Ireland, *Ireland, Knowledge is in Our Nature*, p. 122.
38. This point was made by Declan Kiberd in a recent newspaper column, 'Make Irish a Gift, not a Threat', *Irish Times*, 7 November 2006.
39. 'Ireland's "Tiger" has Devoured our Sense of Culture', *Irish Times*, 8 August 2006.
40. Coleman, M. (2007), *The Best is Yet to Come*, Dublin: Blackhall Publishing.
41. Hiberno-English appears to be suffering the same fate as the Irish language according to Professor Terry Dolan of UCD, the leading authority on Hiberno-English in Ireland. Dolan says, in recent years,

Irish people have started to adopt a flatter, less colourful language. They are taking on the 'Dublin 4 accent' rather than their local 'backward' accent, because it is seen as the way to get ahead. ('Janey-Mac! Irish-English is Banjaxed, so it is…', *Irish Independent*, 9 February 2008).

42. Kearney, R. (1985), 'Introduction: An Irish Intellectual Tradition?' in R. Kearney (ed.), *The Irish Mind: Exploring Intellectual Traditions*, Dublin: Wolfhound Press, pp. 7–14.
43. Moane, G. (2002), 'Colonialism and the Celtic Tiger', in P. Kirby, L. Gibbons and M. Cronin (eds.), *Reinventing Ireland: Culture Society and the Global Economy*, London: Pluto Press, pp. 109–23. See also Kenny, V. (1985), 'The Post-Colonial Personality', *The Crane Bag*, 9(1), pp. 70–8 for an analysis by a psychotherapist on the post-colonial Irish personality.
44. Corkery, D. (1968), *The Fortunes of the Irish Language*, Cork: Mercier Press.
45. 'Regions of Dying Languages Named', *New York Times*, 18 September 2007.
46. 'Native Languages hold the Key to Saving Species', *Independent*, 19 February 2007.
47. Ó Doibhlin, 'An Enterprise of the Spirit'.
48. Delaney, P. (2003), 'A Sense of Place: Travellers, Representation, and Irish Culture', *The Republic*, 3, July, pp. 79–89.
49. O'Toole, F. (1996), *The Ex-Isle of Erin: Images of a Global Ireland*, Dublin: New Island Books.
50. Nash, C. (1999), 'Irish Place Names: Post-Colonial Locations', *Transactions of the Institute of British Geographers*, 24(4), pp. 457–80. The particular intricacies in achieving a shared sense of belonging in Northern Ireland are outlined in Reid, B. (2004), 'Labouring towards the Space to Belong: Place and Identity in Northern Ireland', *Irish Geography*, 37(1), pp. 103–13.
51. Hawkins, M.S.G. (2003), '"We Must Learn where we Live": Language, Identity, and the Colonial Condition in Brian Friel's Translations', *Éire-Ireland*, Spring/Summer, pp. 23–36.
52. Evans, E.E. (1996), 'The Irishness of the Irish' in *Ireland and the Atlantic Heritage: Selected Writings*, Dublin: Lilliput, pp. 31–41 (see p. 38).

53. Tovey, H., Hannan, D. and Abramson, H. (1989), *Why Irish? Irish Identity and the Irish Language*, Dublin: Bord na Gaeilge.
54. 'Dublin Design: Poised to Break Out', *New York Times*, 5 January 2006.
55. Tymoczko, M. and Ireland, C. (2003), 'Language and Identity in Twentieth-Century Ireland', *Éire-Ireland*, Spring/Summer, pp. 4–22.
56. 'Gaeilge Goes Global', *Irish Times*, 5 July 2006.
57. In 'New Irish May Save Language', *Irish Times*, 26 June 2006, John Waters describes a new organisation, called iMeasc, set up by foreign nationals who wish to become fluent in Irish. He says that iMeasc, which has 40 members, confronts one of the central tenets of the ideology of modernity, that progress means standing down or dilution of native cultural values. Waters says the 'utterly spurious idea' that, in order to be welcoming to immigrants, the Irish should put aside elements of its surviving indigenous culture that may create 'discrimination' is based not on 'openness towards outsiders but on hatred for ourselves'.
58. Lillis, S. (2005), 'Realising Community Development's Potential in Ireland through Practice, Learning and Connection', *Perspectives on Community Development*, 1(1), pp. 6–19.
59. Plunkett, H.C. (1904), *Ireland in the New Century*, London: John Murray, p. 245.
60. Feehan, J. (2005), 'Community Development: The Spiritual Dimension', *Perspectives on Community Development*, 1, pp. 64–75.
61. Kennedy, F. (2007), 'The Best of Times, the Worst of Times' in Harry Bohan (ed.), *Freedom – License or Liberty? Engaging with a transforming Ireland,* Dublin: Veritas, pp. 20–32.
62. Hock, D. (2005), *One from Many: VISA and the Rise of the Chaordic Organization*, San Francisco, CA: Berrett-Koehler Publishers.
63. Power, T.M. (1996), *Environmental Protection and Economic Well-Being: The Economic Pursuit of Quality,* 2nd edition, Armonk, New York: M.E. Sharpe, p. 3.

64. Lee, J.J. (ed.) (1985), *Ireland: Towards a Sense of Place*, Cork: Cork University Press, p. x.
65. Sennett, R. (1999), 'Growth and Failure: The New Political Economy and Culture' in M. Featherstone and S. Lash (eds.), *Spaces of Culture: City, Nation, World*, London: Sage Publications, pp. 14–26.
66. Moynihan, M. (ed.) (1980), *Speeches and Statements by Éamon de Valera 1917–1973*, Dublin: Gill and Macmillan, p. 89.
67. Although de Valera's speech does include 'comely maidens' there is no evidence of them dancing at the crossroads or elsewhere.
68. Lee, J.J. (1999), 'A Sense of Place in the Celtic Tiger' in H. Bohan and G. Kennedy (eds.), *Are We Forgetting Something? Our Society in the New Millennium*, Dublin: Veritas, pp. 71–93 (see p. 71).
69. The legacy of de Valera is undergoing a re-examination. A book and radio series called *Judging Dev* by historian Diarmuid Ferriter was published in 2007. The author said at its launch that much scapegoating of de Valera and preponderance of the 'dreary de Valera's Ireland' syndrome was born out of 'intellectual laziness', saying, 'It is legitimate to see it as a product of the critics' frustrations rather than any real engagement with the long and complex career of the man they are determined to dismiss and belittle' (*Irish Independent*, 15 October 2007).
70. Lee, 'A Sense of Place in the Celtic Tiger', p. 72.
71. Lee, 'A Sense of Place in the Celtic Tiger', p. 80.
72. 'A Nation with no Language is Half a Nation', *Irish Times*, 17 March 2003.
73. National Economic and Social Council (2005), *NESC Strategy 2006: People, Productivity & Purpose*, Dublin, p. 81.
74. De Paor, L. (1979), 'Ireland's Identities', *The Crane Bag*, 3(1), 22–29 (see p. 29).
75. Feehan, J. (2005), 'Community Development: The Spiritual Dimension', *Perspectives on Community Development*, 1, pp. 64–75 (see p. 72).
76. Waters, J. (1997), *An Intelligent Person's Guide to Modern Ireland*, London: Duckworth.

77. Lee, J.J. (1999), 'A Sense of Place in the Celtic Tiger' in H. Bohan and G. Kennedy (eds.), *Are We Forgetting Something? Our Society in the New Millennium*, Dublin: Veritas, pp. 71–93 (see p. 74).
78. Praeger, R.L. (2005), 'Our National Trust: Address Broadcast by Radio Éireann, 10 October 1948' in V. Bond, *An Taisce: The First Fifty Years,* Ballivor, Co. Meath: The Hannon Press, pp. 149–55 (pp. 152–3).
79. De Fréine, S. (1978), *The Great Silence*, Cork: Mercier Press.
80. Marshall, J.C., Caldwell, S.D., McKay, L. and Owens, J. (2003), 'Character in our Schools', *Classroom Leadership*, 6(7), April, available at: <http://www.ascd.org/portal/site/ascd/menuitem.29d4046bbea38f2eb85516f762108a0c/>.
81. Plunkett, H.C. (1904), *Ireland in the New Century*, London: John Murray, pp. 152–3.
82. Garvin, T. (2004), *Preventing the Future: Why Ireland was so Poor for so Long,* Dublin: Gill & Macmillan, p. 241.
83. Department of the Taoiseach (2007), *Report of the Taskforce on Active Citizenship*, Dublin: The Stationery Office.
84. Kiberd, D. (1979), 'Writers in Quarantine: The Case for Irish Studies', *The Crane Bag,* 3(1), pp. 9–21.
85. Scalia, A. (1996), 'Commencement Address' at the College of William and Mary, Virginia, USA, May.
86. Coleman, M. (2007), *The Best is Yet to Come*, Dublin: Blackhall Publishing.
87. 'Economic Forces can't Guarantee Solidarity – Bishop', *Irish Independent*, 23 August 2004.
88. Interestingly, the 2007 Christmas/New Year messages of both the Catholic Archbishop of Armagh Cardinal Seán Brady and the Church of Ireland Archbishop of Dublin Dr John Neill echoed each other in warning of Irish society's growing obsession with wealth. Dr Neill said he feared Ireland was 'at risk of losing its way' with a value system increasingly linked to 'wealth, instant gratification and a shallow celebrity culture'. (*Irish Independent*, 31 December 2007).
89. 'What We Own is Who We Are', *Irish Times*, 4 December 2006.

90. 'Society Obsessed with Cash', *Irish Independent*, 24 September 2007.
91. Fallon, B. (1998), *An Age of Innocence: Irish Culture 1930–1960*, New York: St. Martin's Press.
92. Fallon, *An Age of Innocence*, p. 268.
93. Inglis, T. (2008), *Global Ireland: Same Difference*, Routledge: New York.
94. Inglis, *Global Ireland*, pp. 255–6.
95. Inglis, T. (2006), 'From Self-Denial to Self-Indulgence: The Class of Cultures in Contemporary Ireland', *The Irish Review*, 34, Spring, pp. 34–43.
96. 'Ambassador's Jokes get Lost in Translation as "Avaricious" Irish Fail to see the Funny Side', *TimesOnline* (London), 17 September 2007, available at: <http://www.timesonline.co.uk/tol/news/world/europe/article2469335.ece>.
97. 'In the Eye of the Tiger', *Irish Times*, 28 July 2001.
98. 'In the Eye of the Tiger'.
99. 'In the Eye of the Tiger'.
100. 'In the Eye of the Tiger'.
101. Haidt, J. (2006), *The Happiness Hypothesis: Finding Modern Truth in Ancient Wisdom*, New York: Basic Books, p. 176.
102. David Quinn, in the article 'Death of Moral Code no Murder Mystery', *Irish Independent*, 4 January 2008, argues that a combination of free-market ideology that encourages excess, and social liberalism that views social conventions as unwarranted intrusions on personal freedom, have undermined the moral code that once restrained and civilised behaviour. In another piece, 'Why Childhood was Better 30 Years Ago…', *Irish Independent*, 30 November 2007, he argues that Ireland needs a new social revolution to rebalance the scales and return childhood and adolescence to where they were in the 1970s. While the economy was no great shakes at the time, the beauty of that Ireland was that it was nicely poised between old authoritarianism and permissiveness. People still lived within a well-ordered framework that no longer resembled the walls of a prison.
103. The decline in communities is not confined to Ireland. In the UK, for instance, according to a report by the Prince's Trust, a third of

people are predicting the death of their communities. Experts claim that traditional social networks are becoming a thing of the past, as towns and villages across the country adapt to fast changing populations, often from different ethnic groups, that have little in common other than happening to live near one another. See 'Community? We don't know our neighbours', *Independent on Sunday*, 20 January 2008.

104. Haidt, J. (2006), *The Happiness Hypothesis: Finding Modern Truth in Ancient Wisdom*, New York: Basic Books, p. 176.
105. Haidt, *The Happiness Hypothesis*, p. 229.
106. Capra, F. (2002), *The Hidden Connections: A Science for Sustainable Living*, London: HarperCollinsPublishers.
107. Breathnach, A. and Aylward, A. (1983), *Education, Innovation and Entrepreneurship: Lessons to be Drawn from Denmark and Norway*, Dublin: EIE Pilot Research Programme Contract 1983/33/5.

CHAPTER 7

Centenary 2022 – From Independence to Interdependence

> The work of the morrow will largely consist of the impossible of today. If this adds to the difficulty, it also adds to the fun.
>
> Horace Plunkett, 1904[1]

INTRODUCTION

No date in modern Irish history resonates with more meaning than 1916, the year of the Easter Rising. A catalytic moment, its spark led from what seemed a hopeless rebellion to a war of independence and the Treaty of 1921. As the centenary of the Rising approaches, much public attention will focus on it. For many years, the *Proclamation of Independence* read by Pádraic Pearse on the steps of the General Post Office (GPO) assumed the iconic status of a Holy Grail. Even if honoured more in the breach than the observance, it cast a long shadow over Irish life through much of the twentieth century. Derided at the beginning, the 1916 Rising has long had the cultural status of a creation myth, but this status is far less assured in recent years. It could be argued that 2022, centenary of the creation of the Irish Free State, ought to offer more cause for self-reflection, if not for celebration.

After independence, contemporaries of the Revival believed its ideals would be implemented by the Free State. Many were sorely disappointed. This book, which draws so much on the Revival in analysing opportunities in a global Ireland, suggests this period might again provide a source of inspiration on both sides of the border. The intellectual underpinnings of the Revival best capture the potential of the current social, political and economic dynamics of Ireland, North and South. The Revival was a vision never given effect, housed in a society that had not the capability to achieve it. Ireland today has the potential to foster a similar vision, albeit in a very different context. With the political landscape on the island transformed, it is worth considering just what a marriage of capability and vision, the local and the global, innovation and culture, might yield.

The development of the Irish State after independence can be roughly categorised into four phases. The first, identified by laissez-faire policies, ran for about a decade. The second, marked by protectionism and self-sufficiency, lasted a further three. The third, spanning in effect the past five decades or so, is outward oriented but very dependent on inward investment. In a sense, the recent boom could be viewed as a manifestation of Ireland's ability to identify and exploit some key competitive advantages such as an educated young population, low taxes, access to European markets and marketing wizardry at attracting global investment. Yet, as this phase now stutters to a close, several former advantages are no longer unique, distinctive or nearly as valuable as before.

This sets the stage for a fourth phase, characterised by innovation and learning. The focus is turning to the development of indigenous or native-owned enterprise, and niche areas attractive to multinational enterprises, especially in high value-added international traded services. The challenge is to identify what inimitable and valuable characteristics Ireland possesses in this emerging phase.

The best way for Irish businesses to compete globally is to develop learning organisations with Irish identity and sense of place at the core. This can lead to a potent innovative climate, a strong spirit of self-reliance and a vigorous internationally competitive indigenous sector. It should also help expand and embed multinational subsidiaries. Competence to mediate between the local and the global is essential if business is to prosper in Ireland in the years ahead.

Regenerating Vision

Population and Place

Forecasters predict that the population of Ireland will continue its recent record climb into the future. The CSO estimates that the Irish population will be around five million by 2022.[2] It could even be higher. The CSO bases these projections upon relatively optimistic economic forecasts and the presumption that robust levels of net inbound migration will continue. As long as economic growth continues to create jobs, inbound migration will follow suit. If so, what does this imply for Ireland in 2022? It depends, in many respects, on the composition of that inbound migration, and the country these people find when they arrive here.

Several commentators suggest that a critical element in Ireland's future success will be its ability to attract a segment of the Irish Diaspora 'home'. David McWilliams argues:

> The Diaspora is our best economic asset. We have little else. There are 3.5 million Irish citizens living outside the country. But the greater Diaspora is considerably bigger. In economic terms, the 70 million-strong Irish tribe is the 21st century equivalent of a huge oil deposit. In the same way as oil guarantees Saudi Arabia's future, the Irish tribe is the key to Ireland's prosperity in the next century. Unlike oil, because the tribe exists inside the minds of millions of Irish people around the world, if we cultivate it properly, it is a resource that won't run out.[3]

Those members of the widely dispersed 'Irish tribe' who can be coaxed home, says McWilliams, will revitalise the homeland with energy, talent and entrepreneurial drive. Their affection for the 'auld sod' will carry them back, as they search for their roots and an 'authentic' experience of their own ethnicity.[4] This poses a question: aside from some kind of personal and emotional attachment, what exactly will induce them to return? For those of Irish descent who have harboured a romantic image of Irish identity, will Ireland 2022 even be recognisable? But why should Dublin resemble 'dear, dirty Dublin' of the 'rare auld days'? Why can it not be a prosperous, invigorated city with its own distinctive culture and sense of place? McWilliams argues that Ireland should extend the right of citizenship to the Diaspora, and 'give them back that spiritual sense of identity for which they long.'[5] But merely facilitating a return hardly provides a strong impetus for doing so. Surely, there must be something else?

We feel McWilliams a tad over-confident in believing the Diaspora will flock to Ireland's banner as it endeavours to create a successful society. Why cannot such energy, talent and sense of purpose come from the Irish themselves, and from the vast numbers who have already immigrated to an Ireland with which they had no prior connection? Whether by birth or by choice, these already share the geographical and cultural place called Ireland. A common sense of identity, dynamically evolving but rooted in the one place, represents a powerful glue that binds all together.

Coherent National Project

One of McWilliams' conclusions is certainly of great merit: Ireland must 'reinvent a national project for the twenty-first century'.[6] A key theme of this book is that a national project can best encompass the goal of global competitiveness by emphasising meaning, tacit knowledge, culture, identity and a deep pride in place. As other small countries like Finland realised a long time ago, people identify with what they call 'our project'; one founded on shared values and a deeply felt respect for local roots.[7] This empowers individuals in the pursuit of a common purpose invested in community and country. It also fosters inimitable and unique resources, which serve in the innovation age as crucial building blocks for building sustainable competitive advantage. Parenthetically, to the extent that such a national project creates a dynamic Ireland, forward looking *and* authentically rooted in culture and place, the wider Diaspora may be drawn to return 'home'.

A coherent public policy based on a rooted Irish-global identity would be the close equivalent of a national project. Still, it may not be easy to appreciate why thinking of a century and more ago might be relevant in today's learning society. Undeniably, many Irish of the pre-independence era looked to England as the focal point of their culture and lives. Intellectuals during the Revival realised that a better balance in perspective was essential for development. They attempted to do this by emphasising native characteristics, designed to help people appreciate their own history, literature, music, language and community. While remaining open to outside influences, the hope was that the Irish would learn to identify difference and appreciate their own distinctiveness. This would then spur native innovation, as is badly needed today.

Desmond Fennell made a similar call over twenty years ago for what he called a new Irish self-image. He said that this should be based primarily on the country's intellectual resources.[8] As with individuals, it is through the choice and pursuit of a life project that identity or self-image is chosen and forged. Fennell wondered whether wariness towards the promoters of the Revival that developed in the years after independence led to hostility to any notion of a revival today.[9] Fennell alleged that a distorted view of Ireland was fashionable among intellectuals in the eighties.[10] We suspect this still holds sway today. This projects the Irish as conservative and illiberal with life characterised by a traditional and dogged conservatism. Accordingly, Ireland has nothing to teach the world; its role is simply to become liberal like it. According to Fennell, this view condemns its users to emotional antagonism with their own nation and history, making them incapable of looking at either with interest, wonder or a desire to learn. He maintained that, far from being culturally conservative, Ireland was actually the opposite. The Irish progressively ditched almost their entire inherited culture, from language, to dress and even cuisine. They only retained folk music and religion; in religion, only faith and a few pilgrimages have been retained. Fennell said the Irish jettisoned their traditional cultural expressions of religion to a greater degree than virtually any other Catholic country. He argued that liberalism, with its disdain for the traditional, also took root in Ireland only a few years after the word itself reached England:

> Not conservatism, but a rootless, pragmatic and often frenzied grasping at the new, the imported and the trendy – puritanism in Victorian times, consumerism in the Swinging Sixties, cinema, then radio, then air travel, television, mini-skirts, pool tables and disco-dancing – have characterized the Irish since the nineteenth century. Three generations ago they changed the ownership of most of the land; two generations ago they carried out the first anti-imperialist revolution of the twentieth century, founded the first state in the British Isles without a state church, and established more state-run enterprises than 'socialist' Sweden. Today the frankness of Irish radio discussions about sex and contraception shocks French au pair girls trying to learn English.[11]

A new vision of development is critical if Ireland is to move to a successful society. This can only happen if connections with native traditions are renewed and fostered. Vincent Twomey has a similar refrain regarding the Catholic Church. He says only a comprehensive cultural and intellectual renewal will enable it to rise effectively to the challenges posed by modern Ireland.[12] He contends that the Church needs to draw inspiration from its rich Irish heritage if it is to have any hope of prospering in the future. Over the past century or two, it made the fundamental mistake of neglecting the literature and practices of the ancient and medieval Irish Church, both Gaelic and Norman, from the mid-nineteenth century onward, supporting the substitution of a Catholic for a Gaelic identity. At the height of

Church power in 1907, Pádraic Pearse in the Gaelic League newspaper *An Claidheamh Soluis*, criticised the bishops for their refusal to support the recognition of Irish in the National University after the dismissal of language supporter Michael O'Hickey from his professorship at Maynooth for 'indiscipline' in questioning that decision.[13] Yet these were warnings of the coming weakened state of the Catholic Church.

The view of Sir Jonathan Sacks, Chief Rabbi in the UK, who says that without a national culture, there is no nation, is also relevant to Ireland.[14] He maintains that multiculturalism in the UK has led not to integration but to segregation. Such a process has now run its course and it is time to move on. In his opinion, new technologies unite people globally but divide people locally. According to Sacks, 'national cultures make nations; global cultures may yet break them.'[15]

The idea of a new national project is not far-fetched. NESC, for instance, regards the idea of a coherent national purpose or collective national project as important. In its latest *Strategy Report* it remains confident the project of Ireland can still inspire people and instil allegiance:

> There is evidence that the 'project of Ireland' – socially, culturally and economically – still commands allegiance. Ireland's experience since independence suggests that economic dynamism and cultural vitality are positively related. There is evidence that Irish people continue to embrace collective projects that are neither narrow nor focused on material self-interest.[16]

This book's framework, which draws on links between rooted resources and value, parallels how culture, identity, character and commitment to place were driving forces of various self-help movements during the Revival. A core argument is that Ireland can still draw on intellectual strands originating in the Revival. A self-help ethos is perfectly in tune with learning communities, which are crucial for stimulating innovation. Many useful lessons can still be learned from Plunkett or Æ on practical science, character development, independent thinking and social capital; from Hyde on culture, self-confidence and education; from Yeats on imagination and the arts; and from Praeger on place, bioscience and sustainability. Plunkett incorporated self-belief into his co-operative movement and noted that co-operation flourished where the Gaelic League was strong, a view reiterated by Hyde who saw language, a world-view, self-belief and creativity as intertwined. A legacy of the Revival is the impressive performance today of the GAA. Still primarily a grassroots Irish community-centred organisation, it heads a sport practically confined to the island. Yet it vigorously competes for members, advertisers and supporters, holding its own against organisations with massive world-wide appeal.

Valuing Difference

The more Irish society becomes the same as the rest of the West, the more it needs to continually create and maintain difference. Tom Inglis contends that the spatial and temporal compression of the world has led to increasing similarity in everyday life, but there is also increasing emphasis on difference, on uniqueness and on otherness.[17] Increasing sameness produces within itself the need for increasing difference; there is a continual struggle to achieve a balance between the two. However, Inglis argues that, whereas Irish difference was previously created through the reinvention of the past, contemporary individual difference is mainly created in and through the media and the market.

Cultural capital is in this respect crucial for obtaining and growing other forms of capital. Irish cultural capital depends on people *consciously being Irish*; this in turn has value in obtaining other forms of capital. Yet Inglis points out that unless possessing Irish cultural products, such as speaking the language, participating in Gaelic games, listening to Irish music, being knowledgeable about Irish literature and history, and so forth, are seen as important forms of cultural capital, in other words tradable for other forms of capital, Irish cultural capital will decline. This does not mean there is only one way of being Irish. What will keep a strong sense of being Irish alive in an increasingly globalised culture is the number of people and the different ways in which people, not just in Ireland but around the world, use cultural representations as a way of constructing their personal identities.

Even if a country's economy is truly global, independence of mind and character, the basis for innovation, are difficult to attain if a country possesses a narrow identity that lacks depth and breadth. This is compounded if accompanied by a provincial outlook. A rooted Irish-global identity would help Irish people to re-imagine the world in which they live. Pragmatists, naturally, will argue that practical concerns (like the condition of the health service, for example) are more important than focusing on cultural renewal (such as a reinvigorated Irish language). However, the basis for tackling and resolving any problem is human capital, motivation, morale and a sense of purpose. These in turn depend on basic values that inspire a community, the way it sees itself and the objectives it sets itself. As Brendán Ó Doibhlin argues, cultural self-possession is developed by making difficult choices and energetically pursuing purposes.[18] To take the easy way out due to inertia or acceptance of attitudes developed elsewhere from different experiences is ultimately self-corrupting. The moral option is to refuse in the name of human dignity and freedom to acquiesce in what he calls 'the ravishment of the past'. The way Irish people make a genuine contribution to humanity is by evolving an identity and imagining a moral project in continuity with what the past has made them. The loss of the major language and culture of the Celtic group of countries is a tragic impoverishment of all European civilization. The dynamism necessary to reverse such decline cannot be generated merely by establishing the material objectives of economic progress. Countries like Denmark and Finland have recognised this. They have engaged in an effort to end the alienation which colonial exploitation brought upon their societies. Nothing less than rejuvenation of the whole person and culture was necessary to restore their fundamental self-respect and self-reliance.

Public policy does appear to be slowly moving to a less market-oriented perspective. A rooted Irish-global identity appears to be the best way to anchor Ireland's sustainable competitive advantage but the *National Development Plan 2007–2013* does not make this leap in imagination. Despite its subtitle *Transforming Ireland*, it seems to ignore the potential of reinvigorating Irish society through nurturing a sense of identity founded on place.[19] The NESC *Strategy Report* is more imaginative; it accepts that Ireland needs a 'better grasp of how and why the past is valuable to us and how we want to relate to it in ways that enrich our lives and the lives of those who come after us'.[20]

Rooted Diversity

With huge inbound migration a reality, a shared identity based on place offers enormous potential. Immigration itself does not threaten Irish culture and identity; the opposite is more likely true. But as Marc Coleman points out, what happens depends on how committed the Irish themselves are to their own culture.[21] Given the scale of recent immigration, some advocate that Ireland change its own culture to suit immigrants. In Coleman's view, the best response to the stresses and strains of immigration is to do the exact opposite, that is, to strengthen Ireland's own traditions and identity. This makes sense. If the Irish can match their recent economic achievements with determination to retain a unique identity, it could help resurrect one of Europe's oldest cultures.

Privileging place over a common ethnic and cultural identity permits the accommodation of cultural difference, while also working as a welcome antidote to the mantra of globalisation that 'geography doesn't matter.'[22] P.J. Mathews sees such an emerging 'creolisation' of Irish culture as a prospect full of exciting potential, and he predicts the emergence of a vigorous new local Irish identity that might follow the trajectory of the Revival. He puts it:

> It is not difficult to imagine such a culture movement being led by a new generation anaesthetized by Celtic Tiger consumerism, the cultural blandness of global Irishness, and the homogenising pressures of Anglo-American culture. This new local Irishness may also be fuelled by the creative input of recent immigrants. New arrivals are often intensely interested in the dynamics of their new locale and eager to connect with indigenous cultural strands as a way of expressing their commitment to their new homeland. As Douglas Hyde testified, being from a particular ethnic background is not a prerequisite to learn and value the Irish language and its literature – not to mention Irish music and Gaelic games.[23]

Recent political developments and moves towards reconciliation in Northern Ireland have exciting implications for Irish identity, innovation and prosperity. In the 1940s, poet John Hewitt dreamt that Ulster as a region, and not as the symbol of a particular religion, could command the emotional, cultural and even political allegiance of all the inhabitants.[24] For this to happen, Hewitt believed, popular consciousness was necessary, and this had to be facilitated by art and high culture emerging from a rooted sense of Irish identity. At the time, such a dream hardly seemed possible; in today's power-sharing climate, it can become a reality.

Yet, as John Wilson Foster argues, for a Northern Irish or Ulster identity to emerge, it has to be distinct from other regional cultures in the world. While international culture will increasingly render Catholics and Protestants similar, it will not render them distinctive in their mutuality. Wilson Foster's answer is that it is possible to generate a sense that people in Northern Ireland are culturally one people, even if their roots are actually roots of difference. In other words, while the regional identity for many years has been one of negativity and division, it is now possible to forge a positive formation from this. To Wilson Foster, the key is that a nation's consciousness of itself is only authentic when its identity is determined from within or from the self, rather than being from without, the expression of another. There is little dignity, he says, in 'wearing someone else's hand-me-downs'. A cross-community but common commitment to place seems ideal to achieve such self-realisation.

For imagination and innovation to flourish, it is crucial that within the Irish third (and earlier) levels, interdisciplinarity, diversity, identity and a sense of place become central elements in the learning environment. This will require the greatest paradigm shift of all. Opportunities must be grasped which have the potential for rich negotiation of meaning. The overwhelming evidence is that difference or diversity improves performance in companies, schools and in society. While ability, the property of an individual, does matter, what appears to matter *most* is diversity, the property of a collection of people.[25] In other words, progress depends more on collective differences than on individual abilities. Individuals can only achieve so much on their own; collectively, however, there is no such constraint. It is difference, or the capacity to think differently (once there is acceptance of some common community or societal goals) that provides the most powerful culture of innovation. A great benefit of immigrants to a country is that they bring with them different values, experiences and perspectives.[26] They challenge existing patterns of thinking; they look at things in a way that the existing population may never have used when engaging with each other. Experiencing other perspectives and meaning can help a country discover new opportunities, as in new overseas markets, through the exchange of ideas, the fusion of the old with new ideas and the creation of entirely new ones. Differences in human capital offer not only the possibility of a more colourful, vibrant and diverse society but also, ultimately, a more creative and productive economy.

Human behaviour and its manifestations in interpersonal relationships are closely tied to cultural identity. Handled properly, effective management of cultural diversity in Ireland no longer means just along traditional lines of Protestant/Catholic or Gaelic/Anglo-Irish, but would also take account of recent immigration. Having rich multicultural communities could become one of Ireland's core competencies for driving competitive advantage. Each perspective has a part to play in the overall pattern of what Declan Kiberd calls 'a quilt of many patches and colours, all beautiful, all distinct, yet all connected too'.[27]

Evidence shows that greater employee satisfaction, resulting from a more diverse yet cohesive workplace, leads to improved productivity and innovation. A recent discussion paper establishes a strong case for Irish business to invest in managing cultural diversity.[28] However, it also states that awareness of one's own culture is a necessary and enabling step in understanding the culture of others. Research shows that, even in the global age, national culture is still the most potent force influencing business management practices. It is far more important than age, education or indeed the corporate culture within which people employed by multinationals work.[29] An obvious corollary is that the Irish cannot build a vibrant and dynamic multicultural society without a stronger sense of their own cultural identity and place in the world. Yet none of the approaches suggested for managing cultural diversity address the current diffused and incoherent nature of Irish identity, or its even weaker sense of place. However, the paper admits that what is especially lacking in business today is a comprehensive analysis of the specific Irish experience with diversity and its context, which differs from that of other countries. One overall message clearly emerges: Ireland cannot aspire to becoming a leader in cultural diversity management without its own business elite having a rich appreciation of its own cultural heritage and traditions.

There may be a reluctance to accept the framework advocated in this book to take advantage of the country's inimitable resource potential. In Ireland, there sometimes appears to be a deliberate rejection of ideas if too different or ideologically unacceptable. Ex-Senators Brendan Ryan and Joe Lee have long called for radical change in this respect.[30] Ryan points out that many Irish economists appear to put too much faith in the market as the most efficient method to both generate *and* distribute resources. Yet there is evidence from countries like Sweden, Denmark and the Netherlands that, while the market is effective for creating wealth, state-driven redistributive mechanisms are best for promoting development, a concept *different* to growth. The generous unemployment support that individuals receive in these countries goes against Irish economic orthodoxy, which sees people less willing to work if welfare benefits are too high. Yet, by reducing an individual's risk, he or she appears actually more willing to take a job.

The problem perhaps comes down again to learning. Knowing how to learn is the essence of a learning society, and the Irish may not be well equipped in this regard. Joe Lee argues that many Irish intellectuals, due in part to an inadequate education, rely too much on imported ideas. He holds that many do not import ideas properly, or do not adapt them to the particular historical and cultural context of Irish society.[31] While technically well trained, some are more technicians than thinkers, deriving their assumptions from conventional international opinion, invariably Anglo-American. Lee says they often lack perspective, so, when analysing what makes other economies function, they frequently fail to choose the right ones to study. They tend to focus obsessively on the short term, using technique as a substitute for thought. Since economies are an integral part of society, according to Lee they should instead ponder what makes these other *societies* function. This is where culture and meaning play such a crucial role. Unless individuals have the ability to stand back from their own training, they often lack the capacity to assess the assumptions they are using themselves.

Seizing the Opportunity

After almost two decades of exceptional economic growth, Ireland faces serious questions about how success might be sustained and the type of society it wishes to be. This economic success has not been achieved without cost: there have been negative impacts on the quality of many people's lives, the natural environment, a sense of community, and the social and cultural fabric of the nation. In the process of gaining the world, is it losing itself? Perhaps Harry Bohan is right when he says, 'My feeling is that it's actually been more difficult for us to cope with prosperity than it has been for previous generations to cope with poverty.'[32]

The transformation of Ireland over the past two decades is apparent to all, but the odyssey is just beginning. The experiment, whether a small, open, free-market economy can successfully compete in a global economy while retaining, or even enhancing its unique identity, culture and place, has longer to run. Yet the country appears to be at a tipping point. Will it reclaim the spirit, focus and energy of the Revival and achieve the vision of the founders of the State? Alternatively, is it trading away its remaining scraps of identity, language and a host of unique advantages to become a generic way station on a global capital pipeline? Public policy decisions taken over the next decade, coupled with those by enterprises and individuals, will determine Ireland in 2022.

Back in 1968, the late US Senator Robert Kennedy said that GNP measures everything 'except that which makes life worthwhile'.[33] Money simply cannot buy happiness, well-being or contentment. A recent editorial in the *New York Times* stated that 'lining up every policy incentive to strive for higher and higher incomes is just going to make us all miserable.'[34] Happiness appears to have little connection with economic success. Gregg Easterbrook contends in his book *The Progress Paradox* that, while almost all aspects of Western life have vastly improved in the past century, most men and women today feel less happy than in previous generations.[35] In China, for instance, life satisfaction declined between 1994 and 2007, a period that saw average real incomes grow by 250 per cent.

In Ireland, 'happiness levels' have stayed remarkably constant during the boom. According to the *World Database of*

Happiness, Ireland performs relatively well among comparable countries with a score and ranking in 2006 about the same as in 2000.[36] Danny McCoy points out that, while the Irish population honestly reports itself to be among the happiest in the world, the challenge is to ensure that happiness is achieved for the greatest number.[37] He says mental illness, for instance, is the cause of more unhappiness in Ireland than poverty. This is more than a personal issue; it is also an employment and economic issue. While income is important, having a job, regardless of the type or quality, can have latent benefits by providing time structure, regular contact with people outside the nuclear family, involvement in shared goals and a sense of identity. As Tim Kasser and Richard Layard argue, people driven predominantly by extrinsic goals or materialistic values experience a lower quality of life and happiness than those driven by intrinsic goals.[38]

Great disparities of income tend to make people greedier, more socially disruptive and less happy, even if all are better off financially. Economic commentator Colm Rapple is convinced the Irish boom was accompanied by a decline in welfare, although the evidence outlined earlier in this book is somewhat mixed.[39] Rapple argues that public policy objectives must reflect growth in society, encapsulated in the concept of community, rather than growth in economic prosperity per se, which is currently almost an obsession. GNP growth should be the result, not the goal of sound public policies designed to nurture learning, innovation, competitiveness, contentment and well-being.

A society is more than an economy. The contemporary obsession with achieving maximum GNP growth as the overriding policy target is likely to be counterproductive. A learning society is one where shared meaning, a sustainable culture, a common sense of purpose, a service ethic and social relationships all intertwine. The health of a society depends on how (or if) people feel about each other, care about the world and believe in some kind of common purpose. Real progress can only come from shared prosperity, so large disparities in income or perceived inequalities in opportunity for advancement do not foster an innovative climate. A higher GNP means the economy is indeed growing, but this does not necessarily mean the country is becoming more prosperous or the quality of life is improving.[40] Economic performance is not a good indicator of welfare and takes no account of the distribution of income. Yet many Irish people have bought the notion that they now live in a tremendously prosperous society. As Fintan O'Toole puts it, 'some of our politicians have taken to patronising other Europeans as if they're miserable sods without an arse in their collective trousers, and suggesting that if they followed our policies they could be rich like us.'[41]

The mechanical or Cartesian worldview that has driven science and knowledge for centuries, which separates mind from matter and ignores meaning, is increasingly under fire. In reality, a complex relationship exists between national well-being, a successful society, research, innovation, productivity and competitiveness. The 'qualities' of the country, exemplified in its unique cultural, social and natural environments, constitute the crucial elements in Ireland's economic base, innovation strategy and international competitiveness. Ironically, politicians, policy-makers and the public tend to overlook precisely these qualities. International competitiveness has most often been presented as a matter of relative costs. Yet Ireland's competitive position will increasingly be determined by its ability to satisfy international demand through creativity, innovation, meaning, uniqueness, distinctiveness in quality and excellence in service. A potent approach to improve productivity and innovation is to nurture tacit knowledge, heritage and tradition alongside a new emphasis on sustainability, biodiversity and quality of life. If cultural identity and sense of place are central to Ireland's self-image, it will contribute to wholeness, integrity, civic responsibility, aesthetic sensibility and ecological stewardship.

Policies that recognise the nature, emotions and feelings of a people can provide a powerful and inimitable competitive advantage. A grand vision of a successful society, anchored by meaning and practical idealism, and comprising people of different cultural backgrounds who share a communal commitment to place, is a unifying project to drive innovation, transformational learning and sustainable competitiveness. Here is the great opportunity. There is no better time to begin.

Notes

1. Plunkett, H.C. (1904), *Ireland in the New Century*, London: John Murray, p. 183.
2. Central Statistics Office (2004), *Population and Labour Force Projections: 2006–2036*, Dublin: The Stationery Office.
3. McWilliams, D. (2007), *The Generation Game*, Dublin: Gill and Macmillan, p. 245.
4. McWilliams, *The Generation Game*, p. 259.
5. McWilliams, *The Generation Game*, p. 260.
6. McWilliams, *The Generation Game*, p. 260.
7. Oinas, P. (2005), 'Finland: A Success Story?' *European Planning Studies*, 13(8), December, pp. 1227–44.
8. Fennell, D. (1986), 'Creating a New Irish Identity', *Studies: The 300th Issue, 1912–1986 – Towards a New Irish Identity*, 75, Winter, pp. 392–400.
9. Witoszek, N. and Sheeran, P. (1985), 'Giving Culture a Kick – Modern Irish Culture Forum', *The Crane Bag*, 9(1), pp. 94–5.
10. Fennell, D. (1985), 'How Not to See Ireland', *The Crane Bag*, 9(1), pp. 92–3.
11. Fennell, 'How Not to See Ireland'.
12. Twomey, D.V. (2003), *The End of Irish Catholicism?* Dublin: Veritas.
13. Ó Buachalla, S. (ed.) (1980), *A Significant Irish Educationalist: The Educational Writings of P.H. Pearse*, Cork: Mercier Press.
14. 'Wanted: A National Culture', *TimesOnline* (London), 20 October 2007, available at: <http://www.timesonline.co.uk/tol/comment/columnists/guest_contributors/article2697772.ece>.
15. 'Wanted: A National Culture', *TimesOnline*.
16. National Economic and Social Council (2005), *NESC Strategy 2006: People, Productivity & Purpose*, Dublin: NESC, p. 103.
17. Inglis, T. (2008), *Global Ireland: Same Difference*, Routledge: New York.
18. Ó Doibhlin, B. (2004), 'An Enterprise of the Spirit' in C. Mac Murchaidh (ed.) *Who Needs Irish? Reflections on the Importance of the Irish Language Today*, Dublin: Veritas, pp. 140–158.

19. Irish Government (2007), *National Development Plan 2007–2013: Transfoming Ireland*, Dublin: The Stationery Office.
20. *NESC Strategy 2006*, p. 109.
21. Coleman, M. (2007), *The Best is Yet to Come*, Dublin: Blackhall Publishing.
22. Mathews, P.J. (2005), 'In Praise of "Hibernocentricism": Republicanism, Globalisation and Irish Culture', *The Republic,* 4, June, pp. 7–14.
23. Mathews, 'In Praise of "Hibernocentricism"', pp. 12–13.
24. Foster, J.W. (1991), 'Radical Regionalism' in J.W. Foster (ed.) *Colonial Consequences: Essays in Irish Literature and Culture*, Dublin: Lilliput Press, pp. 278–95.
25. Page, S.E. (2007), *The Difference: How the Power of Diversity Creates Better Groups, Firms, Schools and Societies,* Princeton, NJ: Princeton University Press.
26. 'Immigrants Bring Valuable Personal Capital', *Irish Times*, 3 February 2006.
27. Kiberd, D. (1996), *Inventing Ireland: The Literature of the Modern Nation*, London: Random House, p. 653.
28. Crowe, D. (2007), 'Cultural Diversity in the Workplace', Discussion Paper, IMI Bizlab on Cultural Diversity, Dublin: Irish Management Institute.
29. Keating, M. and Martin, G. (2004), *Managing Cross-Cultural Diversity: The Irish-German Experience*, Dublin: Blackhall Publishing. Refer also to Laurent, A. (1983), 'The Cultural Diversity of Western Conceptions of Management', *International Studies of Management & Organization*, 13 (1/2).
30. Ryan, B. (2001), 'Have Intellectuals Failed Ireland' in A. Hoey-Heffron and J. Heffron (eds.) *Beyond the Ivory Tower: The University in the New Millennium*, Cork: Mercier Press, pp. 96–102.
31. Lee, J.J. (1985), 'Centralisation and Community' in J.J. Lee (ed.) *Ireland: Towards a Sense of Place*, Cork: Cork University Press.
32. Bohan, H. (2002) in F. Shouldice (ed.), *Community and the Soul of Ireland: The Need for Values-Based Change,* Dublin: Liffey Press, p. 4.

33. Robert F. Kennedy Address, University of Kansas, Lawrence, Kansas, 18 March 1968, available at: <http://missbitty.blogspot.com>.
34. 'All they are Saying is Give Happiness a Chance', *New York Times*, 12 November 2007.
35. Easterbrook, G. (2004), *The Progress Paradox: How Life gets Better while People Feel Worse*, New York: Random House.
36. National Competitiveness Council (2007), *Annual Competitiveness Report 2007, Volume 1: Benchmarking Ireland's Performance; Volume 2: Ireland Competitiveness Challenge*, Dublin: Forfás.
37. 'Depression Ails our Economy', *Irish Times*, 15 November 2007.
38. Kasser, T. (2002), *The High Price of Materalism,* Cambridge, MA: MIT Press; Layard, R. (2005), *Happiness*, London: Allen Lane.
39. Rapple, C. (2000), 'Beyond the Boom: Towards an Economic Policy for Welfare and Society', *The Republic*, 1, June, pp. 40–9.
40. Reich, R.B. (2005), *Reason: Why Liberals will Win the Battle for America*, New York: Vintage Books.
41. 'So we're Rich, then go Figure', *Irish Times*, 4 January 2005.

Bibliography

Abbott, J. and Ryan, T. (2000), *The Unfinished Revolution: Learning, Human Behaviour, Community and Political Paradox*, Stafford, UK: Network Educational Press.

Abbott, J. and Ryan, T. (1998), 'Upside Down and Inside Out: A Challenge to Redesign Education Systems to Fit the Needs of a Learning Society', *The American Administrator*, January.

Adler, M. (1957), 'The Deterioration of American Education', from a lecture, 'Liberal Education in an Industrial Democracy', presented to the Industrial Indemnity Insurance Company, San Francisco, 1957, available at: <http://radicalacademy.com/adleramericaneducation.htm>.

Advisory Council for Science, Technology and Innovation (2007), *Promoting Enterprise-Higher Education Relationships*, Dublin: Forfás.

Allen, F. and Bradley, F. (2007), 'Transporting Individuals – Transforming Communities', *Studies*, 96(383), Summer, pp. 145–53.

Allen, F. and Bradley, F. (2002), 'The Potential of Public-Voluntary Partnerships for the Delivery of Quality Social Services', *Studies*, 91(364), Winter, pp. 371–80.

Allen, K. (2007), *The Corporate Takeover of Ireland*, Dublin: Irish Academic Press.

Allen, N. (2003), *George Russell (Æ) and the New Ireland, 1905–30*, Dublin: Four Courts Press.

American Chamber of Commerce in Ireland (2007), *Retuning the Growth Engine*, Dublin.

Anderson, R.A. (1935), *With Horace Plunkett in Ireland*, London: Macmillan.

Andrews, C.S. (1982), *Man of No Property,* Cork: Mercier Press.

Attis, D. (2000), 'Science and Irish Identity: the Relevance of Science Studies for Irish Studies' in P.J. Mathews (ed.), *New Voices in Irish Criticism*, Dublin: Four Courts Press.

Aylward, C. and O'Toole, R. (eds.) (2007), *Perspectives on Irish Productivity: A Selection of Essays by Irish and International Economists*, Dublin: Forfás.

Bank of Ireland (2007), *The Wealth of the Nation*, Dublin: Bank of Ireland Private Banking.

Bargh, J.A., Chen, M. and Burrows, L. (1996), 'The Automatic Evaluation Effect: Unconditional Automatic Activation with a Pronunciation Task', *Journal of Personality and Social Psychology*, 71(2), pp. 230–44.

Barney, J.B. (1991), 'Firm Resources and Sustained Competitive Advantage', *Journal of Management*, 17(1), pp. 99–120.

Bawden, R.J. (1992), 'Systems Approaches to Agricultural Development: The Hawkesbury Experience', *Agricultural Systems*, 40(1), pp. 153–76.

Beathnach, C. (1992), *An Fearann Breac*, Dublin: Coiscéim.

Benefiel, M. (2005), *Soul at Work: Spiritual Leadership in Organizations*, New York: Seabury Books.

Bennis, W.G. and O'Toole, J. (2005), 'How Business Schools Lost their Way', *Harvard Business Review*, May, pp. 96–104.

Berry, W. (1995), *Another Turn of the Crank*, Washington, D.C.: Counterpoint.

Bloom, A. (1987), *The Closing of the American Mind: How Higher Education has Failed Democracy and Impoverished the Souls of Today's Students*, London: Penguin Books.

Bohan, H. in F. Shouldice (ed.) (2002), *Community and the Soul of Ireland: The Need for Values-Based Change,* Dublin: Liffey Press.

Bohm, D. (1980), *Wholeness and the Implicate Order*, London: Routledge & Kegan Paul.

Bolger, P. (1977), *The Irish Co-operative Movement: Its History and Development*, Dublin: Institute of Public Administration.

Borish, S.M. (1991), *The Land of the Living: The Danish Folk High Schools and Denmark's Non-Violent Path to Modernization*, Nevada City, CA: Blue Dolphin.

Bowler, P.J. and Whyte, N. (eds.) (1997), *Science and Society in Ireland: The Social Context of Science and Technology in Ireland 1800–1950*, Belfast: The Institute of Irish Studies.

Boyer Commission (2001), *Reinventing Undergraduate Education: Three Years after the Boyer Report*, Stony Brook, New York: State University of New York.

Boyer Commission (1998), *Reinventing Undergraduate Education: A Blueprint for America's Research Universities*, Stony Brook, New York: State University of New York.

Boyer, E. (1990), *Scholarship Reconsidered: Priorities of the Professoriate*, New Jersey: The Carnegie Foundation for the Advancement of Teaching.

Boyte, H.C. (2000), 'The Struggle against Positivism' *Academe*, 86(4), July–August.

Bradley, F. and Allen, F. (2001), 'Value for Money in Public Private Partnerships (PPPs): Myth & Reality', *Administration/Journal of the Institute of Public Administration*, 49(1), Spring, pp. 46–58.

Bradley, J. (2007), 'Small State, Big World: Reflections on Irish Economic Development', *Dublin Review of Books*, 3, Autumn, available at: <http://www.drb.ie/sept_smallstate.html>.

Brealey, R.A., Myers, S.C. and Allen, F. (2006), *Corporate Finance,* 8th edition, New York: McGraw-Hill/Irwin.

Breathnach, A. and Aylward, A. (1983), *Education, Innovation and Entrepreneurship: Lessons to be Drawn from Denmark and Norway*, EIE research programme, Dublin.

Brereton, F., Clinch, J.P. and Ferreira, S. (2006), 'Quality of Life and Environmental Amenities: A Subjective Well-Being Approach', Working Paper, School of Geography, Planning and Environmental Policy, UCD.

Brooks, S. (1907), *The New Ireland*, Dublin: Maunsel & Co.

Brophy, S. (2006), ' "Personal Excellence" as a Value for Health Professionals: A Patient's Perspective', *International Journal of Health Care*, 19(5), pp. 372–83.

Brown, S.J. (1912), 'The Question of Irish Nationality', *Studies*, 1, December, pp. 634–54.

Brown, S.J. (1912), 'What is a Nation?' *Studies*, 1, September, pp. 496–510.

Buckley, V. (1985), *Memory Ireland: Insights into the Contemporary Irish Condition*, Victoria, Australia: Penguin Books.

Cannon, S. (2005), 'Reconciling Local Initiative with National Policy in Teacher Professional Development', unpublished Doctor of Management thesis, University of Hertfordshire, UK.

Canzanelli, G. (2001), 'Overview and Learned Lessons on Local Economic Development, Human Development, and Decent Work', Working Paper, Universitas, ILO, Geneva, October.

Capra, F. (2002), *The Hidden Connections: A Science for Sustainable Living*, London: HarperCollinsPublishers.

Casey, D. and Brugha, C.M. (2005), 'Questioning Cultural Orthodoxy: Policy Implications for Ireland as an Innovative Knowledge-Based Economy', *E:CO*, 7, pp. 2–10.

Castells, M. and Himanen, P. (2002), *The Information Society and the Welfare State: The Finnish Model*, Oxford: Oxford University Press.

Central Statistics Office (2007), *Measuring Ireland's Progress 2006*, Dublin: The Stationery Office, pp. 42–3.

Central Statistics Office (2006), *Census 2006*, Dublin: The Stationery Office.

Central Statistics Office (2004), *Population and Labour Force Projections: 2006–2036*, Dublin: The Stationery Office.

Charles, D. (2005), 'CRITICAL: City Regions as Intelligent Territories: Inclusion, Competitiveness and Learning', conference on 'Intelligent Territories', Employment Research Centre, Trinity College Dublin, 2 December.

Chesbrough, H., Downes, L., Glushko, R.J., Righter, R. and Saxenian, A. (2006), 'Designing a "Services Science, Management and Engineering" Discipline and Curriculum', position paper for workshop: 'Education for Services Innovation', Washington, DC, 18 April.

Chia, R. (1996), 'Teaching Paradigm Shifting in Management Education: University Business Schools and the Entrepreneurial Imagination', *Journal of Management Studies*, 33(4), July, pp. 409–28.

Chickering, A.W. and Reisser, L. (1993), *Education and Identity*, 2nd edition, San Francisco: Jossey-Bass.

Coleman, M. (2007), *The Best is Yet to Come*, Dublin: Blackhall Publishing.

Collis, D.J. and Montgomery, C.A. (1995), 'Competing on Resources', *Harvard Business Review*, July–August, pp. 118–28.

Conference of Religious in Ireland (1997), *Planning for Progress*, Dublin: CORI.

Conference of Religious in Ireland (1996), *Progress, Values and Public Policy*, Dublin: CORI.

Cooley, T.F. (2007), 'The Business of Business Education', *Stern Business*, Fall/Winter, pp. 23–5.

Córas Trachtála (1961), *Design in Ireland*, Dublin: Córas Trachtála.

Corcoran, M., Gray, J. and Peillon, M. (2007), 'Ties that Bind?: The Social Fabric of Daily Life in New Suburbs' in T. Fahey, H. Russell and C.T. Whelan (eds.), *Best of Times? The Social Impact of the Celtic Tiger*, Dublin: Institute of Public Administration.

Corkery, D. (1968), *The Fortunes of the Irish Language*, Cork: Mercier Press.

Cronin, M. (2005), *Irish in the New Century/An Ghaeilge san Aois Nua*, Dublin: Cois Life.

Cronin, M. (2004), 'The Unbidden Ireland: Materialism, Knowledge and Interculturality', *The Irish Review*, 31, Spring/Summer, pp. 3–10.

Cronin, M. (2004), 'Welcoming Address', in C. Nic Pháidín and D. Uí Bhraonáin (eds.), *University Education in Irish: Challenges and Perspectives*, Dublin: Fiontar, DCU, pp. 19–22.

Cullen, C. (2007), 'The Museum of Irish Industry: Robert Kane and Education for all in the Dublin of the 1850s and 1860s', *History of Education*, July, pp. 1–14.

Curley, M. (2004), *Managing Information for Business Value*, Oregon, USA: Intel Press.

Darwin, C. (1873), *The Expression of the Emotions in Man and Animals*, New York: D. Appleton.

Darwin, C. (1966, 1859), *The Origin of the Species*, Cambridge, MA: Cambridge University Press.

Davies, G.H. (1985), 'Irish Thought in Science' in R. Kearney (ed.), *The Irish Mind*, Dublin: Wolfhound Press, pp. 294–310.

De Fréine, S. (1978), *The Great Silence*, Cork: Mercier Press.

Delaney, P. (2003), 'A Sense of Place: Travellers, Representation, and Irish Culture', *The Republic*, 3, July, pp. 79–89.

De Paor, L. (1979), 'Ireland's Identities', *The Crane Bag*, 3, pp. 22–9.

Department of Finance (1999), *Proposed Working Rules for Cost-Benefit Analysis*, Dublin: CSF Evaluation Unit.

Department of the Taoiseach (2007), *Report of the Taskforce on Active Citizenship*, Dublin: The Stationery Office.

Dewey, J. (1938), *Experience and Education*, New York: Touchstone/Simon & Schuster.

Dewey, J. (1897), 'My Pedagogic Creed', *The School Journal*, 54, January, 77–80.

Dierickx, I. and Cool, K. (1989), 'Asset Stock Accumulation and Sustainability of Competitive Advantage', *Management Science*, 35(12), December, 1504–11.

Dinnie, K. (2007), *Nation Branding: Concepts, Issues, Practice*, Oxford: Butterworth-Heinemann.

Donnelly, W.J. (2000), 'Public Research: Managing the Innovation Process', *International Journal of Dairy Technology*, 53, November, pp. 149–55.

Dorgan, S. (2006), 'How Ireland Became the Celtic Tiger', *Backgrounder*, The Heritage Foundation, Washington, DC, No. 1945, 23 June.

Downey, L. and Purvis, G. (2005), 'Building a Knowledge-Based Multifunctional Agriculture and Rural Environment' in Mollan, C. (ed.), *Science and Ireland – Value for Society*, 2, Dublin: RDS, pp. 121–39.

Dunleavy, J.E. and Dunleavy, G.W. (1991), *Douglas Hyde: A Maker of Modern Ireland*, Berkeley, CA: University of California Press.

Dunne, J. (1999), 'Professional Judgment and the Predicaments of Practice', *European Journal of Marketing*, 33(7/8), pp. 707–19.

Easterbrook, G. (2004), *The Progress Paradox: How Life gets Better while People Feel Worse*, New York: Random House.

Economist Intelligence Unit (2007), 'Sharing the Idea: The Emergence of Global Innovation Networks', Dublin: EIU for IDA Ireland.

Economist Intelligence Unit (2004), *Quality-of-life Index:The World in 2005*, London: EIU.

Eisner, E.W. (2002), *The Arts and the Creation of Mind*, New Haven: Yale University Press.

Elias, R. (1998), 'Game Models' in S. Mennell and J. Goudsblom (eds.), *Norbert Elias: On Civilization, Power and Knowledge*, Chicago: The University of Chicago Press, pp. 113–38.

Enterprise Ireland (2007), *Transforming Irish Industry: Enterprise Ireland Strategy 2008–2010*, Dublin.

Enterprise Strategy Group (2004), *Ahead of the Curve: Ireland's Place in the Global Economy*, Dublin: Forfás.

Environmental Protection Agency (2006), *Environment in Focus 2006: Environmental Indicators for Ireland*, Johnstown Castle Estate, Wexford: EPA.

Esty, D.C. and Porter, M.E. (2001), 'Ranking National Environmental Regulation and Performance: A Leading Indicator of Future Competitiveness?' in *The Global Competitiveness Report, 2001–2002*, New York: Oxford University Press.

Evans, E.E. (1996), 'The Irishness of the Irish' in *Ireland and the Atlantic Heritage: Selected Writings*, Dublin: Lilliput Press, pp. 31–41.

Evans, E.E. (1984), *Ulster: The Common Ground*, Dublin: Lilliput Pamphlets.

Evans, E.E. (1982), *The Personality of Ireland*, Dublin: Lilliput Press.

Fahey, T., Russell, H. and Whelan, C.T. (eds.) (2007), *Best of Times? The Social Impact of the Celtic Tiger*, Dublin: Institute of Public Administration.

Fahy, J. (2000), 'The Resource-Based View of the Firm: Some Stumbling-Blocks on the Road to Understanding Sustainable Competitive Advantage', *Journal of European Industrial Training*, 24, pp. 94–104.

Fallon, B. (1998), *An Age of Innocence: Irish Culture 1930–1960*, New York: St. Martin's Press.

Farrell Grant Sparks and Goodbody Economics Consultants, in association with Chesterton Consulting (1998), *Public Private Partnerships*, Dublin: FGS.

Featherstone, M. and Lash, S. (eds.) (1999), *Spaces of Culture: City, Nation, World*, London: Sage Publications, pp. 14–26.

Feehan, J. (2005), 'Community Development: The Spiritual Dimension', *Perspectives on Community Development*, 1, pp. 64–75.

Fennell, D. (1986), 'Creating a New Irish Identity', *Studies: The 300th Issue, 1912–1986 – Towards a New Irish Identity*, 75, Winter, pp. 392–400.

Fennell, D. (1985), 'How Not to See Ireland', *The Crane Bag*, 9(1), pp. 92–3.

Fitzpatrick, R. (1989), *God's Frontiersmen: The Scots-Irish Epic*, London: Weidenfeld and Nicolson.

Foley, A. (2008), 'Service Export Performance', *Business & Finance*, 15 February, pp. 56–7.

Forfás (2008), *The Higher Education R&D Survey 2006 (HERD)*, March, Dublin: Forfás.

Forfás (2007), 'Council Highlights Areas Vital to Enhancing Ireland's Competitiveness', 29 November, available at: <http://www.competitiveness.ie>.

Forfás (2007), *Ireland's Co-operative Sector*, Dublin: Forfás.

Forfás (2007), *Tomorrow's Skills: Towards a National Skills Strategy*, 5th Report of Expert Group on Future Skills Needs, Dublin: Forfás.

Forfás (2007), *Towards Developing an Entrepreneurship Policy for Ireland*, Dublin: Forfás.

Forfás (2006), 'Services Innovation in Ireland – Options for Innovation Policy', September, Dublin: Forfás.

Forfás (2005), *Making Technological Knowledge Work: A Study of the Absorptive Capacity of Irish SMEs*, report conducted by Technopolis, February, Dublin: Forfás.

Foster, J.W. (1991), 'Natural Science and Irish Culture', *Éire-Ireland*, 26, pp. 92–103.

Foster, J.W. (1991), 'Radical Regionalism' in J.W. Foster (ed.), *Colonial Consequences: Essays in Irish Literature and Culture*, Dublin: Lilliput Press, pp. 278–95.

Foster, J.W. (1990), 'Natural History, Science and Irish Culture', *The Irish Review*, 9, pp. 61–9.

Foster, J.W. and Chesney, H.C.G. (eds.) (1997), *Nature in Ireland: A Scientific and Cultural History*, Dublin: Lilliput Press, pp. 573–96.

Frank, R.H. (1988), *Passions within Reason: The Strategic Role of the Emotions*, New York: W.W. Norton.

Friberg, E. (trans.) (1988), *The Kalevala – Epic of the Finnish People*, Helsinki: Otava Publishing Company.

Fuscaldo, D. (2008), 'Innovation: Corporations Embrace Social Networking', Fox Business, 8 February, available at: <http://www.foxbusiness.com/story/markets/innovation/innovation-corporations-embrace-social-networking/>.

Futures Academy (2008), *Twice the Size? Imagineering the Future of Irish Gateways*, Dublin Institute of Technology, Report for the Urban Forum.

Gardner, H. (1993), *Frames of Mind: The Theory of Multiple Intelligences*, New York: Basic Books.

Garvin, T. (2004), *Preventing the Future: Why was Ireland so Poor for so Long?* Dublin: Gill & Macmillan.

Gilmor, D.A. (ed.) (1979), *Irish Resources and Land Use*, Dublin: Institute of Public Administration.

Glassick, C.E. (1999), 'Ernest L. Boyer: Colleges and Universities as Citizens' in R.G., Bringle, R. Games and E.A. Malloy (eds.), *Colleges and Universities as Citizens*, Boston: Allyn & Bacon, pp. 17–30.

Goleman, D. (1996), *Emotional Intelligence: Why it Can Matter More than IQ*, London: Bloomsbury.

Government of Ireland (2007), *National Development Plan 2007–2013: Transforming Ireland*, Dublin: The Stationery Office.

Government of Ireland (2006), *Strategy for Science, Technology and Innovation, 2006–2013*, Dublin: The Stationery Office.

Government of Ireland (2006), *Towards 2016: Ten-Year Framework Social Partnership Agreement 2006–2015*, Dublin: The Stationery Office.

Government of Ireland (in association with OECD) (1965), *Investment in Education: Report of the Survey Team appointed by the Minister of Education in 1962*, Dublin: The Stationery Office.

Government of Ireland (in association with OECD) (1965), *Science and Irish Economic Development: Report of the Research and Technology Survey Team appointed by the Minister for Industry and Commerce in 1963*, Dublin: The Stationery Office.

Government of Ireland (1958), *Economic Development*, Dublin: The Stationery Office.

Government of Ireland (1958), *Programme for Economic Expansion*, Dublin: The Stationery Office.

Graddol, D. (2006), *English Next*, London: British Council.

Graeber, D. (2001), *Toward an Anthropological Theory of Value*, New York: Palgrave.

Grant, R.M. (1991), 'The Resource-Based Theory of Competitive Advantage: Implications for Strategy Formulation', *California Management Review*, 33, pp. 114–35.

Greene, D. (1972), 'The Founding of the Gaelic League' in S. Ó Tuama (ed.), *The Gaelic League Idea*, Cork: Mercier Press, pp. 9–19.

Gunnigle, P., Heraty, N. and Morley, M.J. (2006), *Human Resource Management in Ireland,* 3rd edition, Dublin: Gill & Macmillan.

Haidt, J. (2006), *The Happiness Hypothesis: Finding Modern Truth in Ancient Wisdom*, New York: Basic Books.

Hart, K. (1999), *The Memory Bank: Money in an Unequal World*, London: Profile Books.

Hart, T. (2001), *From Information to Transformation: Education for the Evolution of Consciousness*, New York: Peter Lang.

Hawken, P., Lovins, A.B. and Lovins, L.H. (1999), *Natural Capitalism: The Next Industrial Revolution*, London: Earthscan.

Hawkins, M.S.G. (2003), '"We Must Learn where we Live": Language, Identity, and the Colonial Condition in Brian Friel's Translations', *Éire-Ireland*, Spring/Summer, pp. 23–36.

Hock, D. (2005), *One from Many: VISA and the Rise of the Chaordic Organization*, San Francisco, CA: Berrett-Koehler Publishers.

Hofstede, G. (1997), *Cultures and Organizations: Software of the Mind*, New York: McGraw-Hill.

Hogan, P. (1995), *The Custody and Courtship of Experience: Western Education in Philosophical Perspective*, Dublin: The Columba Press.

Honohan, P. (1998), *Key Issues of Cost-Benefit Methodology for Irish Industrial Policy*, ESRI, General Research Series, No. 172, November.

Hopwood, A.G. (1988), 'Production and Finance: The Need for a Common Language', Proceedings of the 1st Industrial Summit on New Manufacturing Imperatives, 12–15 January, London.

Horgan, J. (1997), *Seán Lemass: The Enigmatic Patriot*, Dublin: Gill & Macmillan.

Hughes, C. (2000), *The Evolution of the Worker Co-operative Concept in Ireland*, unpublished MSc thesis, NUI Cork.

Hyde, D. (1894), 'The Necessity for De-Anglicising Ireland' in *The Revival of Irish Literature: Addresses by Sir Charles Gavan Duffy, Dr George Sigerson and Dr Douglas Hyde*, London: Fisher Unwin, pp. 117–61.

IBM Institute for Business Value (2006), 'The Power of Many', Somers, NY: IBM Global Business Services, available at: <http://www.935.ibm.com/services/us/gbs/bus/pdf/g510-6335-00-abc.pdf>.

IDA Ireland (2006), *Ireland: Knowledge is in Our Nature*, Dublin: IDA.

Information Society Commission (2005), *Learning to Innovate: Re-perceiving the Global Information Society*, Dublin: Department of the Taoiseach.

Information Society Commission (2002), *Building the Knowledge Society: Report to Government*, Dublin: Department of the Taoiseach.

Information Society Council (2006), *Report to the Finnish Government – Efficiency and Vitality in Future Finland*, February, Finland: Prime Minister's Office.

Inglis, T. (2008), *Global Ireland: Same Difference*, New York: Routledge.

Inglis, T. (2006), 'From Self-Denial to Self-Indulgence: The Class of Cultures in Contemporary Ireland', *The Irish Review*, 34, Spring, pp. 34–43.

Institute of Management Development (2007), *World Competitiveness Yearbook*, IMD, Lausanne, Switzerland.

Irish Council for Science, Technology and Innovation (2004), *ICSTI Statement – Sustainable Development in Ireland: The Role of Science and Technology*, Dublin: Forfás.

Irish Universities Association (2005), 'Reform of Third-Level and Creation of Fourth-Level Ireland: Securing Competitive Advantage in the 21st Century', Dublin: IUA.

Jaruzelski, B., Dehoff, K. and Bordia, R. (2005), 'The Booz Allen Hamilton Global Innovation 1000 – Money Isn't Everything', *Strategy & Business*, 41, Winter, Booz Allen Hamilton, New York, available at: <http://www.boozallen.com/media/file/151786.pdf>.

Johnston, R. (1983), 'Science and Technology in Irish National Culture', *The Crane Bag*, 7, pp. 58–63.

Johnston, R.H.W. (2003), *A Century of Endeavour*, Dublin: Tyndall Publications/The Lilliput Press.

Jordan, D. and O'Leary, E. (2007), 'Is Irish Innovation Policy Working?: Evidence from Irish High-Technology Businesses', paper presented to a meeting of the Statistical and Social Inquiry Society of Ireland (SSISI), Dublin, 25 October.

Jordan, D. and O'Leary, E. (2005), 'The Roles of Interaction and Proximity for Innovation by Irish High-Technology Businesses: Policy Implications', *Quarterly Economic Commentary*, Summer, pp. 86–100.

Kandybin, A. and Kihn, M. (2004), 'Raising your Return on Innovation Investment', *Strategy & Business*, 35, Summer, Booz Allen Hamilton, New York, available at: <http://www.strategy-business.com/media/file/rr00007. pdf>.

Kane, R. (1844), *The Industrial Resources of Ireland*, Dublin: Hodges and Smith.

Kasser, T. (2002), *The High Price of Materalism,* Cambridge, MA: MIT Press.

Kearney, R. (1985), 'Introduction: An Irish Intellectual Tradition?' in R. Kearney (ed.) *The Irish Mind: Exploring Intellectual Traditions*, Dublin: Wolfhound Press, pp. 7–14.

Keating, M. and Martin, G. (2004), *Managing Cross-Cultural Diversity: The Irish-German Experience*, Dublin: Blackhall Publishing.

Keating, P. and Desmond, D. (1993), *Culture and Capitalism in Contemporary Ireland*, Aldershot: Avebury.

Kelleher, D. (1985), 'The Alienation of Science: An Irish Cultural, Industrial and Political Problem', *The Crane Bag*, 9(1), pp. 63–9.

Kelly, S. (2006), 'The GAA – Reflecting all that is Good in Irish Culture' in J. Mulholland (ed.), *The Soul of Ireland: Issues of Society, Culture and Identity*, Dublin: Liffey Press.

Kennedy, F. (2007), 'The Best of Times, the Worst of Times' in Harry Bohan (ed.) *Freedom – Licence or Liberty? Engaging with a Transforming Ireland,* Dublin: Veritas, pp. 20–32.

Kennedy, J. (2004), 'Code Warrior', *Silcon Republic.com*, 15 December 2004, available at: <http://www.siliconrepublic.com/news/news.nv?storyid=single4192>.

Kennelly, B. (2002), *The Little Book of Judas*, Tarset, Northumberland, UK: Bloodaxe Books.

Kenny, V. (1985), 'The Post-Colonial Personality', *The Crane Bag*, 9(1), pp. 70–8.

Ketels, C.H.M. (2006), 'Michael Porter's Competitiveness Framework – Recent Learnings and New Research Priorities', *Journal of Industry, Competition and Trade*, 6, pp. 115–36.

Keynes, J.M. (1933), 'National Self-Sufficiency', *The Yale Review*, 22(4), June, pp. 755–69.

Kiberd, D. (2003), 'Republicanism and Culture in the New Millennium' in R.J. Savage (ed.), *Ireland in the New Century: Politics, Culture, Identity*, Dublin: Four Courts Press, pp. 84–5.

Kiberd, D. (1996), *Inventing Ireland: The Literature of the Modern Nation,* London: Random House.

Kiberd, D. (1993), 'Douglas Hyde: A Radical in Tory Clothing?' *Irish Reporter*, 11, pp. 18–20.

Kiberd, D. (1979), 'Writers in Quarantine: The Case for Irish Studies', *The Crane Bag*, 3, pp. 9–21.

Kinsella, T. (trans.) (1969), *The Táin*, Dublin: Dolmen Press.

Kirby, P. (1997), *Poverty Amid Plenty*, Dublin: Trócaire/Gill & Macmillan.

Kirby, P., Gibbons, L. and Cronin, M. (eds.) (2002), *Reinventing Ireland: Culture, Society and the Global Economy*, London: Pluto.

Kreisler, H. (1999), 'Adaptation and Change in the American University', conversation with Frank H.T. Rhodes, in *Conversations with History Series*, Institute of International Studies, UC Berkeley, 31 March, available at: <http://globetrotter.berkeley.edu/people/Rhodes/rhodes-con0.html>.

Lambooy, J. (2005), 'Innovation and Knowledge: Theory and Regional Policy', *European Planning Studies*, 13(8), December, pp. 1137–52.

Landes, D. (1998), *The Wealth and Poverty of Nations*, London: Little, Brown and Co.

Laurent, A. (1983), 'The Cultural Diversity of Western Conceptions of Management', *International Studies of Management & Organization*, 13(1/2).

Layard, R. (2005), *Happiness: Lessons from a New Science*, London: Allen Lane.

Layte, R., Nolan, A. and Nolan, B. (2007), 'Health and Health Care' in T. Fahey, H. Russell and C.T. Whelan (eds.), *Best of Times? The Social Impact of the Celtic Tiger*, Dublin: Institute of Public Administration, p. 114.

Lee, J.J. (1999), 'A Sense of Place in the Celtic Tiger' in H. Bohan and G. Kennedy (eds.), *Are we Forgetting Something? Our Society in the New Millennium*, Dublin: Veritas, pp. 71–93.

Lee, J.J. (1989), *Ireland 1912–1985: Politics and Society*, Cambridge: Cambridge University Press.

Lee, J.J. (ed.) (1985), *Ireland: Towards a Sense of Place*, Cork: Cork University Press.

Lee, J.J. (1985), 'Centralisation and Community' in J.J. Lee (ed.) *Ireland: Towards a Sense of Place*, Cork: Cork University Press.

Lester, R.K. (2005), 'Universities, Innovation and the Competitiveness of Local Economies', *Summary Report from the LIS Project-Phase 1*, MIT Industrial Performance Centre, Working Paper 05-010.

Lester, R.K. and Piore, M.J. (2004), *Innovation – The Missing Dimension*, Boston, MA: Harvard University Press.

Levitt, T. (1983), 'The Globalization of Markets', *Harvard Business Review*, May/June, pp. 92–102.

Lillis, S. (2005), 'Realising Community Development's Potential in Ireland through Practice, Learning and Connection', *Perspectives on Community Development*, 1(1), pp. 6–19.

Lillis, S. (2001), 'An Inquiry into the Effectiveness of my Practice as a Learning Practitioner-Researcher in Rural Development', unpublished Ph.D. thesis, University College Dublin.

Lindeman, E.C. (1926), *The Meaning of Adult Education*, New York: New Republic.

Lynch, P. (1979), 'Whither Science Policy?' Seventh Kane Lecture, Science Policy Research Centre, UCD.

Lynch, P. (1972), 'Interdisciplinarity in the Universities', *Irish Journal of Education*, 6(1), pp. 3–8.

Lyons, F.S.L. (1963), *Ireland Since the Famine*, London: Fontana Press.

Lysaght, S. (1998), *Robert Lloyd Praeger: The Life of a Naturalist*, Dublin: Four Courts Press.

Lysaght, S. (1996), 'Themes in the Irish History of Science', *The Irish Review,* 19(1), 87–97.

Lysaght, S. (1989), 'Heaney vs. Praeger: Contrasting Natures', *The Irish Review*, 7(1), 68–74.

McCarthy, P. (2000), *McCarthy's Bar: A Journey of Discovery in the West of Ireland*, New York: Martin's Press.

McCraw, T.K. (2007), *Prophet of Innovation: Joseph Schumpeter and Creative Destruction*, Cambridge, MA: Belknap Press/Harvard University Press.

McDonagh, E. (2005), 'University Reform in Ireland', unpublished manuscript, St. Patrick's College, Maynooth.

McDonald, F. (2000), *The Construction of Dublin,* Kinsale: Gandon Editions.

McDonald, F. (1989), *Saving the City*, Dublin: Tomar Publishing.

McDonald, F. (1985), *The Destruction of Dublin*, Dublin: Gill & Macmillan.

McDonald, F. and Nix, J. (2005), *Chaos at the Crossroads,* Kinsale: Gandon Editions.

McGeachy, C. (2001), *Spiritual Intelligence in the Workplace*, Dublin: Veritas.

McIver Consulting (2004), *Software Industry Training Study*, prepared for FÁS, Dublin.

McKenna, L. (1912), 'The Educational Value of Irish', *Studies*, 1(2), pp. 307–26.

MacTighearnáin, E. (1987), '*Is Treise Dúchas ná Oiliúint*' ('Tradition is Stronger than Learning'), Comharcumann Íde Naofa, Faing, Co. Luimnigh, Méan Fómhair.

McWilliams, D. (2007), *The Generation Game,* Dublin: Gill & Macmillan.

McWilliams, D. (2006), *The Pope's Children: Ireland's New Elite*, Dublin: Gill & Macmillan.

Magee, B. (1973), *Popper*, London: Fontana Press.

Maillat, D. (2001), 'Territory and Innovation: the Role of the Milieu' in G. Sweeney (ed.), *Innovation, Economic Progress and the Quality of Life*, Cheltenham: Edward Elgar, pp. 137–43.

Matthews, P.J. (2005), 'In Praise of "Hibernocentricism": Republicanism, Globalisation and Irish Culture', *The Republic,* 4, June.

Matthews, P.J. (2003), *Revival: The Abbey Theatre, Sinn Féin, The Gaelic League and the Co-operative Movement*, Notre Dame, IN: University of Notre Dame Press.

Maume, P. (1995), *D.P. Moran*, Dundalk: Dundalgan Press, Life and Times: No. 4, for the Historical Association of Ireland.

Mays, M. (2005), 'Irish Identity in an Age of Globalisation', *Irish Studies Review*, 13 February, pp. 3–12.

Mintzberg, H. (2004), *Managers, Not MBAs,* London: FT/Prentice Hall.

Mjøset, L. (1992), *The Irish Economy in a Comparative Institutional Perspective*, Dublin: NESC.

Moane, G. (2002), 'Colonialism and the Celtic Tiger', in P. Kirby, L. Gibbons and M. Cronin (eds.), *Reinventing Ireland: Culture Society and the Global Economy*, London: Pluto Press, pp. 109–23.

Moloney, M. (2006), 'Re-Imagining Irish Music and Dance' in A.H. Wyndham (ed.) *Re-Imagining Ireland*, Charlottesville, VA: University of Virginia Press.

Moore, M.H. (1995), *Creating Public Value: Strategic Management in Government*, Cambridge, MA: Harvard University Press.

Mortiboys, A. (2005), *Teaching with Emotional Intelligence*, Oxford, UK: Routledge Falmer.

Moynihan, M. (ed.) (1980), *Speeches and Statements by Éamon de Valera 1917–1973*, Dublin: Gill & Macmillan.

Mulreaney, M. (1999), 'Cost-Benefit Analysis' in M. Mulreaney (ed.) *Economic and Financial Evaluation: Measurement, Meaning and Management*, Dublin: Institute of Public Administration, pp. 177–204.

Murphy, S. (1997, 1966), *Stone Mad*, Belfast: Blackstaff Press.

Nalebuff, B.J. and Brandenbuger, A.M. (1997), *Co-opetition*, London: HarperCollinsBusiness.

Nash, C. (1999), 'Irish Place Names: Post-Colonial Locations', *Transactions of the Institute of British Geographers*, 24(4), pp. 457–80.

National Competitiveness Council (2007), *Annual Competitiveness Report 2007, Volume 1: Benchmarking Ireland's Performance/Volume 2: Ireland Competitiveness Challenge*, Dublin: Forfás.

National Competitiveness Council (2007), *Review of International Assessments of Ireland's Competitiveness*, Dublin: Forfás.

National Economic and Social Council (2005), *NESC Strategy 2006: People, Productivity and Purpose*, Dublin.

National Economic and Social Development Office (2006), *Learning Society Foresight Project: Delivery of Consultancy Services – Call for Outline Proposals*, Dublin: NESDO.

National Economic and Social Forum (2003), *The Policy Implications of Social Capital: Forum Report Number* 28, Dublin: NESF.

Nattrass, B. and Altomare, M. (1999), *The Natural Step for Business: Wealth, Ecology and the Evolutionary Corporation*, Gabriola Island, British Columbia, CA: New Society Publishers.

Nic Eoin, M. (2004), '*Idir Dhá Theanga*: Irish Language Culture and the Challenges of Hybridity' in C. Mac Murchaidh (ed.), *'Who Needs Irish?' Reflections on the Importance of the Irish Language Today*, Dublin: Veritas, pp. 131–2.

Norberg-Hodge, H., Merrifield, T. and Gorelick, S. (2002), *Bringing the Food Economy Home: Local Alternatives to Global Agribusiness,* London: Zed Books.

Norman, R. and Ramirez, R. (1993), 'From Value Chain to Value Constellation: Designing Interactive Strategy', *Harvard Business Review*, 71, July–August, pp. 65–77.

Ó Buachalla, S. (ed.) (1980), *A Significant Irish Educationalist: The Educational Writings of P.H. Pearse*, Cork: Mercier Press.

O'Connor, N. (2007), 'Industry-Academia Collaboration: A Competence Centre Approach for Ireland?' *Studies in Public Policy*, No. 22, The Policy Institute, Trinity College Dublin.

Ó Doibhlin, B. (2004), 'An Enterprise of the Spirit' in C. Mac Murchaidh (ed.) *'Who Needs Irish?' Reflections on the Importance of the Irish Language Today*, Dublin: Veritas, pp. 140–58.

O'Donnell, I. (2007), 'Crime and its Consequences' in T. Fahey, H. Russell and C.T. Whelan (eds.) *Best of Times? The Social Impact of the Celtic Tiger*, Dublin: Institute of Public Administration, pp. 245–64.

Ó Dúshláine, T. (2007), 'Breandán Ó Doibhlin: Pathfinder' in *Breandán Ó Doibhlin: Saol agus Saothar*, Dublin: Coiscéim, pp. 1–25.

Ó Gráda, C. (1977), 'The Beginnings of the Irish Creamery System 1880–1914', *The Economic History Review*, 30(2), pp. 284–305.

Ó Lúing, S. (1973), 'Douglas Hyde and the Gaelic League', *Studies*, Summer, pp. 123–38.

O'Neil, D. (1987), 'Explaining Irish Underdevelopment: Plunkett and Connolly Prior to 1916', *Éire-Ireland*, 22(4), Winter, pp. 47–71.

Ó Riain, S. (2008), 'Competing State Projects in the Contemporary Irish Political Economy', in M. Adshead, P. Kirby and M. Miller (eds.), *Contesting the State*, Manchester: Manchester University Press, pp. 165–85.

Ó Riain, S. (2006), 'Nurturing Many Knowledges to Grow Ireland's Knowledge Society', paper delivered at Irish Universities Association (IUA), Humanities and Social Sciences Conference, Dublin, 23–24 October.

O'Rourke, K.H (2007), 'Culture, Conflict and Co-operation: Irish Dairying before the Great War', *The Economic Journal*, 117(523) October, pp. 1357–79.

O'Sullivan, M. (2006), *Ireland and the Global Question*, Cork: Cork University Press.

O'Toole, F. (1996), *The Ex-Isle of Erin: Images of a Global Ireland*, Dublin: New Island Books.

Ó Tuama, S. (1972), 'The Gaelic League Idea in the Future' in S. Ó Tuama (ed.) *The Gaelic League Idea*, Cork: Mercier Press, pp. 98–109.

Oinas, P. (2005), 'Finland: A Success Story?' *European Planning Studies*, 13(8), December, pp. 1227–44.

Organisation for Economic Co-operation and Development (2004), *Examiner's Report – Review of National Policies for Education: Review of Higher Education in Ireland*, Paris: OECD.

Organisation for Economic Co-operation and Development (1996), *Territorial Development and Human Capital in the Knowledge Economy: Towards a Policy Framework*, LEED Notebook No. 23, Paris: OECD.

Outram, D. (1986), 'Negating the Natural: Or Why Historians Deny Irish Science', *The Irish Review*, 1, pp. 45–9.

Page, S.E. (2007), *The Difference: How the Power of Diversity Creates Better Groups, Firms, Schools and Societies*, Princeton, NJ: Princeton University Press.

Palmisano, S.J. (2006), 'Globally Integrated Enterprise', *Foreign Affairs*, 85(3), pp.127–36.

Pearce, D.R. (ed.) (2001), *The Senate Speeches of WB Yeats*, London: Prendeville Publishing.

Pirsig, R.M. (1974), *Zen and the Art of Motorcycle Maintenance*, London: Vintage.

Plunkett, H.C. (1904), *Ireland in the New Century*, London: John Murray.

Polanyi, M. (1974), *Personal Knowledge: Towards a Post-Critical Philosophy*, Chicago: University of Chicago Press.

Polanyi, M. and Prosch, H. (1975), *Meaning*, Chicago: University of Chicago Press.

Porritt, J. (2006), *Capitalism as if the World Matters*, London: Earthscan.

Porter, M.E. (1998), 'Clusters and the New Economics of Competition', *Harvard Business Review*, November–December, pp. 77–90.

Porter, M.E. (1990), *The Competitive Advantage of Nations*, New York: Free Press.

Porter, M.E. (1990), 'The Competitive Advantage of Nations', *Harvard Business Review*, March–April, pp. 73–93.

Porter, M.E. and Van der Linde, C. (1995), 'Green and Competitive', *Harvard Business Review*, September–October, pp. 120–34.

Posner, E. (ed.) (1997), *The Essential Holmes: Letters, Speeches, Judicial Opinions and Other Writings of Oliver Wendell Holmes Jr.*, Chicago: University of Chicago Press.

Postman, N. (1996), *The End of Education: Refining the Value of School*, New York: Vintage Books.

Power, T.M. (1996), *Environmental Protection and Economic Well-Being: The Economic Pursuit of Quality*, 2nd edition, Armonk, New York: M.E. Sharpe.

Praeger, R.L. (2005), 'Our National Trust: Address Broadcast by Radio Éireann, 10 October 1948' in V. Bond (ed.) *An Taisce: The First Fifty Years*, Ballivor, Co. Meath: The Hannon Press, pp. 149–55.

Prahalad, C.K. and Hamel, G. (1990), 'The Core Competence of the Corporation', *Harvard Business Review*, May–June, pp. 79–91.

Preston, P. (2005), 'The Cultural Turn versus Economic Returns: The Production of Culture in an Information Age', *The Republic*, 4, June, pp. 60–79.

Rapple, C. (2000), 'Beyond the Boom: Towards an Economic Policy for Welfare and Society', *The Republic*, 1, June, pp. 40–9.

Read, C., Ross, J., Dunleavy, J., Schulman, D. and Bramante, J. (2001), *eCFO: Sustaining Value in the New Corporation*, Chichester, UK: John Wiley & Sons.

Reich, R.B. (2005), *Reason: Why Liberals will Win the Battle for America*, New York: Vintage Books.

Reid, B. (2004), 'Labouring towards the Space to Belong: Place and Identity in Northern Ireland', *Irish Geography*, 37(1), pp. 103–13.

Ridley, M. (1996), *The Origins of Virtue*, London: Penguin Books.

Rogers, J.S. (2004), 'A Monument More Lasting than Bronze: Eoin McKiernan, 1915–2004', *New Hibernia Review*, 8, Autumn, p. 9–11.

Royal Irish Academy (2005), *School Science Infrastructure: Can Ireland Deliver?* RIA Workshop, Dublin, May 2005.

Russell, G.W. (1916), *The National Being*, Dublin: Maunsel and Company.

Ryan, B. (2007), *Corporate Finance*, London: Thomson.

Ryan, B. (2001), 'Have Intellectuals Failed Ireland?' in A. Hoey-Heffron and J. Heffron (eds.), *Beyond the Ivory Tower: The University in the New Millennium*, Cork: Mercier Press, pp. 96–102.

Ryan, É. (2007), 'Commercialising our R&D', *Business & Finance*, 25 January.

Sabau, G. (2003), 'The Knowledge-Based Economy – Sustainable Development Nexus', paper presented at the Conference, 'The Knowledge-Based Economy and Regional Economic Development', St. John's Newfoundland, CA, 3–5 October.

Salmi, J. (2001), 'Tertiary Education in the 21st Century: Challenges and Opportunities', *Higher Education Management*, 13(2), pp. 105–31.

Seely Brown, J. and Duguid, P. (2000), *The Social Life of Information*, Boston: Harvard Business School Press.

Senge, P. (1990), 'The Leader's New Work: Building Learning Organizations', *Sloan Management Review*, 32(1), pp. 7–23.

Senge, P.M. (1990), *The Fifth Discipline: The Art and Practice of the Learning Organization*, London: Random House.

Sennett, R. (2008), *The Craftsman*, London: Penguin/Allen Lane.

Sheeran, P. (1988), '*Genius Fabulae*: The Irish Sense of Place', *Irish University Review*, 18, pp. 191–206.

Skilbeck, M. (2002), *The University Challenged: A Review of International Trends and Issues with Particular Reference to Ireland*, Dublin: HEA/CHIU.

Smith, A. (1910, 1776), *The Wealth of Nations*, New York: Everyman's Library.

Smith, A. (1966, 1759), *The Theory of Moral Sentiments*, New York: Kelley.

Smyth, E., McCoy, S., Darmody, M. and Dunne, A. (2007), 'Changing Times, Changing Schools? Quality of Life for Students' in T. Fahey, H. Russell and C.T. Whelan (eds.), *Best of Times? The Social Impact of the Celtic Tiger*, Dublin: Institute of Public Administration,

Smyth, W.J. (1985), 'Explorations of Place' in J.J. Lee (ed.) *Ireland: Towards a Sense of Place*, Cork: Cork University Press, pp. 1–20.

Snow, C.P. (1998), *The Two Cultures*, Cambridge: Cambridge University Press.

Spenser, E. (1970, 1596), *A View of the Present State of Ireland*, Oxford: Oxford University Press.

Stacey, R. (2006), 'Ways of Thinking about Public Sector Governance' in R. Stacey and D. Griffin (eds.), Complexity and the Experience of Managing in Public Sector Organizations, London: Routledge, pp. 15–42.

Sterne, J. (2004), *Adventures in Code*, Dublin: Liffey Press.

Stirling, S. (2001), *Sustainable Education: Re-Visioning Learning and Change*, London: Green Books.

Sturt, G. (1993), *The Wheelwright's Shop,* Cambridge, UK: Cambridge University Press.

Sugarman, B. (2000), 'A Learning-Based Approach to Leading Change', The PriceWaterhouseCoopers Endowment for the Business of Government, December.

Suri, J.F. and Howard, S.G. (2006), 'Going Deeper, Seeing Further: Enhancing Ethnographic Interpretations to Reveal More Meaningful Opportunities for Design', *Journal of Advertising Research*, September, pp. 246–50.

Sustainable Energy Ireland (2004), 'Investing in Energy: A Practical Guide to Preparing and Presenting Energy Investment Proposals', Dublin.

Sutherland, P. (2008), 'A Golden Mean between Multiculturalism and Assimilation', *Studies*, 97(385), Spring, pp. 73–86.

Sweeney, G. (2002), 'The Skilbeck Report and the Need for Change', *Céide*, April/May, pp. 18–20.

Sweeney, G. (2001), 'Introduction: Innovation and Innovation Policy: the Need for Re-Examination' in G. Sweeney (ed.), *Innovation, Economic Progress and the Quality of Life*, Cheltenham, UK: Edward Elgar.

Sweeney, G. (2001), 'Social Capital: The Core Factor in Economic Resurgence' in G. Sweeney (ed.), *Innovation, Economic Progress and the Quality of Life*, Cheltenham, UK: Edward Elgar.

Sweeney, P. (ed.) (2007), *Ireland's Economic Success: Reasons and Lessons,* Dublin: New Island Books.

Sykes, C.J. (1990), *ProfScam: Professors and the Demise of Higher Education*, New York: St. Martin's Griffin.

The Bell (1942), 'The Gaelic League', 4(2), pp. 77–86.

The Futures Academy (2005), *Imagineering Ireland: Future Scenarios for 2030*, October, Dublin: Dublin Institute of Technology.

'The Globalization Index 2007' (2007), *Foreign Policy*, November/December, available at: <http://www.foreignpolicy.com/story/cms.php?story_id=3995>.

Throsby, D. (2001), *Economics and Culture*, Cambridge, UK: Cambridge University Press.

Tidd, J., Bessant, J. and Pavitt, K. (2005), *Managing Innovation: Integrating Technological, Market and Organizational Change*, 3rd edition, Hoboken, NJ: John Wiley & Sons.

Tiernan, C. and Peppard, J. (2004), 'Information Technology: of Value or a Vulture?' *European Management Journal*, 22(6), December, pp. 609–23.

Tierney, M. (1944), 'M. Maritain on Education', *Studies*, 33(129), March, pp. 21–9.

Tovey, H., Hannan, D. and Abramson, H. (1989), *Why Irish? Irish Identity and the Irish Language*, Dublin: Bord na Gaeilge.

Trench, B. (2007), 'Irish Media Representations of Science' in J. Horgan, B. O'Connor and H. Sheehan (eds.), *Mapping Irish Media: Critical Explorations*, Dublin: University College Dublin Press, pp. 128–41.

Trench, B. (2003), 'Science, Culture and Public Affairs', *The Republic*, 3, July, pp. 53–63.

Tuohy, B. (2002), 'A Liberal Education for a Technology World', paper presented at the Conference on Values in Education and Public

Policy, University of Limerick, Centre for Culture, Technology and Values, April.

Turner, F.M. (ed.) (1996), *The Idea of a University – John Henry Newman*, New Haven, CT: Yale University Press.

Twomey, D.V. (2003), *The End of Irish Catholicism?* Dublin: Veritas.

Tymoczko, M. and Ireland, C. (2003), 'Language and Identity in Twentieth-Century Ireland', *Éire-Ireland*, Spring/Summer, pp. 4–22.

Uí Bhraonáin, D. (2007), *500 Seanfhocal/Proverbs/Refranes/Przyslów*, Dublin: Cois Life.

United Nations Development Program (2006), *Human Development Report 2006,* data from the period 1994–2002, New York.

Vargo, S.L. and Lusch, R.F. (2004), 'Evolving to a New Dominant Logic for Marketing', *Journal of Marketing*, 68, January, pp. 1–17.

Verganti, R. (2003), 'Design as Brokering of Languages: Innovation Strategies in Italian Firms', *Design Management Journal*, Summer, pp. 34–42.

Verhelst, T.G. (1990), *No Life without Roots: Culture and Development*, London: Zed Books.

Viney, M. (1986), 'Woodcock for a Farthing: the Irish Experience of Nature', *The Irish Review*, 1, pp. 58–64.

Walley, P. (1993), *Learning the Future – A Brief Guide to the Knowledge Society*, Galway: Meitheal Mhaigheo, City of Galway VEC.

Walsh, J.P., Weber, K. and Margolis, J.D. (2003), 'Social Issues and Management: Our Lost Cause Found', *Journal of Management*, 29(6), pp. 859–81.

Waters, J. (1997), *An Intelligent Person's Guide to Modern Ireland*, London: Duckworth.

Watson, I. (2008), 'The Irish Language and Identity' in C. Nic Pháidín and S. Ó Cearnaigh (eds.) (2008), *A New View of the Irish Language*, Dublin: Cois Life, pp. 66–75.

Wenger, E. (1998), 'Communities of Practice: Learning as a Social System', *Systems Thinker*, 9(5), June, available at: <http://www.co-i-l.com/coil/knowledge-garden/cop/lss.shtml>.

Wenger, E. (1998), *Communities of Practice: Learning, Meaning and Identity*, Cambridge: Cambridge University Press.

Wernerfelt, B. (1984), 'A Resource-based View of the Firm', *Strategic Management Journal*, 5, pp. 171–80.

Wheeler, T.S. (1944), 'Sir Robert Kane: Life and Work; Part I: 1809–1844', *Studies*, 33(130), June, pp. 158–68

Wheeler, T.S. (1944), 'Sir Robert Kane: Life and Work; Part II: 1844–1890', *Studies*, 33(131), September, pp. 316–20.

Whelan, K. (1992), 'The Power of Place', *The Irish Review*, 12, pp. 13–20.

Whitaker, T.K. (1983), *Interests*, Dublin: Institute of Public Administration.

Whitehead, A.N. (1932), *The Aims of Education*, London: Williams & Norgate.

Whyte, N. (1999), *Science, Colonialism and Ireland*, Cork: Cork University Press.

Williams, G. (2007), 'From Media to Multimedia: Workflows and Language in the Digital Economy' in M.J. Cormack and N. Hourigan (eds.), *Minority Language Media: Concepts, Critiques and Case Studies*, Clevedon, UK: Multilingual Matters, pp. 88–106.

Witoszek, N. and Sheeran, P. (1985), 'Giving Culture a Kick – Modern Irish Culture Forum', *The Crane Bag*, 9(1), pp. 94–5.

World Economic Forum (2007), *The Global Competitiveness Report 2006–2007*, Cologny/Geneva: WEF.

Young, P., O'Donnell, I. and Clare, E. (2001), *Crime in Ireland: Trends and Patterns, 1950–1998*, Dublin: The Stationery Office.

Zimmermann, E.W. (1933), *World Resources and Industries: A Functional Appraisal of the Availability of Agricultural and Industrial Resources*, New York: Harper and Brothers.

Zinsmeister, K. (1997), 'Tradition Works', *The American Enterprise Online*, March/April, available at: <http://www.taemag.com/issues/articleid.16200/article_detail.asp>.

Index